MoSO

A Model of Sustainable Organisation

Antony Aitken

Tony Brown

Ray Charlton

Alan Clark

Malcolm Gall

Fabian Hiscock

Alan Hodges

Tony Korycki

Kevan Leach

Terry Peterson

Will Pollard

Derek Richings

Esther Ridsdale

Terry Rose

Mike Upstone

Edited by Peter Leeson

ISBN: 9798861760041

Foreword

Several different people wrote the following pages at various times. They worked together to help develop a practical and straightforward approach to building, managing and leading a sustainable organisation based on the principles laid out by many professional consultants, advisors and teachers, and Dr Deming.

These individuals collaborated and reviewed each other's work. As active members of the Chartered Quality Institute (CQI), they formed the "Deming Special Interest Group". Their work was first published on the website of the CQI. Like all websites, this one evolves and changes, breaking links and references over time. Therefore, it was time to reorganise the information in a more permanent structure.

It was my privilege to edit, format and update these documents. I also felt it necessary to add some explanations and chapters within the document to introduce concepts to readers who may be less familiar with the history of professional quality management.

In the first section of this little book, I have taken it upon myself to attempt to introduce and clarify some critical components and aspects of the quality principles.

However, before that, I need to thank the original authors (in alphabetical order):

Antony Aitken

Tony Brown

Ray Charlton

Alan Clark

Malcolm Gall

Fabian Hiscock

Alan Hodges

Tony Korycki

Kevan Leach

Terry Peterson

Will Pollard

Derek Richings

Esther Ridsdale

Terry Rose

Mike Upstone

Peter Leeson, June 2023

Antony Aitken

Tony Brown

Ray Charlton

Alan Clark

Malcolm Gall

Fabian Hiscock

Alan Hodges

Tony Korycki

Kevan Leach

Terry Peterson

Will Pollard

Derek Richings

Esther Ridsdale

Terry Rose

Mike Upstone

Peter Leeson, June 2023

Foreword

Several different people wrote the following pages at various times. They worked together to help develop a practical and straightforward approach to building, managing and leading a sustainable organisation based on the principles laid out by many professional consultants, advisors and teachers, and Dr Deming.

These individuals collaborated and reviewed each other's work. As active members of the Chartered Quality Institute (CQI), they formed the "Deming Special Interest Group". Their work was first published on the website of the CQI. Like all websites, this one evolves and changes, breaking links and references over time. Therefore, it was time to reorganise the information in a more permanent structure.

It was my privilege to edit, format and update these documents. I also felt it necessary to add some explanations and chapters within the document to introduce concepts to readers who may be less familiar with the history of professional quality management.

In the first section of this little book, I have taken it upon myself to attempt to introduce and clarify some critical components and aspects of the quality principles.

However, before that, I need to thank the original authors (in alphabetical order):

Table of Contents

Table of Figures

Section 1.Some Fundamental Concepts

Introducing Dr Deming[1]

Doctor W. Edwards Deming (1900-1993) was an American engineer, statistician and consultant who devoted his life to the systematic improvement of quality and the consequent improvement of both efficiency and effectiveness. A key turning point in Dr Deming's career was probably in 1950 when he trained engineers and senior executives in statistical process control and quality concepts in Japan. This education was foundational in helping Japan move from a destroyed militaristic empire to a leading global economy.

Dr Deming is probably most often misquoted by people who are randomly using the PDCA concept. Anyone who confuses PDCA and Deming demonstrates a lack of understanding of both elements.

Some of the more important creations of Dr Deming include:

- Plan-Do-Study-Act;
- The 7 Deadly Diseases;
- The 14 Points for Management;
- The System of Profound Knowledge.

I am briefly detailing these concepts hereunder for those who are not familiar with them. If you wish to learn more about them, these (and many

---

[1] More about Dr Deming in "The Deming Approach", page 280.

more) are treated in depth in Dr Deming's literature. As one becomes acquainted with these principles, it becomes evident that, whatever progress technology has made, these concepts are as valid today as they were when he first formalised them in the middle of the twentieth century.

At their most simple, I would abbreviate Dr Deming's guiding principles appear to the following:

1. Quality is designed, developed and delivered by individuals;
2. Individuals want to take pride in the quality of their work and cannot perform at their best unless they feel some level of job satisfaction;
3. The effectiveness and performance of individuals are limited by the system in which the organisation has locked them;
4. Senior management remains ultimately responsible for the system put in place to manage the work of the individuals concerned.

In other words, there is no point in measuring the productivity of an individual if you are constraining that person's work in a system that does not allow them to operate at optimum capacity.

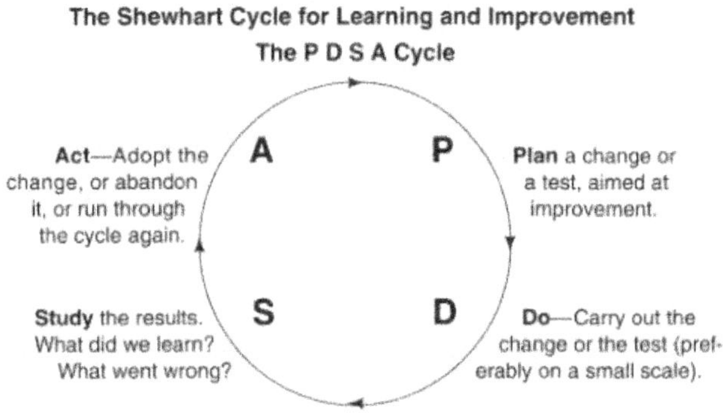

The Shewhart Cycle for Learning and Improvement
The P D S A Cycle

Act—Adopt the change, or abandon it, or run through the cycle again.

Plan a change or a test, aimed at improvement.

Study the results. What did we learn? What went wrong?

Do—Carry out the change or the test (preferably on a small scale).

Figure 1: PDSA

PDSA[2]

Dr Deming developed and pushed PDSA (also known as the Deming Cycle) and not the PDCA[3] cycle used by many people. The emphasis on the need to Study rather than Check stresses understanding the root causes of failure or success rather than checking the result. Based on Walter Shewhart's three-step approach of planning and designing, building and selling, and measuring the market feedback, Deming's approach focused more on predicting the results of any improvement effort to update or adapt any ideas or theories that led to the planning phase.

Dr Deming defines PDSA as:[4]

---

[2] More on PDSA on page 139
[3] Dr Deming stated that "Check" implies to hold back, while "Study" means to actively learn lessons from successes and failures.
[4] Deming, W. Edwards. "The New Economics for Industry, Government, Education", third edition. MIT Press, 2018 (First edition 1993).

Step 1. PLAN. Somebody has an idea for an improvement of a product or of a process (This is stage 0, embedded in Step 1). It leads to a plan for a test, comparison, and experiment. Step 1 is the foundation of the whole cycle. A hasty start may be ineffective, costly, and frustrating. People have a weakness to short-circuit this step. They cannot wait to get into motion, to be active, to look busy, move into Step 2.

The planning stage may start with a choice between several suggestions. Which one can we test? What may be the result? Compare the possible outcomes of the possible choices. Of the several suggestions, which one appears to be most promising in terms of new knowledge or profit? The problem may be how to achieve a feasible goal.

Step 1. PLAN. Somebody has an idea for an improvement of a product or of a process (This is stage 0, embedded in Step 1). It leads to a plan for a test, comparison, and experiment. Step 1 is the foundation of the whole cycle. A hasty start may be ineffective, costly, and frustrating. People have a weakness to short-circuit this step. They cannot wait to get into motion, to be active, to look busy, move into Step 2.

The planning stage may start with a choice between several suggestions. Which one can we test? What may be the result? Compare the possible outcomes of the possible choices. Of the several suggestions, which one appears to be most promising in terms of new knowledge or profit? The problem may be how to achieve a feasible goal.

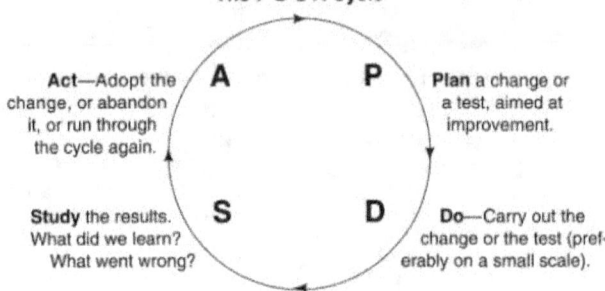

Figure 1: PDSA

PDSA[2]

Dr Deming developed and pushed PDSA (also known as the Deming Cycle) and not the PDCA[3] cycle used by many people. The emphasis on the need to Study rather than Check stresses understanding the root causes of failure or success rather than checking the result. Based on Walter Shewhart's three-step approach of planning and designing, building and selling, and measuring the market feedback, Deming's approach focused more on predicting the results of any improvement effort to update or adapt any ideas or theories that led to the planning phase.

Dr Deming defines PDSA as:[4]

---

[2] More on PDSA on page 139

[3] Dr Deming stated that "Check" implies to hold back, while "Study" means to actively learn lessons from successes and failures.

[4] Deming, W. Edwards. "The New Economics for Industry, Government, Education", third edition. MIT Press, 2018 (First edition 1993).

Step 2. DO. Carry out the test, comparison, or experiment, preferably on a small scale, according to the layout decided in Step 1.

Step 3. STUDY. Study the results. Do they correspond with hopes and expectations? If not, what went wrong? Maybe we tricked ourselves in the first place, and should make a fresh start.

Step 4. ACT. Adopt the change. or Abandon it. or Run through the cycle again, possibly under different environmental conditions, different materials, different people, different rules.

The reader may note that to adopt the change, or to abandon it, requires prediction."

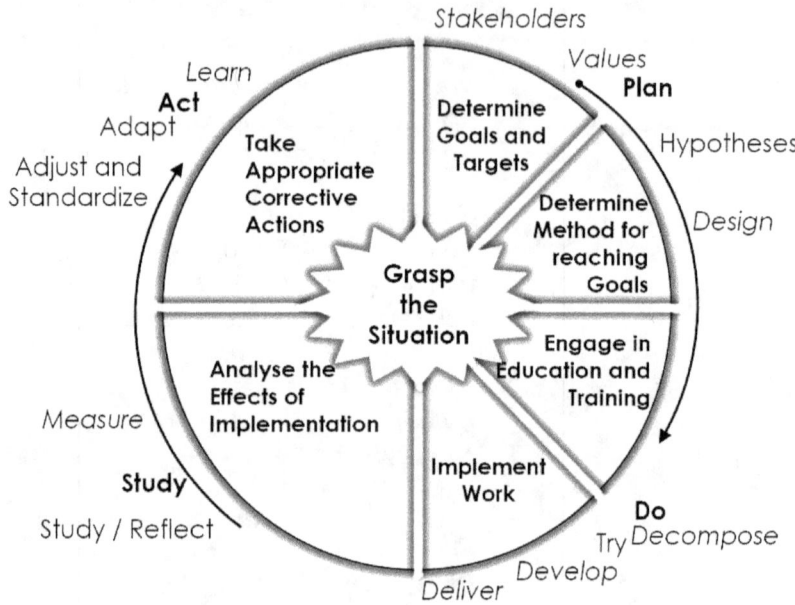

Figure 2: SAPDo

Subsequent variations to PDSA have included additional steps that seek to clarify missing concepts. An example is "SAPDo" (Figure **Error! Reference source not found.**).

The Seven Deadly Diseases

The seven deadly diseases of Western management are failures and bad habits that impede progress, efficiency and quality improvement in most industries. The diseases listed by Dr Deming are:

1. *A lack of constancy and purpose to plan products and services that will have a market, keep the company in business, and provide jobs;*

2. *An emphasis on short-term profits and short-term thinking fed by fears of an unfriendly takeover and push from bankers and owners for regular dividends;*

3. *The evaluation of performance, merit rating or annual review;*

4. *The mobility of management and general job hopping;*

5. *Management based only on visible figures with little or no consideration of figures that are currently unknown or unknowable;*

6. *Excessive medical costs;*

7. *Excessive cost of liability swelled by lawyers that work on contingency fees.*

In his book "Out of the Crisis[5]", Dr Deming explains the five first elements in this list. The last two are identified as being specific to the USA only and are not discussed in detail.

The Fourteen Points for Management

In the same volume ("Out of the Crisis"), Dr Deming defined the 14 points to help with the transformation of American industry beyond solving the existing problems. Their goal is to demonstrate management's intention to stay in business and aim to protect both investors and jobs. They are:

> 1. *Create constancy of purpose toward improvement of product and service, with the aim to become competitive and to stay in business, and to provide jobs.*
>
> 2. *Adopt the new philosophy. We are in a new economic age. Western management must awaken to the challenge, must learn their responsibilities, and take on leadership for change.*

---

[5] Deming, W. Edwards. "Out of the Crisis". MIT Press, 1986

3. *Cease dependence on inspection to achieve quality. Eliminate the need for inspection on a mass basis by building quality into the product in the first place.*

4. *End the practice of awarding business on the basis of price tag. Instead, minimise total cost. Move toward a single supplier for any one item, on a long-term relationship of loyalty and trust.*

5. *Improve constantly and forever the system of production and service, to improve quality and productivity, and thus constantly decrease costs.*

6. *Institute training on the job.*

7. *Institute leadership (see Point 12). The aim of supervision should be to help people and machines and gadgets to do a better job. Supervision of management is in need of overhaul, as well as supervision of production workers*

8. *Drive out fear, so that everyone may work effectively for the company.*

9. *Break down barriers between departments. People in research, design, sales, and production must work as a team to foresee problems of production and in use that may be encountered with the product or service.*

10. *Eliminate slogans, exhortations, and targets for the workforce asking for zero defects and new levels of productivity. Such exhortations only create adversarial relationships, as the bulk of the causes of low quality and low productivity belong to the system and thus lie beyond the power of the workforce.*

11. *(a) Eliminate work standards (quotas) on the factory floor. Substitute leadership.*

11. *(b) Eliminate management by objective. Eliminate management by numbers, numerical goals. Substitute leadership.*

12. *(a) Remove barriers that rob the hourly worker of his right to pride of workmanship. The responsibility of supervisors must be changed from sheer numbers to quality.*

12. (b) Remove barriers that rob people in management and in engineering of their right to pride of workmanship. This means, inter alia, abolishment of the annual or merit rating and of management by objective.

13. Institute a vigorous program of education and self-improvement.

14. Put everybody in the company to work to accomplish the · transformation. The transformation is everybody's job.

Reading through this list, one must wonder at the obsession with managers today, all over the world, to continue to manage by numbers and objectives, frequently pitting teams against each other in their efforts to win that first prize, best team, employee of the month recognition and bonus.

A System of Profound Knowledge[6]

The competition between teams, departments and employees was another aspect of modern management that Dr Deming decried. He successfully demonstrated that organisations were being led into creating negative results for the whole organisation to create more profit for a department. The most obvious example is the sales department, where sales continue to make more promises to potential clients and sign more contracts without regard for the engineering department's capacity to deliver. As engineering falls behind and fails to deliver the promised specifications, senior management traditionally blames the engineers for not meeting their objectives rather than the sales department for generating too much revenue by promising unrealistic features and deadlines.

The System of Profound Knowledge (referenced as SPoK from here on) states that senior management needs to understand how the whole organisation works and an understanding of the interactions between the different components of the system. It is expectable that one department will make a loss if that allows the entire organisation to produce better customer satisfaction.

There are four critical components to the SoPK:

- Appreciation for a system
- Knowledge of variation

---

[6] More information on the System of Profound Knowledge on page 323

- Theory of knowledge
- Psychology.

These components form a holistic framework for improving organisations. They are based on Deming's belief that organisations must continually strive for improvement to remain competitive and relevant in a rapidly changing world.

Too frequently, organisations focus on assigning blame and rewards to individuals rather than considering the system as a whole: the system that allowed the error to occur or enabled the success. Rarely does success or failure depend on a single individual or event.

Similarly, when variations occur, the temptation to assign the change to a cause can create more trouble than one might expect. Reshaping a process due to an exceptional cause of variation can produce a significant loss of effectiveness; however, creating a spot-fix for a defect emanating from a common cause of variation can be just as useless or even destructive.

The organisational and leadership knowledge must be built through observation and testing. These

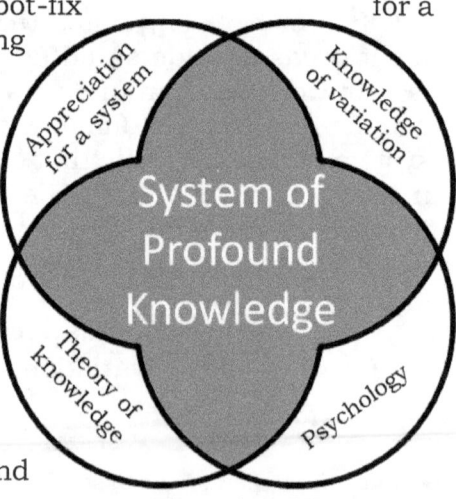

Figure 3: SoPK

16

activities can lead to the creation of a theory that might be acceptable but needs to be tested to ensure its validity. You must be ready to discard your theory once contradictory evidence comes to your attention.

Moreover, we must remember a fact that I have personally been repeating for many years and in many contexts: quality is created by motivated and happy people. Understanding what produces the right level of motivation in your key people is critical to any successful leadership.

None of these components is sufficient, you need all four, and you need to understand the interactions between all four components.

Defining Sustainability

For the past few decades, the word "sustainability" has gained popularity, and it seems everyone wants to claim it. However, few agree on an actual definition.

Organisations claim to be sustainable while doing everything to promote continuous growth; governments believe that growth is required to be sustainable. They do not appear to understand the apparent contradiction in these attitudes. No economist or government wants to show the consequences of continuous growth over the long term; they like to show measurable growth in the past and the next decade but avoid the question of the natural effects.

At government levels, growth is usually measured in terms of "Gross Domestic Product" or GDP. GDP measures the money flow in the nation without interest in the value or quality of what is produced. If you build a poorly designed product and consumers need to replace it after a few months or years, that is good for the GDP. Of course, you are wasting precious natural resources, building frustration in your customers and generating more landfill material and pollution, all items that are not measured in the GDP, so they do not matter.

Sustainability should require an understanding of how to combine three elements:

- Produce something, a product or service, that fulfils a purpose or a need;

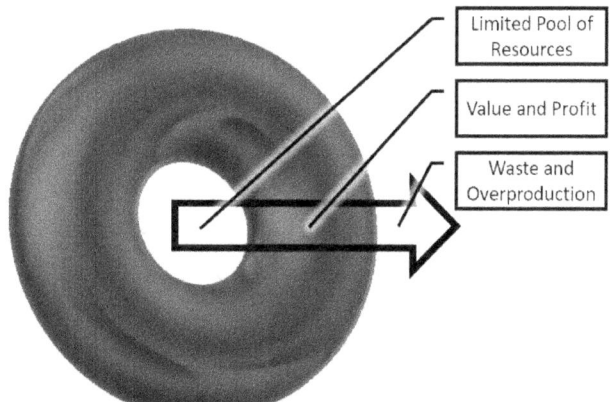

Figure 4: The Doughnut

- Eliminate waste due to over-production, misuse, or failures;
- Use as few resources as possible, always keeping an eye on whether these are re-plenished faster than you are depleting them.

Kate Raworth explains this in more detail in her brilliant book on "Doughnut Economics."[7]

Ms Raworth's message focuses on national and global economics. Let me try to simplify this somewhat to explain how it pertains to commercial operations.

The doughnut's centre represents your limited resources; we find natural resources here, such as wood, water, oil, and metal. It also includes specific resources such as the labour market, money available, and customer potential.

---

[7] Cornerstone Publications, 2018, ISBN 978-1-84794-137-4

Outside the doughnut, we find waste, over-production, defects and anything that we have produced that does not aim at satisfying the organisational goals. Waste may be extended to include bureaucracy, wasted office hours, heating empty buildings and more.

Being sustainable signifies surviving and growing within the doughnut's body. Without depleting your resources, without creating waste.

For clarity, I have included the doughnut graphic as illustrated in Ms Raworth's book on page 22.

The idea of moving from a linear growth mindset to a doughnut one involves several changes that are found in greater detail in Ms Raworth's book. However, I am listing here as they pertain to some extent to the organisational level, just as they do to the global level.

1. Embrace the 21st-century goal: aim to meet the needs of all people within the means of the planet.
2. Seek the big picture: recognise the potential, the means and the synergies that allow transformation.
3. Nurture human nature: promote diversity, participation, collaboration, reciprocity, and networks of trust.
4. Think in systems: experiment, adapt, evolve, and be aware of feedback loops, dynamic effects and tipping points.
5. Be distributive: work in the spirit of open design, share the value created with the co-creators, and redistribute power to improve stakeholder equity.

6. Be regenerative: be a sharer, repairer, re-generator, steward.
7. Aim to thrive rather than to grow: do not let growth become the goal.
8. Be strategic in practice: always ask whose voice is left out, share back learning and innovation, and unleash peer-to-peer inspiration.

Most of these concepts are already present in the texts produced by Dr Deming over half a century ago. The main difference here is that with "doughnut economics", Ms Raworth is seeking to reach a new public: that of politicians who have never considered the writings of a man interested in manufacturing.

I wanted to share this reference because I believe it is crucial to understand the concept of sustainability, and the doughnut (see Figure 5: Doughnut Economics, page 22) explains it in simple, clear and correct terms.

"Sustainable" does not mean that we need to continue to grow our business forever to reach world domination; it means recognising our limits and working within those.

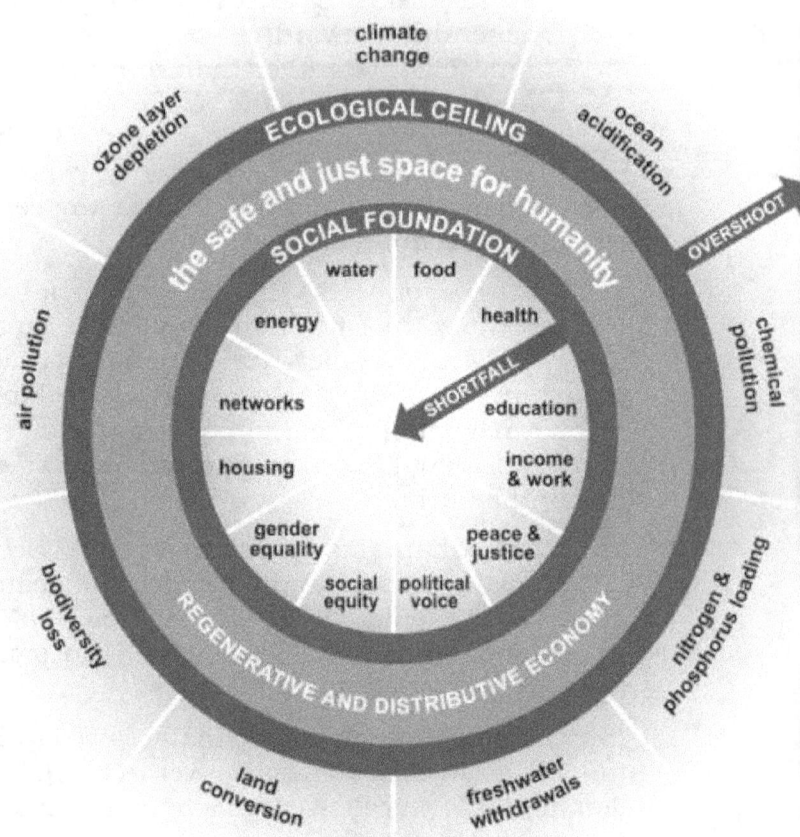

Figure 5: Doughnut Economics

Section 2.Introduction to MoSO

Suggestions for how to use this book

This book is set out in what the authors called

- 'bite',
- 'snack', and
- 'meal'.

That is to say:

- Section 3 (the bite) can easily be swallowed in one gulp, giving a taste of MoSO.
- Section 6 to Section 6 (the snacks) give more detail or flavour to MoSO and take longer to digest.
- Section 7 and following (the meal) give in-depth information about particular subject areas in easy-to-read, stand-alone articles.

This structure was chosen because a detailed understanding of every aspect of MoSO is not required to get started. You can typically get a general understanding and then build knowledge and experience over time and in a sequence unique to you and your organisation's needs. The bite, snack, and meal arrangement allows users to 'dip into' the information as and when required.

A word about Section 9

An essential aspect of MoSO is developing and using powerful self-examing questions to understand an organisation better. Section 9 compiles questions throughout the book into one place for easy access.

Special Note

When reading the various sections of this book, you will notice that the same (or similar) topics are discussed from different perspectives and, in some cases, by different authors who have put forward their understanding or interpretation. We think this is a real strength of MoSO: in most cases, there is no 'right' or 'wrong' way. However, care has been taken (through peer review) to ensure that the information given is not contradictory. In other words, whilst there may be differing viewpoints, there is general agreement that the information given is valid and worthy of consideration in the view of the MoSO Cooperative.

What is MoSO?

This section aims to give a general outline of MoSO, including some background and context.

MoSO is a new way to look at organisations and addresses the needs and aspirations of our time. At its heart is a model, yet it is so much more than that.

MoSO is a holistic or Systems-Thinking approach that shows that all organisations of any type or size exist within a context bounded by the environment, society in which they live and work, culture, and leadership style. These all influence the organisation's operational performance and its effect on the environment.

The Genesis of MoSO

MoSO was started in 2008 by members of the Deming Special Interest group (DemSig) of the Chartered Quality Institute.

The group wanted to make Dr Deming's work more accessible to today's world, explaining why it was so instrumental in transforming Japanese and American industry in the second half of the 20th century. Deming himself was a lifelong learner and would undoubtedly have continued to enhance and update his work. In so doing, the group embraced the work of other significant thinkers on subjects such as organisational development and leadership.

We call this approach "Deming ++".

The group penned the term **"Sustainable Organisation"** as a focus for their work, having decided that societal and environmental concerns were a logical extension of Deming's latter-day thinking.

The Sustainable Organisation

A "Sustainable Organisation" in the language of MoSO meets current needs and aspirations, emphasising more than just the financial aspects. The Sustainable Organisation includes its operations' social and environmental management as a coherent strategy for long-term success.

> *A "Sustainable Organisation" is an organisation of any type or size which strives to build a sustainable long-term future by positively impacting the society and the environment in which it lives and works.*

It should be understood that managing societal and environmental impacts is not purely altruistic (as valuable as that may be) - they are seen as essential elements of organisational learning and, therefore, of long-term success.

The words "*society*" and "*environment*" are used in their broadest sense – the precise meaning should be determined by individual organisations.

Two important thoughts at the heart of a sustainable organisation are *long-term* and *collaboration*.

- *Long-term* (success): When people believe that an organisation has a long-term future, they are more likely to want to contribute their resources (including, among others, skills, enthusiasm and energy, and financial support) and want to play a part in that future.

- ***Collaboration:*** Rarely can anything substantive be achieved in isolation – whether it is as individuals, departments, functions, or even organisations. Some degree of collaboration (toward a common aim) is essential. A sustainable organisation extends collaboration into the society where it lives and works and into the environment. Collaborating with a network of other organisations (private, public and voluntary) allows one to achieve substantive benefits, learning from the experience and bringing new ideas and skills to play in its success.

Why do we need Sustainable Organisations?

There are three compelling reasons.

1. Today's business environment is becoming ever more complex.
2. Existing 'models' focusing on short-term 'financials' and shareholder value at any cost fail to meet society's and individuals' aspirations and needs.
3. We live in an era of harsh economic realities epitomised by "cuts-cuts-cuts" and "do more with less", not to mention big questions about the Big Society and its impact on organisations.

In the face of these compelling reasons, leaders and individuals in organisations that aspire to do more than survive are asking for a better way to build a sustainable long-term future.

MoSO can be a crucial stepping stone in setting out this 'better way'.

Organisational Sustainability - a challenge and a journey, not a prize

Organisational sustainability cannot be 'won', like a prize or a certificate on the wall. It is a journey, a direction of travel.

It is a challenge and a provocation – it is certainly not a prescription. It requires 'joined-up' thinking, engaged people and sustained committed leadership.

What are the benefits of accepting the MoSO challenge?

1. It promotes a fresh and innovative way to lead and manage an organisation.
2. It provides new insights into the way that organisations work.
3. All stakeholders (employees, suppliers, customers, community and the environment) benefit long-term.
4. It stimulates improved motivation by giving everyone a stake in the organisation's future success.

The Model of a Sustainable Organisation (MoSO)

At the heart of the thinking that underpins MoSO and organisational sustainability is a generic model (some use the word framework) that gives a visual image of the essential elements of a sustainable organisation and how they fit together to form a cohesive whole.

However, this is not a 'conventional' or linear input-output process type model. Today's organisations do not work like that – they are more complex and unique. However, MoSO in itself is not complex, but it looks different at first sight.

The generic MoSO is the starting point for organisations to develop their unique model – letting them see the big picture and join the dots. It is the act of mapping strategies and relationships onto your own MoSO that identifies your organisation's path towards sustainability.

MoSO challenges you to ask powerful questions

For example,

- To what extent is our organisation sustainable?
- What would our MoSO look like?
- What strategies do we have in place for each of the elements?
- Do they work together as a whole, focused on a common aim?

- Are there gaps and inconsistencies?

Individuals and organisations should draw their own unique conclusions: MoSO **is not a prescription**. It is not the perfect model.

> *The goal is to encourage people to use it, join in the thinking and contribute.*

Section 3. Understanding The Model And Its Essential Elements

The Model

This section aims to give a flavour of what MoSO is about by understanding the model and its essential components.

Figure 6: MoSO

At the heart of the thinking that underpins MoSO and organisational sustainability is a generic model (or framework) that gives a visual image of the essential elements of a sustainable organisation and how they fit together to form a cohesive whole. The model highlights the importance of relationships between all the elements in any situation.

MoSO is a holistic (or Systems-Thinking) approach that shows that all organisations, of whatever type or size, exist within a context bounded by the environment, the society in which they live and work, their culture and culture and leadership style. These influence the organisation's operational performance and its effect on the environment.

Our working definition:

> *A model is a simplification of reality intended to promote understanding and learning.*

Therefore, the model is neither intended to be prescriptive nor perfect. As George Box said, *all models are wrong, but some are more useful than others - so mind the gap!*

The generic MoSO is intended as the starting point for organisations to develop their own unique model – letting them see the big picture and join the dots. It is the act of mapping strategies and relationships onto your own MoSO that identifies your organisation's path towards sustainability.

MoSO can be used at any level in an organisation:

- overall organisation level
- department/functional entity level
- individual level.

There are two versions of the model

- The BASIC model
- The ENHANCED model is built upon the basic model.

The Essential Elements of the model and your personal journey to sustainability are:

- Your Customers,
- Your Operations,
- Your People, Culture, Leadership and Management,
- Your Societal Influences / Learning,
- Your Environment,
- Your Continual Improvement and Innovation, and
- Your Essential interactions/communication and collaboration.

The Enhanced Model incorporates *The Three Voices*:

- Voice of the Customer,
- Voice of the People,
- Voice of the System.

Building The Basic Model – Element By Element

Customers

Customers are the fundamental element of every business or public sector organisation. They are the reason it exists. Meeting or exceeding the needs and expectations of customers is essential for sustained success and, consequently, for jobs, profits or dividends.

The Customers element is split into two parts rec-

Figure 7: MoSO Customers

ognising that all work, whether commercial or improvement, starts and finishes with the customer. Customers are the only ones to have a vote on quality: it is whatever they think it is.

Expectations inevitably rise over time as 'exciting features' become the norm, and the norm is taken for granted. This expectation increase gives rise to the need to continually improve and innovate, especially in today's dynamic environments.

Customers are a distinct element in MoSO:

- They provide **the** unique focus for the organisation
- They provide alignment for everyone within all organisations.
- They are a unique sub-set of society (one of the other essential elements of MoSO) and, in turn, of the external environment in which businesses or public sector organisations operate.

In recent times, the needs and expectations of other stakeholders have rightly become more fully recognised; however, this should never diminish the customer's pre-eminence.

Operations

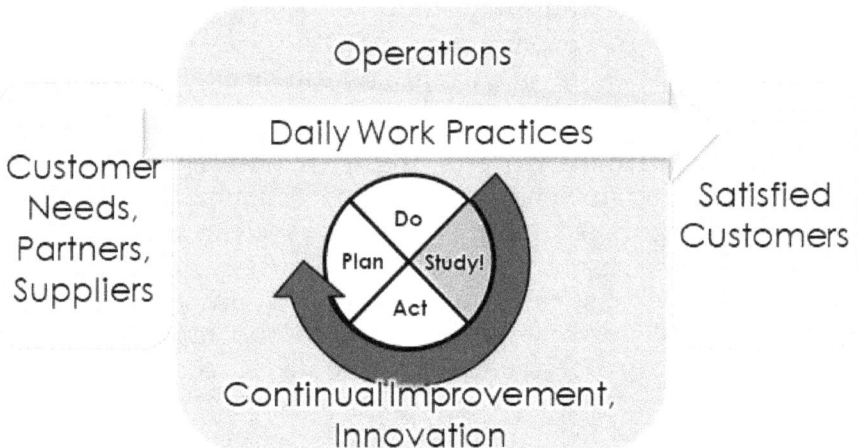

Figure 8: MoSO Operations

Joining the two "Customer" sides, MoSO places 'operations' to describe all work performed by your organisation to provide products and services that satisfy and exceed customer expectations. Every organisation's operations (ways of working) are unique, differentiating them from each other.

Continually evolving customer needs and expectations must be satisfied for any organisation to continue to exist and prosper. Consequently, MoSO has two key features related to *your* operations:

1. Work processes are viewed as an **end-to-end** flow or system, from "customer needs" to "satisfied customers", creating a seamless, rapid flow of work and information throughout the organisation;
2. An embedded method to **systematically** drive continual improvement and innovation, keeping pace with the ever-evolving demands of current and future customers.

Compare this approach to the often inefficient, wasteful, and torturous circuit the work must follow through departmental and functional silos working in isolation, without any clear view of customer expectations and needs. How often do customer issues (whether raised by internal or external customers) fall through the organisational gaps between departments or corporate functions?

In addition, organisations often fail to implement effective and systematic ways to improve and learn from mistakes and customer feedback continually and rapidly.

MoSO shows that operations do not work in a vacuum: people, culture, leadership and management all have a profound, if not fully appreciated, influence on the structure and effectiveness of an organisation. The converse is also true.

In the bigger MoSO picture, societal and environmental influences impact customer needs and expectations concerning the products and services provided and how an organisation is expected to operate.

Continual Improvement And Innovation (PDSA)

A Plan, Do, Study, Act (PDSA) 'learning' cycle is shown at the heart of the model because it is how organisations continuously improve and innovate towards a single aim: customer satisfaction.

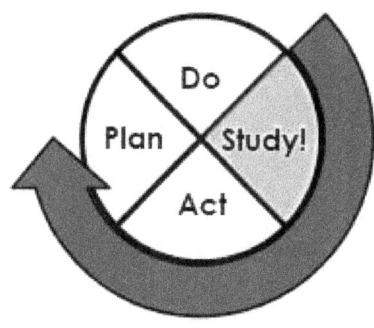

Figure 9: PDSA!

PDSA is a generic cyclical four-stage improvement process based on the scientific methodology that uses feedback to enable systemic changes to be measured and improved over time. Experience has shown that applying a methodical sequence of stages to any problem-solving, experimentation or design activity contributes to achieving the best results.

43

There are many versions and interpretations of what is known as Deming's PDSA cycle. The intent is not to be prescriptive as to which interpretation to use but to show that having a systematic way, or ways, of improving is an essential element of a sustainable organisation.

The PDSA cycle is at the heart of MoSO because the improvement activity applies equally to all activities and elements of the model.

Innovation

Proper engagement with innovation is inescapable for a sustainable organisation, but what is innovation? Innovation is not invention, nor is it just improvement or novelty. Practical innovation creates value, both social and economic. For our purposes, we say that:

- **Improvement** is doing existing things better,
- **Invention** is finding or creating a new thing,
- **Innovation** is doing or using new things to change for the better.

Every organisation today is pressured into increased effectiveness to pursue its aims and do more with less. Without innovation in an organisation, customers and stakeholders can be expected to drift away.

When addressing the role of management's responsibility in securing its organisation's future by pursuing innovation, Deming used to say:

> *Improvement is essential but*
> *relatively unimportant.*

Deming gave Four Prongs of Quality, starting with the most important:

1. Innovation in product and service
2. Innovation in process
3. Improvement of existing product and service
4. Improvement of the existing process.

However, the importance of starting with improvement activities, or at least working on improvement activities in parallel with innovations, cannot be understated. From a customer or market perspective, there can be little appetite for new products and services if existing offerings are (say) unreliable, the organisation is unresponsive, or it cannot get to the root cause of problems. From an organisational standpoint, problem-solving skills associated with implementing effective improvements are an essential platform for launching new products and services.

People, Culture, Leadership And Management

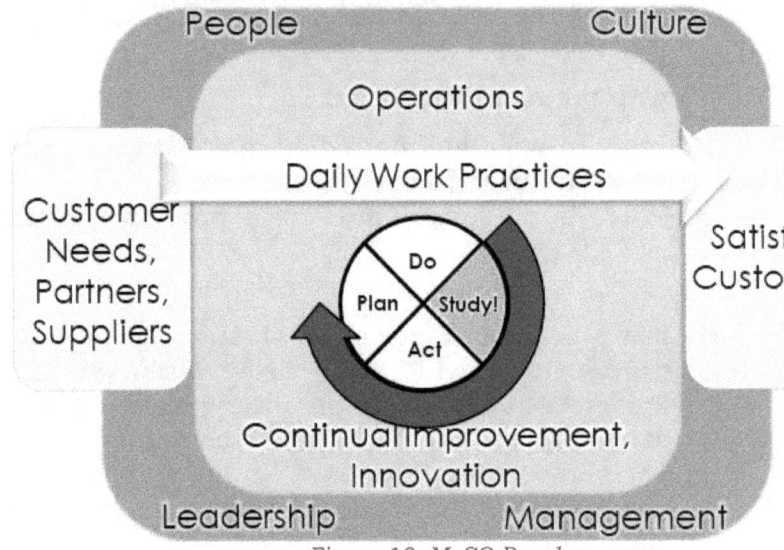

Figure 10: MoSO People

People, culture, leadership and management are influential interacting constituents of any organisation. We have brought them together because of their profound effect on how an organisation works and the results it sets out to achieve.

As you look at the expanded model, visualise all the permeations of interactions that can take place: there are no 'hard' barriers between the elements. Each element can influence the others; each element can influence the system as a whole (as indicated in the model by the absence of boundaries between elements). As the model builds, you will see that societal influences and the environment may impact all the elements shown so far.

46

People

In any organisation:

- The customers for products or services are people;
- People provide the vision;
- People do the work and improve things;
- People need to be engaged: they have needs, as does the organisation.

Understanding what happens in an organisation (and outside it) requires a detailed understanding of how people work together and why they do not.

Culture

"*The way we do things around here*" is a simple description of the culture. We must look below the surface to work with it rather than being frustrated by culture's seeming intransigence.

An organisation's culture has been described as the emergent result of continuing negotiations about values, meanings and proprieties between the members of that organisation and its environment.

Hofstede describes Culture as

> *the collective programming of the mind which distinguishes one human group from another.*

Culture can also be described as

- The way team members act when they are not being observed;
- The common wisdom that allows the group to take correct and appropriate actions

when facing the unknown and the unexpected.

Culture is about paradigms – assumptions of thinking that create advantageous shortcuts in static situations but which need questioning and changing for dynamic environments.

Leadership

Leadership has been described as the capacity to release the collective intelligence and insight of groups and organisations. It involves helping people to find their own answers. There are things that leaders need to know if they are to be credible, but there are moments when they need to say *"I do not know"* if others are to confront complex issues and learn how to overcome them.

Leadership by each individual or as a group is responsible for creating the vision (to see beyond today's difficulties) and the culture (that sustains the organisation for the longer term)[8].

Management

Management is responsible for ensuring efficient implementation of the organisation's daily work and continually improving outcomes to meet and exceed customer expectations. Management, therefore, has the job of ensuring that the organisation gets better at getting better. Of course, this cannot be achieved without a thorough and

---

[8] Living Leadership a practical guide for ordinary heroes, Binney, Wilke & Williams 2005 Prentice Hall

up-to-date understanding of customer expectations[9]).

The top management is responsible for quality. Quality cannot be delegated. Quality improvement increases productivity and reduces waste (financial, human, material and environmental).

The goal of management is to improve quality and reduce costs simultaneously.

Management systems should ensure pride in achievement for everyone and give people joy in their work. When you look after your people, your people look after your customers.

Managers need to develop a correct understanding of data and information in a scientific context. For this, they need to ask what they are learning about the organisation's performance from the measurements they collect[10].

It is essential to have an ongoing commitment to continual improvement and innovation in design, product and process, i.e. having a planned approach to improvement, innovation and learning.

---

[9] The Voice of the Customer is covered in The Enhanced Model, page 22

[10] The wisdom of numbers can be understood through the Voice of the System in the Enhanced Model, page 23.

Societal Influences and Learning

The next element represents the broad society in which an organisation operates and from which it learns.

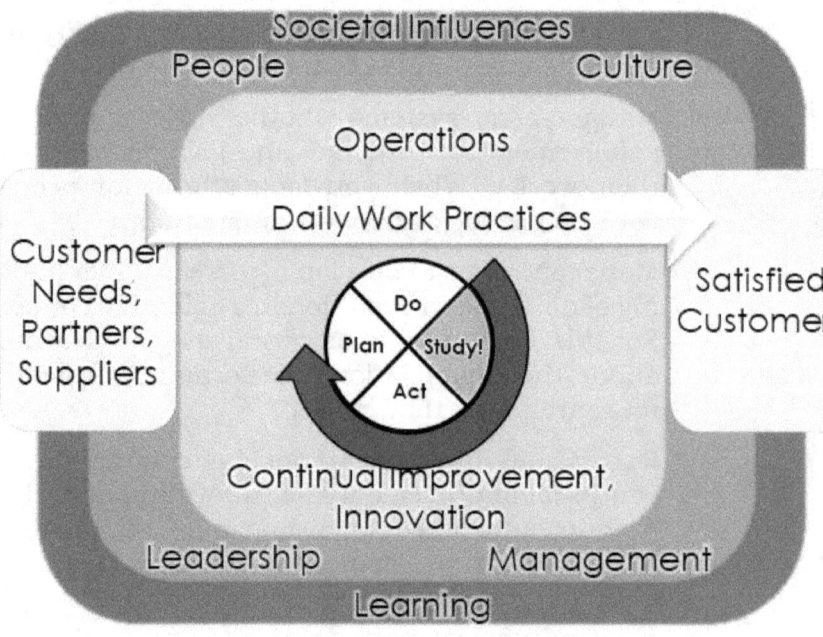

Figure 11: MoSO Society

The precise interpretation of each organisation's 'society' needs to be defined as part of their interpretation of MoSO. However, it should probably include the market sector, societal and business interactions, and corporate social responsibility.

In its totality, this element represents the learning environment in which an organisation lives and works.

50

The broad society in which we live and work has a profound and ever-changing effect on us as consumers and workers. It affects our lifestyles, expectations of the products and services we buy, and the types of opportunities available to us as 'workers'.

This element is intended to highlight some aspects of the influence on the sustainable enterprise influences of the societies in which it exists and question how the enterprise can use or meet these influences to ensure that it is genuinely sustainable.

The Environment

The Environment forms the outermost element and completes the basic MoSO model.

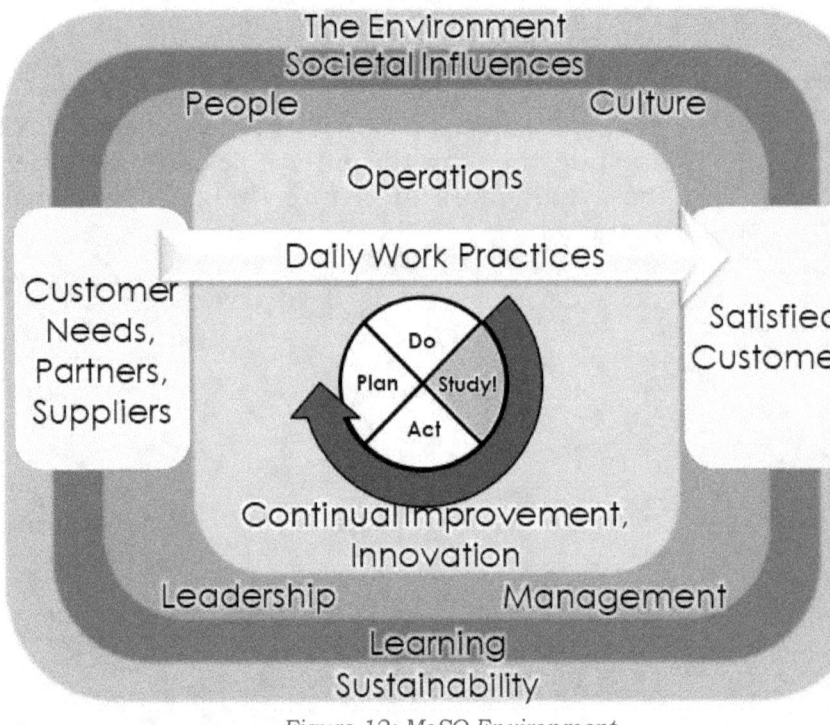

Figure 12: MoSO Environment

The environment bounds us all together. It expresses the need for everyone, and all organisations, to actively play whatever role they can to promote environmental sustainability. The environment sets the agenda for market and consumer requirements regarding product and service offerings and how organisations are expected to operate.

52

> *The environment is everything*
> *that isn't me.*
> *(Albert Einstein)*

Dr Deming pointed out that "any defects within a process contribute to poor environmental performance for a company.

Managing environmental sustainability provides profound insights into an organisation's external and internal environments. Sustainability emphasises system optimisation, stability, logic, and understanding of processes.

Internal and external environments are shaped by the organisation's interaction with its surroundings. Deming stated that he viewed good stewardship as leaving a better world behind for our children than the one we inherited. In his intellectual approach, he subscribed to Einstein's view that "Problems cannot be solved by the same level of thinking that created them": bad stewardship simply transfers costs to future generations.

MoSO is about creating enduring, sustainable, balanced systems that develop in an organic way to eliminate waste naturally. To do this, we must strive to improve everything continually through a holistic understanding of organic systems and a constancy of purpose.

Essential Interactions and Communications And Collaboration

Communication and interactions, whether social or through processes, formal or informal, are the lifeblood that pumps brings life to any organisation – no matter what type or size.

In MoSO, all elements have the potential to influence each other. This openness is symbolised by the absence of lines that separate the elements. For example, thoughts and actions about minimising the effect on the environment permeate the design and operation of daily work processes.

Collaboration

An organisation's aims are best achieved through collaboration – both internally to the organisation and externally to the society and the environment in which it lives and works. Rarely can anything substantive be achieved in isolation – whether as individuals, departments, functions, or even companies. Some degree of collaboration (toward a common aim) is essential.

A sustainable organisation extends collaboration into the society in which it exists and into the environment. For this, it may collaborate with a network of other organisations (private, public and voluntary) to achieve substantive benefits – all the time learning from the experience and bringing new ideas and skills to play in its success.

For a sustainable organisation, collaboration is essential to achieving long-term success – it is part of a coherent long-term strategy.

When looking beyond the organisation, important decisions must be made about

- what should be achieved,
- with whom to collaborate,
- how best to collaborate and
- when to collaborate.

A collaboration strategy aims:

1. To make a positive impact on the society in which the organisation exists – typically in some specific area of interest;
2. To have a positive impact on the future success of the organisation. Examples could include
   a. obtaining additional skills brought about by the collaboration;
   b. having a positive impact on the culture of the organisation;
   c. bringing new ways of doing things into the organisation.

Section 4. The Enhanced Model

Primary Activities

The Enhanced Model adds more understanding of how an organisation operates as a self-sustaining system.

Sustainable organisations can be said to have three Primary Activities:

- Income generation,
- Support and Regulatory activities, and

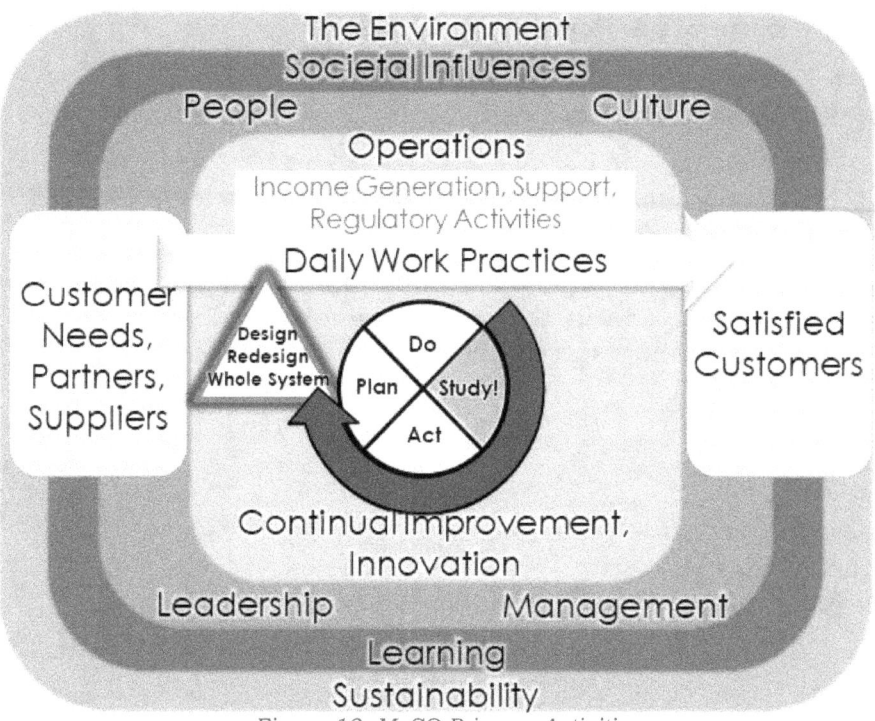

Figure 13: MoSO Primary Activities

- Continual Improvement and Innovation, driven by the Three voices: Customer, People, and System.

This additional level of detail is shown on the MoSO Enhance model.

Income Generation

This group includes what the organisation does to provide products or services for which customers are willing to pay (or that someone funds in the case of not-for-profit organisations).

Support & Regulatory Activities

These activities include all the organisation does to keep itself in existence and legally compliant.

Continual Improvement & Innovation (renewal)

The unyielding and continual improvement effort by everyone in the organisation to understand, meet, and exceed the expectations of their customers.

The Three Voices

The Culture of an organisation (influenced by Societal and Environmental trends and issues) expects and supports its People and Leadership to continually drive innovative improvements using The Three Voices:

- Voice of the Customer (VoC),
- Voice of the People (VoP), and
- Voice of the System (VoS).

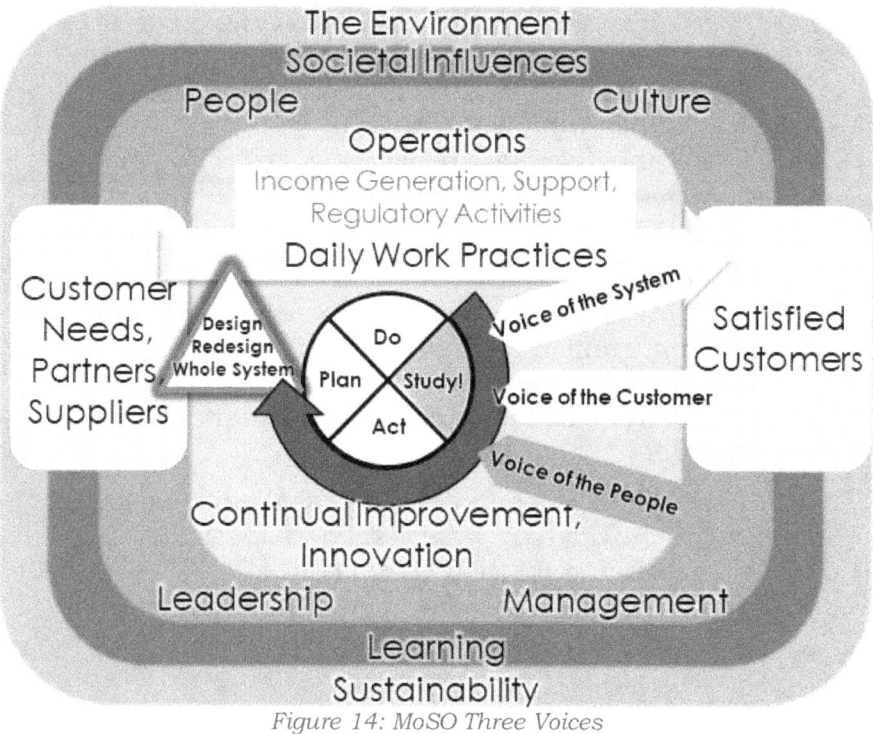

Figure 14: MoSO Three Voices

The voices feed into the Plan Do Study Act (PDSA) learning cycle at the heart of the model and represent the self-renewing and self-sustaining element of MoSO.

The three voices must be requested, heard, listened to and understood systematically for any organisation to continue to prosper.

Voice of the Customer

The expression *"voice of the customer"* (VoC) is typically used in two ways:

1. We refer to VoC as the data that defines or describes customer needs and expectations. These data can be in numbers, language, or both. In other words, VoC defines what is wanted.
2. An organisation may also have VoC processes to systematically capture and analyse VoC data and drive product, service, and process improvements.

The VoC should integrate the feedback from existing customers, but also that of potential and missed customers. Why people do not buy into your work is as important as understanding why they do.

It should be noted that some organisations, such as the providers of public services, have little to no feedback from their consumers.

Voice of the People

The Voice of the People (VoP) is essential in assessing the health and capability of any organisation. Leaders must recognise the differences between what people can and will do. However, too many organisations allow their people to be transient and uncommitted or treat them as 'all the same', simply a collective resource of 'manpower'.

Nevertheless, the contribution of people to organisational performance is vital as it generates aspects of products and services that are often of critical value to customers. People are usually the primary way customers experience an organisation. Failing to listen to the VoP leads to leaders misunderstanding how their staff interact with customers at critical moments of truth.

So you might ask, how well does your organisation:

- Structure an approach to capturing feedback from its people?
- Actively deploy that approach, seeking out and acting upon feedback?
- Capture data and knowledge about its people's morale, attitude and capability?
- Communicate issues, progress, success and learning from failures?

Voice of the System

Voice of the system (VoS) is used to describe the use of a simple process behaviour chart (a form of control chart) to characterise the performance of a process or system over time.

By interpreting the process behaviour chart, it is possible to determine, with a high degree of certainty,

- What level of performance the process or system can achieve;
- What type of action can best be taken to improve performance.

Do not be deceived; VoS is more than a simple yet powerful technique. It is a way of thinking that drives continual performance improvement instead of only taking (often inappropriate, knee-jerk) actions when a target or expectation has not been met: so-called fire-fighting.

It is necessary to use the VoS to provide relevant information on how the operational processes are functioning, and whether changes are required due to internal or external (environmental or social) changes – in short, the VoS is about measurement and relating this measurement to a dynamic environment.

When used effectively, VoS helps to prevent and pre-empt firefighting and other short-term measures through its ability to define system performance, especially in dynamic environments.

VoS is absolutely *not* a measure of the performance of individual people.

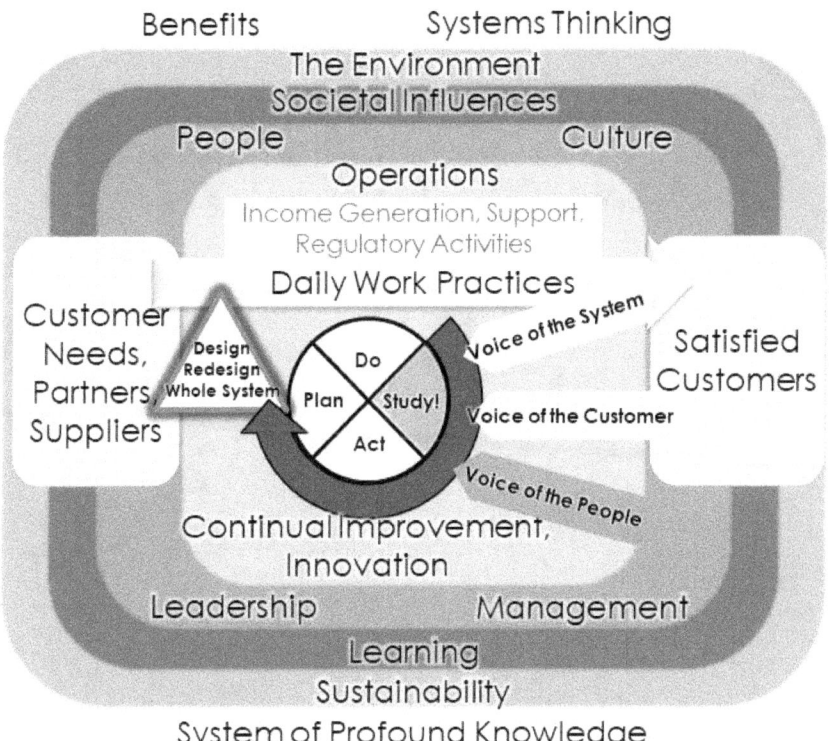

Figure 15: The Enhanced MoSO

Section 5. Fundamental Thinking That Supports MoSO

The 8 Core MoSO Principles

This section explores the background or fundamental thinking that informed the team's work in developing MoSO.

We suggest that a sustainable organisation operates on the following set of eight guiding principles.

> *Principle #1: Customer focus put into practice through quality - an understanding of customer needs and expectations.*

Customer focus is **the** primary principle, for the organisation has no purpose without customers. Quality is what the customer says and provides a constant reference point for every part of the organisation.

> *Principle #2: Systems-Thinking, taking the approach to understand the whole situation in perspective – the woods and the trees.*

The essence of Systems-Thinking is that everything is connected; therefore, it is worth understanding the most critical connections for any given situation.

> *Principle #3: Everyone's daily work is viewed as a seamless flow through the organisation to produce outcomes valued by customers with minimal waste.*

The organisation's daily work is to transform the inputs of customer needs and resources into outcomes valued by customers. Daily work needs to be timely, efficient and productive to minimise waste (human, material and environmental)

> *Principle #4: Wisdom from data (both numbers and language) - guided by actions.*

Knowing when and how to act requires wisdom from data of all types to deal with complexity and balance human nature. These data require measurement and methods to deal with the variation present in messy real-world data.

> *Principle #5: Leadership that is Inspiring, visionary and guides change.*

Leadership must synthesise and communicate a vision of a better future that inspires organisations to respond in a changing world. This long-term philosophy is at the core of any sustainable organisation.

> *Principle #6: An openness to learning that drives continual improvement and innovation.*

Learning, continual improvement and innovation are essential to everyone's daily work to achieve the vision of a better future.

> *Principle #7: Protection of the natural environment.*

The resources of the natural environment are finite and held in trust for future generations. Consideration should also be given to other external environments that are part of the operating context and have been created by global society. Examples are the finance and built environments.

> *Principle #8: Respect for people.*

Organisations consist of people who are part of a global society. Therefore, *Respect for people* is the starting point and guiding light underpinning MoSO. It is both the foundation for growth and the basis on which you need to treat everyone to develop

The intent is that users take these principles and build on them to make them their own – perhaps by using different wording that has a better meaning within the organisation or sector.

Some Benefits Of Sustainable Organisations

Looking at organisations, we see changes happen when obstacles are removed and enablers are implemented. The removal of waste in these organisations and their processes allows them to survive and prosper.

Dr Deming first spelt out this principle for manufacturing processes from the 1950s to the 1980s. Since then, the removal of waste in service operations has been similarly studied; the results show that the benefits of a sustainable organisation reach more widespread areas than is conventionally imagined.

Taking a sustainable approach (such as MoSO) can:

1. Promote a fresh and innovative way to lead and manage an organisation.
2. Provide new insights into the way that organisations work.
3. Allow all stakeholders, employees, suppliers, customers, community and the environment to benefit over the long term.
4. Stimulate improved motivation by giving everyone a stake in the organisation's future success.

Sustainability

Sustainability results from activities that:

- Develop and maintain enterprises that maximise people's capability effectively and efficiently,
- Enhance the planet's ability to maintain and renew the viability of sustained life on earth,
- Enhance society's ability to maintain itself and solve its significant problems,
- Enhance the useful life of organisations by innovation, maximising resources and focusing on all stakeholders, and
- Recycle all aspects of an enterprise's life cycle activities, from design through recycling the product in the field.

The rapidly increasing rate of change in society has led to the demise of more enterprises than ever in human history.

Whether in financial management, banks, automotive or other industries, the rate of decline, job loss and industrial infrastructure loss has accelerated with the current recession.

The rate of technological progress continues to accelerate.

Globalisation has seen the government helpless to prevent the flight of capital and industries.

Outsourcing to low-cost countries is rampant.

The prospects for the future look grim.

Survival of the organisation for all stakeholders is management's number one task. Sustainability has to be the number one item on every CEO's agenda. Dr Deming's track record with companies that have stood the test of time is convincing. His legacy, philosophy, the System of Profound Knowledge (SoPK), and other teachings provide a platform for survival and a bedrock for building a sustainable enterprise.

Transformation

For MoSO, transformation is seen as an existing organisation's journey to always becoming more sustainable. Transformation is the journey of change to an organisation's

- Systems,
- Policies,
- Values, and
- Processes.

In other words, changing anything can help an organisation perform better and be more sustainable.

The gap between where we are today (the current state) and our vision of us as a sustainable organisation (the destination) represents this journey's length and difficulty. While every organisation's journey is different, there are likely to be some generic steps or milestones that can help signpost the way forward.

Experience shows that although the journey includes dead-ends and wrong turns, it is typically an iterative, challenging and hugely enjoyable process. There is great value to be had in the journey itself.

> *There is as much pleasure to be had in the journey as in the destination.*

Systems-Thinking

Systems-Thinking seeks to understand the totality of the situation: what the various active components are and how they interact. This approach enables effective action based on the broadest possible understanding of potential influences while minimising undesirable unintended consequences. It is genuine joined-up thinking guided by a long-term unifying aim.

Systems-Thinking is a holistic approach based on the idea that everything is connected, and outcomes emerge from the multiple interactions of this connectedness. It provides a perspective so that both 'the forest and the trees' can be seen, i.e. the whole situation and the related detail.

Organisations are defined by purpose and boundaries, the latter defining an area of interest. As shown in the MoSO model, the boundaries are porous. Connections and two-way interactions occur within and without the organisation, including individuals, organisations, communities and the environment.

Effective organisational action applies to daily work, continual improvement, innovation and problem-solving. Effective action often means working on, facilitating, and improving the real world of cooperative relationships and associated processes.

Systems-Thinking is fundamental to MoSO: customers, the organisation, its people, management, leadership and culture are related to external society and the environment. A sustainable organisation lasts while minimising its environmental impact by implementing Systems-Thinking at every level. Systems-Thinking, and therefore MoSO, enables people aiming to make their organisation more sustainable to identify the potential connections and interactions to ask better questions in their search to understand the whole situation, leading to more effective decision-making and action.

The Deming Approach

Dr Deming's approach to management in private, public and not-for-profit sectors of society continues to be relevant to today's leaders and managers. It has been central to the thinking that underpins MoSO.

The Deming approach is a wide-ranging, reasoned management system that delivers consistently high performance over the long term. It views an organisation as a complete system focused on meeting the needs of customers and other stakeholders; this means quality is the central value. Improving quality reduces waste and cost and, therefore, improves productivity.

Deming was possibly one of the world's most influential 20th-century figures, as we know it economically and organisationally. His contribution continues long after his death in 1993 through his thinking about management.

System Of Profound Knowledge

Dr Deming's System of Profound Knowledge is the thought processes we use to help us understand:

- The world in which we live,
- The family to which we belong,
- The organisation in which we work,
- The team in which we work.

Fundamentally it is about viewing any organisation from the outside through four lenses which often interact with one another:

1. Appreciation of a system.
2. Knowledge of variation.
3. Theory of knowledge.
4. Psychology.

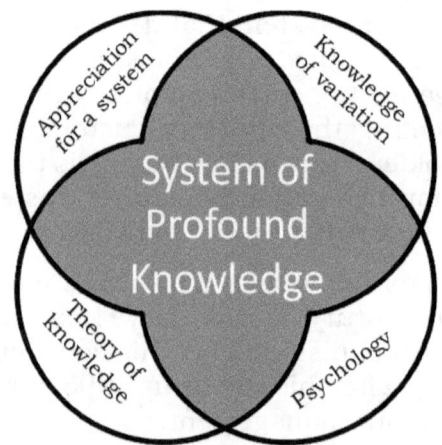

Values

Values (some would include ethics) apply to all aspects of organisational conduct and are relevant to individuals and organisations.

Values remain consistent over the long term, even as markets, strategies and goals change. Values might be thought of as representing that for which the people in the organisation stand.

Values that support MoSO

Several values could be listed by most, if not all, organisations, such as honesty, integrity, trustworthiness and respect. However, our focus here is to ask what specific values support MoSO. Some possible examples are listed below as a basis for discussion. What do you think?

- Respect for people;
- Customers can count on us;
- Openness to learning;
- Transparency;
- Sharing success equally;
- Respect for the environment in which we live and work.

The list can go on; however, it is essential for organisations, particularly their people, to develop their own sustainable values.

Section 6. Using MOSO

Using MoSO in Your Organisation

This section aims to set out an approach to using MoSO. It is not the only way to use MoSO, as seen from the case studies in this section. The intent is to enhance and expand ways of using MoSO based on practical experience.

Now that you understand MoSO, it is time to consider how you might use it in your organisation.

> *Your organisation is unique.*

Recognising and valuing your uniqueness may mean you want to retain and build on it. MoSO can help by providing new perspectives to study your organisation, plus new knowledge and information.

Your Learning Journey

Using MoSO is a learning journey that will almost certainly lead to organisational change or even radical change, referred to as transformation. Change takes time. There will be some quick wins; there will be occasional tough battles; there will be some rare brilliant flashes of insight.

By transformation, we mean a radical change in how individuals and organisations perceive themselves and how they lead, manage and work with each other. The people enable an organisation to become genuinely sustainable, achieving lasting success whilst engaging positively with the society where you live and work and minimising the impact on the natural environment.

Steps to Change

The following steps form a possible outline plan that can be used or adapted to your unique situation.

Step 1. What is your vital need or imperative?

Since everyone's learning journey differs, start anywhere that works for you. One thing is essential: that is some business imperative, a pain or burning platform that makes you say,

> *"We really must do something!"*

It may also be a passion within the organisation to move forward. Otherwise, it rapidly degrades to become something nice to do and never really happens or is not sustained. Be honest: will this carry you through when the going inevitably gets tough?

Step 2. Understand how MoSO looks at organisations differently

Get a clear and shared understanding of both the basic and enhanced models. At this early stage, it is essential to have a good overview of the model, know how the elements fit together, the likely interactions, and the importance of the MoSO principles. Practice using the self-examination questions.

Step 3. Make MoSO your own

Put yourself and your team at the centre of the Model. Ask yourself:

- To what extent does the generic MoSO work for my/our organisation?
- What new questions arise from this different way of looking at your organisation?
- At what level do you want to use MoSO, the whole organisation, your part of it or for yourself?
- While maintaining the MoSO structure, would different words to describe the main elements better represent your organisation and increase understanding?
- How do the elements of your MoSO work together as a continually improving or self-sustaining system?
- What are the areas for improvement?

Step 4. Consider the MoSO principles

Any organisation needs to have some clearly understood principles which inform people's actions and behaviours.

Compare your organisation's principles (which may be unspoken)[11] with those of MoSO; develop a set of principles that fit your current situation and organisational aims. If you cannot achieve a consensus on some, leave them out. However,

---

[11] Ask team members what they believe are the true principles. What stories would they tell a friend or relative who might apply for employment?

you should return to them later to see whether you are ready to adopt them.

Step 5. Identify benefits and gaps

Identify and document the potential benefits of changing how we work, making it consistent with our adopted version of MoSO.

It may help to better understand your current operating system in the context of MoSO by coming down to a level of detail which can be readily understood.

Ask to what extent the operational processes work together as a continually improving end-to-end system.

Overlay current processes onto the MoSO elements and look for areas not currently covered or performing to the expected standard.

Step 6. Decide to take action and make a plan – remember PDSA

Next, you must develop a plan to start working with these ideas and new insights. Here, one of the central ideas behind MoSO is indispensable: PDSA.

Take a methodical approach to learning and building knowledge about your organisation, customers, and the whole situation. Understand your needs, strengths, weaknesses and potential.

Section 7. Case Studies

Introduction to Case Studies

The following case studies have been selected to illustrate the successful application of one or more of the MoSO principles or, conversely, the consequences of not applying them.

We have provided some long case studies and some short ones. The longer studies include a case where a MoSO system was set up within an organisation's culture, with its own values, aims and vocabulary. The short ones are structured with narrative, learning points and resource references if you want to pursue the example further.

> *Examples without theory teach nothing: they invite mindless copying.*

Check the learning points against the MoSO principles and see whether you agree with our analysis or have found different insights.

Using MoSO With A Senior Leadership Team

Sector	Global customer support and medical devices manufacturer
Author	Terry Rose

Introduction

The Senior Leadership Team (SLT) of the Global Customer Services group of a major worldwide Medical Devices company wanted my help to develop a Management Framework to map out a future direction and to help them improve as a management team. A framework based on MoSO seemed to fit the bill perfectly – and so it proved.

Background

Early in 2009, there had been yet another round of organisational changes plus pressure from 'corporate' to implement additional processes and initiatives, including Six Sigma – but the group had been there, done it, got the T-shirt.

The SLT felt uncomfortable. They were doing many good things – but as the Senior VP said, "Not everything we are doing fits together, and we no longer have a map to guide us and set a direction – our True North."

The SLT was looking to develop a Management Framework to help them lift their eyes from the daily work and see the big picture. It would 'join the dots' of their current management processes and, at the same time, identify gaps in their thinking and in their implementation. An off-the-shelf solution did not fit the bill - and there was certainly no interest in certification, plaques on walls and award schemes. The SLT were determined to improve as a leadership team and saw a framework that could evolve with the needs of the business as critical to achieving this.

How MoSO was used

Having introduced the model to the Senior VP and gained his confidence, the next step was to get the buy-in of the rest of the SLT. They were very hands-on, wanting to understand and further develop the principles on which MoSO is based and to make the model their own. This was achieved through facilitation and frank, open discussion in working sessions. The following paragraphs give a brief outline of *their* MoSO.

Operating System	It was decided to embrace all thoughts about the group's Operations into a single aim – **Operational Excellence** –defined as 'predictably and consistently exceeding customer expectations with optimal organisational efficiency'. Operational Excellence (OE) was bounded on the input side by 'Customer Expectations' and 'Loyal Customers' as the

output. This interpretation captured many important principles agreed upon by the SLT.

OE put added emphasis on some existing processes (e.g. a customer loyalty programme) plus highlighting areas of concern that the SLT were determined to tackle, e.g. the need to organise processes as a continually improving end-to-end system without departmental 'silos of self-interest' driven by sub-optimal operational and financial goals.

People, Culture, Leadership, Management	The emphasis here was placed on Leadership, specifically setting strategic direction and how to organise and encourage individuals and teams to take leadership roles within the organisation. Also, 'Talent Management' emerged as a priority.
Societal Influences & Learning	This element was re-defined as *The Market Place & External Influences*. Focus was placed on Service Marketing & Communications, Third Party Performance.

Management and an Online Self-Service project (a response to customer feedback). External Influences included the 'imposition' of potentially unwelcomed corporate initiatives. How best to influence rather than being the victims?

Environ-
ment

Re-defined as *The Environment and Blue Sky* (as in blue sky thinking). Environmental (green) issues were not initially on the SLT's agenda. This began to change as a greater awareness of its influence on market/customer requirements emerged, both in terms of product and service offerings and how organisations are expected to operate. Areas under discussion included: Remote service, Energy consumption of equipment, Installation, disposal and recycling of gas and waste material, and Equipment scrappage policy.

Blue Sky thinking would be required to develop entirely new products and working methods.

What Happened Next?

An interactive presentation was developed, which allowed the SLT to personally cascade the resulting set of values, principles, and the model (shown below) throughout the organisation to

Figure 16: The Environment and Blue Sky

communicate the way forward and capture suggestions for improvement. At the time of writing, this is an ongoing process.

Lessons Learned

From the client's perspective:

1. It was stated in the **Background** that the SLT members were initially uncomfortable (because they no longer felt fully in control). This was explored during one of the facilitated team discussions. The Senior VP expressed that it was important for the

SLT to be 'comfortable with being uncomfortable', to which an immediate retort was, "We also need to be 'uncomfortable with being comfortable'."

2. The methods used to manage 'daily work' differ from those required to handle 'improvement work'. For employees to be fully involved, there needs to be an infrastructure in place to make it happen and to sustain it over time. The SLT decided to explore using the 7 Infrastructures described in the Transformation article (see MoSO Supporting Information).

From the consultant's perspective:

1. MoSO can be confusing at first sight if presented in one go. By design, there are no obvious start- or end-points and no flow. Building the model one element at a time worked in this case – it let the users soak in the significance of each component and begin to relate the model to their situation.

2. When working with a client, your own interpretation of the model is only a starting point. What matters is how the user interprets MoSO. It is like a composer with a piece of music. Once written, there is no way of controlling how others interpret and arrange it.

3. Self-Examining Questions played an essential role in helping the SLT embrace and internalise the model. A few 'starter' questions helped, but it was important for the team to formulate and begin to answer their own open-ended questions.

Conclusion

In this case, a very experienced Senior Leadership Team successfully used MoSO as a starting point to develop a management framework as a roadmap to improving the business. Initially, the term 'MoSO' was not used because the S-word[12] was not part of the SLT's common language. Discussions about the principles which underpin the framework (MoSO Principles) convinced this operations-focused team (notice the importance placed on Operational Excellence) to move from a *show-and-tell* style of management to an *involved* style summed up in the following Confucius (dated to 452 BCE) quotation:

> *Tell me and I will forget,*
> *Show me and I may remember,*
> *Involve me and I will*
> *understand.*

---

[12] Sustainability

Brief Case Studies

1. Ford Motor Company

What Happened

In 2006, the CQI Deming Special Interest Group reviewed the transformation and decline of the Ford Motor Company at the end of the 20th century. This review inspired the MoSO project.

By 1980, Ford Motor Company was turning in a $1.5 billion loss. In 1981 it called in the renowned Dr W Edwards Deming for help. Deming worked directly with Ford CEO Donald E Peterson facilitating a turnaround in the company's fortunes that saw it delivering a $5.4 billion profit before the decade's end.

Management took time to develop its 'Mission Statement', but by the early/mid-1990s, Ford was back in a loss-making situation, having moved away from the principles that had transformed it. These principles (which align with MoSO) were behind the transformation.

Ford went back to basics, reducing the emphasis on financial-led management.

Learning Points

- The consultant (Deming) worked with the CEO, who led the transformation;
- The company developed a clear set of principles, which included:
    - o Quality is job one,
    - o Employee involvement.

- SPC, including the appointment of Dr Bill Scherkenbach as Director of Quality;
- When they stopped doing it, poor results followed:
  - o Return to finance-led management/growth,
  - o Succession planning/failed to embed the principles after Peterson left.

Resources:

- W E Deming, The New Economics, 1994
- W E Deming, Out of the Crisis, 1986
- W W Scherkenbach, The Deming Route to Quality and Productivity, 1986
- W W Scherkenbach, Deming's Road to Continual Improvement, 1991
- www.scherkenbach.com

2. Toyota Motor Corporation

What happened

Toyota Motor Corporation has long been held up as a pioneer and world leader in manufacturing excellence, quality and financial performance. It had grown to become the largest vehicle manufacturer in the world.

Its principles and methods have been studied, and many have attempted to emulate it by applying so-called "lean thinking and manufacturing".

The Principles

However, towards the end of the first decade of the 21st century, problems began to appear. In 2006, product quality and safety problems began surfacing. By the decade's end, it had turned in two successive annual losses, the first for sixty years.

Learning points

Finance and growth-led goals do not work.

Resources

- H T Johnson & A Broms, Profit Beyond Measure, 2000
- J K Liker, The Toyota Way, 2004

3. Department 13

What Happened

Don Wheeler has been a consultant for many years, applying statistical methods to many different types of organisations to promote innovation and improvement. This is an example from his practice.

An organisation that made articles through a succession of manufacturing processes sought to set up an improvement culture by encouraging each department to initiate and carry out improvement projects and ideas.

- Each department made a monthly report of management data used by the organisation at its top level.
- Key performance indicators were production volume, material costs, person-hours, energy and fixed costs and total production.
- The organisation sponsored a company-wide improvement programme based on its departments.

Department 13 concentrated on material costs, initially comprising three-quarters of its costs. Department 13 made four changes to material selection and handling in three years. This resulted in lower material costs. The other indicators were up and down; some months were better than others.

Detailed examination of material costs on process behaviour charts showed reductions after each project initiative. So much so that Department

13 was awarded the company's improvement prize in one year!

However, the success of Department 13 came at a price. Their output is fed into the following department, Department 14, for further processing. From the start of the improvements in Department 13, Department 14 experienced progressively higher levels of difficulty, and scrap, in using their precursor's output. In fact, during the improvement project initiative, Department 13 caused more significant losses throughout the company than its own local gains. They provided an example of sub-optimization.

Learning Points

- Looking at data is good, but focus on the useful data
- Sub-optimization occurred because local departments used the KPIs appropriate to the organisation as a whole but not its constituent departments.
- It is dangerous to run a company on visible figures alone.

Resources:

1. DJ Wheeler, Understanding Variation – The key to managing chaos, 1993
2. DJ Wheeler, Twenty things you need to know, 2008
3. www.spcpress.com

4. Interface Carpets

What Happened

In 1994 Ray C Anderson, Founder, Chairman and CEO of Interface Carpets, realized how environmentally unsustainable his successful business was: all his products were destined for the incinerator or landfill.

In other words, they were to be waste.

From 1994 to 1998, Interface made many changes in its structure to develop and realize new sustainable thinking.

One of the elements was the adoption of The Natural Step framework: a systematic approach to business, which has four system conditions:

- There should not be systematically increasing concentrations in nature of substances extracted from the Earth's crust;
- There should not be systematically increasing concentrations of substances produced by society;
- There should not be systematically increasing degradation of nature by physical means;
- Development should not be made at the expense of human needs worldwide.

Interface has worked in areas that it calls its Seven Fronts

1. Elimination of waste
2. Benign emissions
3. Renewable energy
4. Closure of the loop (i.e. cyclical flows)

5. Resource efficient transportation
6. Sensitivity hookup (i.e. work with the supply chain etc.)
7. Redesign of commerce (i.e. the delivery of service, not just product).

At the time of writing, Interface is still a successful company and a leader in sustainable business. Its activities are reported on the Interface website, as are its detailed past and present performance.

Learning points

- It is possible to show leadership in environmental, financial and social sustainability together
- A logical framework for a multifaceted change in a business is essential; it must recognize the systemic nature of the business and its environments
- Active leadership is necessary to get change throughout a company. Innovation must be encouraged, or people will quickly revert to old practices
- An organisation's people are essential to its development of sustainable conduct.

Resources

1. www.interfaceglobal.com
2. B Nattrass & M Altomare, *The Natural Step for Business*, 1999

5. People Management In Healthcare

What Happened

The job of a medical records supervisor, whom we shall A included ordering stationery. The use of necessary forms had to continue if the organisation was to function continuously, even in the absence of administrative staff.

A's line manager (whom we shall call B) discovered that on one occasion, when they were absent from the site, A had written B's signature in the approval box of an order for a set of forms. B did not see this as keeping essential supplies available but as a breach of trust.

The personnel department advised B to conduct an investigatory hearing. At this and another hearing, A admitted to having written B's name, in their absence, on order sets on more than ten other occasions; this was to keep the flow of forms and other items maintained. More hearings followed into what was becoming regarded as fraudulent behaviour, although no motives of personal gain seemed apparent. If anything, A had a reputation among colleagues for doing extra work to keep the department running smoothly; they were reported to have received a written warning for not keeping to contractual hours by starting work at 6.00 am rather than the formal 8.30 am.

B's manager considered that because it had taken so long for the facts to emerge, A had shown some serious misconduct.

A few months later, A was ordered to attend another hearing in a letter which raised the possibility of dismissal.

A did not attend the hearing, having committed suicide in the grounds of the facility on the day appointed.

At the subsequent enquiry, it emerged that the organisation would have accepted A's own signature or a 'pp' with the line manager's name on the order form. The organisation did not have a written procedure covering the ordering of stationery when the line manager was away. The organisation had not taken legal advice on whether the supervisor's actions were fraudulent.

Learning Points

- Conscientious people should not be wasted.
- The opportunity to build a team that could cover absences and unforeseen circumstances was not realized.
- Parts of the organisation had lost sight of its aim, namely, the welfare of patients.

Resources

1. PR Scholtes, The Team Handbook, 1997
2. PR Scholtes, The Leaders Handbook, 1997

6. Herald Of Free Enterprise

What Happened

The *MV Herald of Free Enterprise* cross-Channel car ferry left the port of Zeebrugge on 6 March 1987. On a calm day, it heeled over and sank, killing 186 people. The vessel was a roll-on roll-off ferry and had been sailing with its bow doors open. In a slight swell, it started to take on water. With the ship's rolling, it took in water faster and sank within four minutes.

The vessel had been designed for the Dover-Calais run, but the Zeebrugge docks were different. The ship had to increase its forward ballast to lower its front so the pier and main vehicle deck were in line. There was an absence of bulkheads so that the loading and unloading of vehicles could be hastened. There was easy access for passengers to get up from the vehicle decks to the (profitable) refreshment facilities.

Previous vessels had visor doors, and it was evident from the bridge whether they were open, i.e. up or not. The new design of clamshell doors, vertically mounted, meant they were invisible from the bridge.

In addition, the vessel had to be backed away from the Zeebrugge dock before the door closure could start. There had been previous occasions when other ferries in the fleet had got underway without the doors being closed. Requests from captains for an indicator light to be installed on the bridge were refused on three occasions.

The assistant bosun was responsible for closing the doors. His trigger to act was an announcement over the ship's loudspeaker system. After closure, he did not have to report that the doors were shut. He was asleep in his cabin on this occasion and did not hear the departure announcement.

The ship's bosun took a literal view of his duties, which did not include supervising the assistant bosun's duties.

The officer loading the main vehicle deck was supposed to ensure the doors were 'secure when leaving port'. This was generally ignored. Here the officer believed he saw the assistant bosun moving forward to close the doors (this is now thought to have been a lorry driver in overalls returning to his vehicle). The officers and crew worked different shifts and did not know each other.

Learning points
- The management did not understand their business (the maritime transport of people and not the floating cafe business).
- The daily work of the organisation paid insufficient attention to safety.
- Written instructions were unclear and contradictory.
- There was a lack of leadership; responsibilities for safety at the Board level were unclear.
- Advice from men on the job was ignored.

Resources

- T Kletz, Learning from Accident.

Section 8. Supporting Articles

This section aims to give more in-depth information about the fundamental thinking that underpins MoSO; this is achieved through a series of easy-to-read, stand-alone articles written by various authors. Due to the variety of authors, you will find these articles written in different styles and with varying grammatical styles.

The information given is, by its very nature, the author's interpretation or understanding of complex subject areas. A system of peer reviews was used to ensure a good degree of cohesion in thinking and about the various subjects. In many cases, peer reviews added to individual and group understanding.

Whilst a good deal of leeway was given to authors as to how each article was written, in general, and where appropriate, a Bite, Snack, Meal structure has been used (see page 25 "Suggestions for how to use this book"):

Bite	Introduction or Overview.
Snack	Main Content – split into appropriate headings or sections.
Meal	References to further reading / recommended books for those who wish to get a deeper understanding or perhaps a different perspective of the subject area.
Self-examining Questions	Some 'powerful' questions individuals and organisations may ask themselves to better understand either 'Your MoSO' or your unique journey

towards being a sustainable organisation.

List Of Articles

MoSO Principles

Author   Terry Peterson

Reviewers   Alan Clark, Terry Rose, Tony Brown, Malcolm Gall

How Do You Ensure The Organisation Is Sustainable?

By supporting the people in their daily work and managing change in a way that ensures the organisation continues to provide a valuable and sustainable service and has a valuable and sustainable place in the world.

This provides a means to understand the sustainable organisation as a system, an organisation in a context that makes what it does meaningful.

This is core, consisting of eight principles which underpin MoSO.

Eight Core MoSO Principles

1. Customer Focus

Customer focus put into practice through quality - an understanding of customer needs and expectations.

Customer focus is **the** primary principle, for the organisation has no purpose without customers.

Quality is what the customer says it is and provides a constant, ever-changing reference point for the whole organisation.

Taking care of customers will serve the organisation's financial goals, but the reverse is untrue. If you look after your customers, your customers will look after your profits.

2. Systems-Thinking

Systems-Thinking means taking the approach to understanding the whole situation in perspective – the woods and the trees.

The essence of Systems-Thinking is that everything is connected; therefore, it is worth understanding the most critical connections for any given situation.

3. Seamless Daily Work

Everyone's daily work is viewed as a seamless flow through the organisation to produce outcomes valued by customers with minimal waste.

The organisation's daily work is to transform the inputs of customer needs and resources into outcomes valued by customers. Daily work needs to be timely, efficient and productive to minimise cost waste (human, material and environmental) and, therefore, costs.

An organisation is a network of interdependent components (processes) that work together to achieve the system's aim. Without that aim, there is no system. Cooperation, not competition, is required between the parts of the system.

Managers must understand, take responsibility for, and ensure the implementation of the organisation's work. Quality is determined by top management. It cannot be delegated.

4. Wisdom from Data

Wisdom from data includes both numbers and language and is guided by actions.

Knowing when and how to act requires wisdom from data of all types to deal with complexity and balance human nature; this includes the measurement and methods to deal with the variation in messy real-world data.

Everyone, especially managers, needs to develop a correct understanding of data / information in a scientific context to understand what the things they measure tell them about how they are performing against their purpose.

5. Leadership

Leadership that is Inspiring, visionary and guides change.

Leadership must synthesize and communicate a vision of a better future that inspires organisations to respond in a changing world. This long-term philosophy is at the core of a sustainable organisation.

6. An Openness to Learning

An openness to learning that drives continual improvement and innovation.

Learning, continual improvement and innovation are essential to everyone's daily work to achieve the vision of a better future.

7. Protection of the natural environment.

The resources of the natural environment are finite and held in trust for future generations. Consideration should also be given to other external environments that are part of the operating context and have been created by global society. Examples are the finance and built environments.

8. Respect for people.

Organisations consist of people who are part of a global society. Respect for people is, therefore, the value that underpins MoSO.

Leaders and managers must develop a system of management that will ensure pride in achievement for everyone. Give people joy in work. If you look after your people, your people will look after your customers.

The intent is that users take these core principles and build on them to make them their own – perhaps by using different wording that has a better meaning within the organisation or sector.

Organisational Purpose

The Organisational Purpose is best defined from a customer's point of view. Your purpose is related to the benefits and capabilities your customers acquire due to their interaction with you. A purpose based on customer capability can provide a beacon of stable focus and direction during turbulent technological or market changes.

Profits or return on investments are a necessary means to an end. When they become an end in themselves, however, a business is likely to begin hurting its customers, its employees, the quality of its goods and services, the community, the environment, and its own long-term survival.

When a business is committed to serving customers and society, such a purpose can create and sustain excitement and commitment among leaders, managers, employees, stockholders, and — most importantly — customers. The purpose of the organisation must describe "work worth doing." Such a business, if it is well-led, is also likely to prosper.

Collins and Porras studied the characteristics of the world's most enduring and successful organisations. They did not find that maximising shareholder wealth or profit maximisation were dominant forces or primary objectives throughout the history of visionary companies. This focus did not mean that the successful organisations did not pursue profits but that they also pursued more meaningful ideals. For them, profitability is necessary for existence and the means to more important ends, but not the end itself.

The Voice Of The Customer

In sustainable organisations, strategy is aligned with their values and their core purpose, and they achieve consistent execution in the way they carry out their business to ensure they meet their strategic goals.

They design their structures and procedures to meet customer requirements efficiently. Management, marketing, sales, customer service, R&D, production, shipping, training, purchasing, and the customer all become part of the same smooth continuous system, ensuring that customers get the value they are looking for in every transaction.

The "customer-in" mentality is outward-focused and is characterised by customer focus and responsiveness. If you understand the day-to-day experiences of your customers, you can imagine products and services that they might not even think of. Customer-in thinking increases the likelihood that customers get what they need and need what they get.

In a customer-in organisation, marketing becomes focused on actual customer research: research not just on sales strategies but also on customers and their needs and experiences.

Daily Work

Managers must understand, take responsibility for, and ensure the implementation of the organisation's work. In other words, they must take responsibility for maintaining and improving how work is done daily.

Poor quality results from management failing to carry out this responsibility, not poor workmanship or laziness. **Quality is determined by top management**. It cannot be delegated. All activities that relate directly to making a product or providing a service should be the key focus of management attention. They must "make the work work".

Management exists to provide the necessary support to the daily work. Therefore, management must maintain close contact with the realities of work to solve whatever problems arise there. To put it differently, whatever assistance management provides should start from the specific needs of the worksite.

Management is responsible for the system. This concept is the basis of providing quality to the customer.

> *Make the work work.*

Improved Quality Reduces Waste

Focusing on Quality translates into making improved products and providing better services. The result is a chain reaction — lower costs, better competitive position, happier people on the job, jobs, and more jobs. This is a management responsibility.

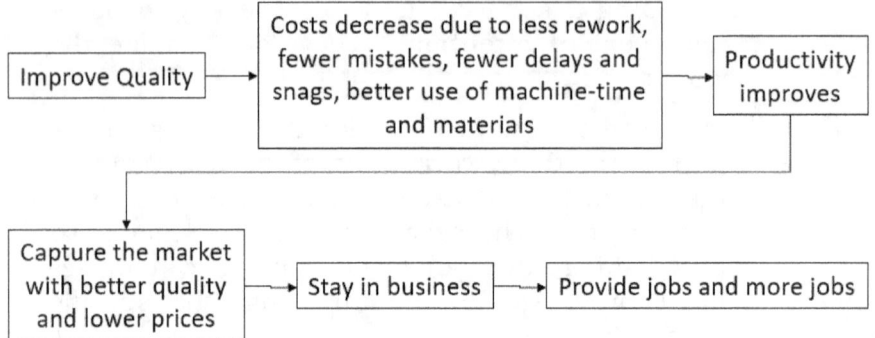

Figure 17 Quality Chain

Figure 17 is a diagram of this chain reaction that was on the board of every meeting Deming had with top management in Japan from July 1950 onward.

Improving quality and reducing cost are compatible objectives. Quality is the foundation upon which both cost and delivery can be built. Without a firm system to assure quality, there can be no hope of building effective cost management and delivery systems.

Not only is it possible to improve quality and reduce cost simultaneously, but we must do both to meet today's customer requirements.

Wisdom From Numbers

Managers need to develop a correct understanding of data and information in a scientific context.

Managers need to understand what the things that they measure tell them about how they are performing against their purpose. We must have an operational definition of the context in which data and information were obtained.

What reliance can we put on the data? All data varies; we need to know what this **variation** tells us about the system; by distinguishing between common and special causes of variation.

We need an **operational definition** of the context in which data and information were obtained, including how they were obtained, to what accuracy and using which standards. What reliance can we put on the data?

Measurement is a critical component of any system. It is essential to collect the right data about how the system achieves its customer-focused goals.

Managers need to understand what the things that they measure tell them about how they are performing against their purpose. Data collection requires careful thought and planning. Once gathered, there are ways to present it in a way that makes it easier to use well to support the achievement of the organisation's purpose.

All data varies; we need to know what this **variation** tells us about the system; by distinguishing between common and special causes of variation.

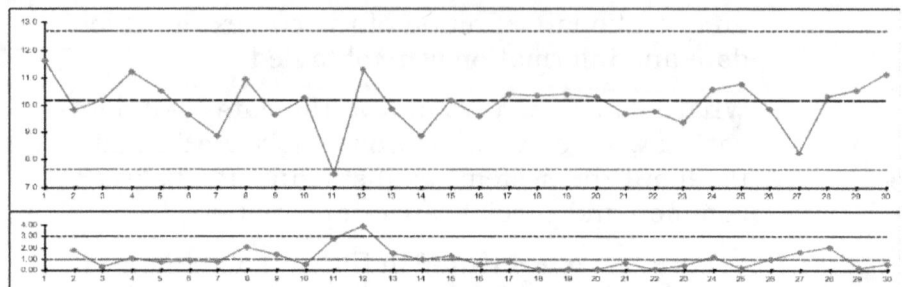

Figure 18. A Process Behaviour Chart

This understanding can help managers and staff reduce variation, improve the stability and predictability of their processes and, thereby, improve quality. Knowing a process is stable enables managers to assess systematically the effects of changes.

Not all data contain information that leads to change and improvement. Many elements of the organisation cannot be defined in strictly numerical terms — for example, customer loyalty or the benefits of training may be difficult to quantify — yet they can still be managed *and* improved.

We can use this to predict their processes' stability and improve the system's efficiency and quality by reducing variation.

We need to understand the dangers of tampering with the system without appropriate knowledge of its stability.

We need to understand the wisdom of numbers.

Continual Improvement And Innovation

There should be a **planned approach** to improvement, innovation and learning. Customers and competition impose constant pressures to change. There needs to be a culture of learning that accepts change, fosters the exploitation of new ideas from all sources and encourages a strong team approach to managing change.

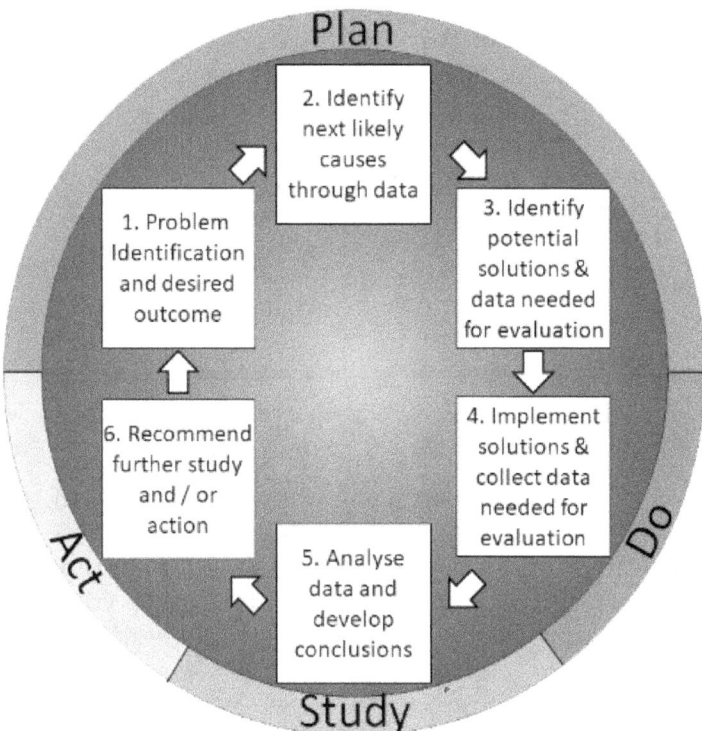

Figure 19: Plan, Do, Study, Act

Managers understand that customers and competition impose constant pressures to change.

121

They are committed to ongoing improvements to all business processes, systems and procedures; they have adopted a planned approach to continual improvement and learning - involving teamwork and well-tried process improvement methods.

Improvement and learning are directed not only toward better products and services but also toward being more responsive, adaptive, and efficient — giving the company additional marketplace and performance advantages. There is a focus on how learning in one process or company unit is replicated and added to the knowledge base of other projects or company units. Methods are in place that encourages all staff to make creative and innovative suggestions for improvement.

People

Develop a system of management that will ensure pride in achievement for everyone.

In an efficient workplace, people accept control of their processes, are **intrinsically motivated** to do their best and get true satisfaction from their contribution. Give people **joy** in work. If you look after your people, your people will look after your customers. If managers adopt Deming's way, they will understand that they need the workers - not just as arms and legs to do what they are bid, but as intelligent human beings who can provide insights into how to improve the output and efficiency of the place.

Sustainable organisations define their purpose in a way that inspires whole-hearted commitment by all who are valuable to the company's success; in particular, they support employees in their efforts to satisfy customers. If an organisation wants to keep its customers, it needs committed staff. Staff are crucial to customer satisfaction; they are the organisations' primary point of contact with the outside world. Innovative companies invest in workforce development through education, training, and opportunities for continuing growth. Training and development of all staff should be integrated with business development.

It is now commonplace that *People are our most important asset,* and it has been suggested that, in many organisations, this is honoured more in the breach. Managers understand the system's effect on people's behaviour and performance. They recognise that intrinsic motivation is the only sort worth having and create situations that allow staff to realise true satisfaction from their contribution. They understand that they need the workers - not just as arms and legs to do what they are bid, but as intelligent human beings who can provide insights into how to improve the output and efficiency of the place.

These organisations inspire whole-hearted commitment; their systems support employees in their efforts to satisfy customers. They invest in workforce's development through education, training, and opportunities for continuing growth. Training and development of all staff are integrated and aligned with the development of the business.

A small example might be in order. You are look-ing at some management data showing unex-pected or undesirable behaviour; it is possibly in-consistent. Invoking the Compound Lens, you would wonder what system generated these data. At this point, your mind would speculate upon the behaviour and motivations of the people who asked for the data, the people who collected the data and the people whose work is represented in the data. Finally, you would be trying to sur-face/recognise your assumptions and theories as to what is causing the phenomenon character-ised by the data.

You might very well be doing this with frontline people or listening to the frontline people them-selves go through this analysis. The focus would be on the work and the impact on the customer.

This approach radically differs from traditional destructive management behaviours, including "shooting from the hip" and "endless politically charged management meetings".

Leadership

Organizations are human achievements based on cooperation.

The job of a leader is to accomplish the transfor-mation of the organisation:

- Understanding what change is needed and
- how it will affect the organisation and the people involved.
- By leading the transformation and
- having a step-by-step plan.

For our purposes, **transformation** is seen as a journey that an existing organisation may take to become ever more sustainable. The 'gap' between "Where we are today" and "Our vision of us as a sustainable organisation" (the destination) represents the length of the journey and its degree of difficulty.

Regardless of type or size, organisations need a strategy and structure for introducing and managing change initiatives. Strategies typically have three integral parts:

1.   **Leader as driving force for change:** this involves high visibility involvement - hands-on participation; making decisions; evaluating the change process and results; leading from the front - not delegating to 'experts' but becoming the expert.

2.   **Strategies for introduction:** chosen to suit the style and culture of the organisation. Many different models are available, but typically phases include:

- **Initiating:** Goal setting; telling people what is coming and why; initial training;
- **Empowering or Mobilising:** Giving people the ability to act – setting to work; further training as required (e.g. action learning); organising teams;
- **Aligning:** Ensuring all the work is aligned to the required results.

3.   **Organisational infrastructure:** put in place to manage (govern) the transformation and beyond; this typically includes the management

team structure, teams to organise training programs, promotion of success stories, etc.

Organizational Capabilities / System Thinking

The first step in the transformation is to define a clear purpose for the organisation.

A purpose is essential as it defines the system. Once explicit, building consensus around it and a vision of the organisation's direction and character is possible. Organisations that have sustained profitable businesses over a long period generally have a well-defined core purpose. The organisation's aim is typically outside-in, reflecting a deep understanding of the value customers look for in every transaction with the organisation.

In a sustainable organisation, the strategy is aligned with values and core purpose. And actions are aligned with all three. Structures and procedures are designed to align efforts to deliver customer requirements; this helps the customers realise the value they look for in every transaction.

This purposeful alignment of the system elements inspires whole-hearted commitment by those critical to the company's success, balancing the needs of owners, employees, customers, community and other stakeholders.

Viewing the organisation as **a system** allows the creation of a network of sub-groups, departments, activities, processes, procedures, sub-

126

processes and components *and* the connections between them *that work together* to meet the **aim** or **purpose** of the organisation.

Any organisation — a department, a division, a multinational — is a complete system in which every part is dependent on and affected by every other part. Thus the performance of any part of an organisation is best judged in terms of its contribution to the aim of the total system. Optimisation of one component in isolation can cause sub-optimisation of the whole — and everyone loses in the long term.

> *Cooperation (not competition) is required between the parts of the system.*

Benefits Of MoSO – A Chain Reaction

Author	Malcolm Gall
Reviewers	Terry Rose, Alan Clark

Executive Summary

If you look at organisations, you can see that changes happen when obstacles are removed, and enablers are put in place. The removal of waste in these organisations or their processes allows them to survive and prosper.

This concept was first spelt out for manufacturing processes from the 1950s through to the 1980s by Deming. Since then, waste removal in service operations has been similarly studied. This section examines how the benefits of a sustainable organisation can reach more widespread areas than is conventionally imagined.

A Chain Reaction Of Benefits For Manufacturing Organizations

There used to be a pearl of received wisdom that Quality and Productivity existed in a trade-off relationship. If you want high quality, you cannot have high output rates. You had to manufacture more slowly and inspect the output more thoroughly. Any dubious material had to be reworked. It was obvious this added to costs. So, higher quality goods had to be more expensive.

Those who could bring their production into 'statistical control' were the first to invalidate this view. In practical terms, this meant the measures of the output showed no signals on process behaviour charts. In conventional terms, this meant less scrap and less rework. It also resulted in fewer failures in the customers' hands, so claims and complaints were reduced. This enhanced reputation enabled the producer to keep business in bad times and to grow the business in good times.

Deming summed this up in his "Chain Reaction". A simplified version is given in figure Figure 20.

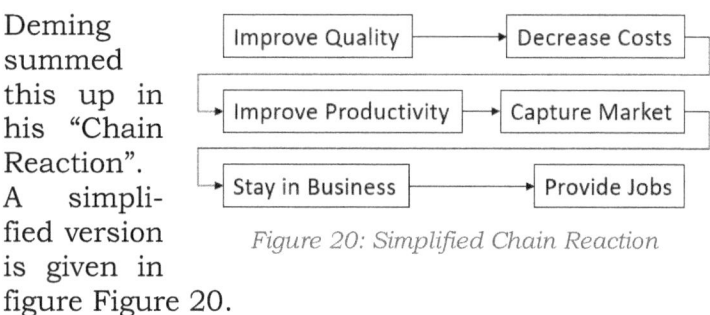

Figure 20: Simplified Chain Reaction

Some companies took changes further by actively seeking changes that reduced waste and increased efficiency. The next generation of process and product improvement was achieved by considering customer needs. If part of the process did not produce value for the customer, then its presence was questioned, and it was removed or minimised. Herein lies the start of 'Lean' production.

Deming's full chain reaction (see Figure 17, page

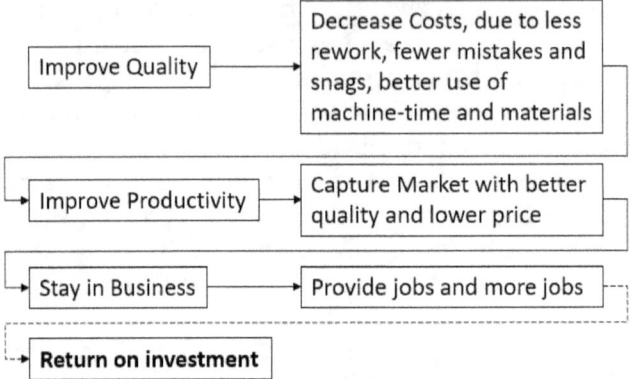

Figure 21: Extended Quality Chain

118), with a final box added by Brian Joiner, is shown in Figure 21.

Providing meaningful jobs aids social cohesion while lacking jobs promotes social breakdown. If an organisation's time is less taken up with corrective actions and repair, then it has time to innovate.

This is a chain. It is essential to start at the beginning. Not starting with Quality Improvement means the organisation will not sustainably deliver a Return on Investment. Starting by Cutting Costs will seldom bear continuing benefits because complexity and waste are not systematically removed and will reappear in the future.

Advantages to People in the organisation.

Taking the broader view, people in an improving organisation can acquire new skills, not least learning how to learn. This ability generates confidence and self-regard. They are more widely employable if the economic climate turns very bleak. Finally, while not loudly acknowledged, all this contributes to management's education.

Advantages to Society.

At the very least, a surviving organisation pays taxes to its community. The members of the organisation participate, at the very least financially, in their community. The organisation can support the community in many ways, such as sponsorship of culture or learning.

Advantages to the Environment.

The physical environment needs nurture, not waste. Not all forms of environmental damage carry clearly associated costs, though some, such as toxic discharge cleanup or fuel costs, do.

Sustainable Development can only be pursued by organisations that can understand its requirements. To do so, these organisations have to find the resources (time, facilities and people). They can achieve this when they start upon the chain reaction to become sustainable in all senses, namely economic, social and environmental.

Thus the Chain Reaction provides an Organisation and its Customer with a **WIN-WIN** situation.

However it can go further; it provides the Organisation, its Customer, its People, its Society and its Environment with advantages. It creates a **WIN-WIN-WIN** situation.

A Chain Reaction Of Benefits For Service Organizations

With a service operation, an even more significant number of challenges can be present than in manufacturing cases.

More stakeholders can be involved. Those impacted can provide feedback at different times and in different ways. Complexity can be easily generated. Often no one has the authority to remove complexity. These additional complexities can lead to chaos and a focus on different parts of the operation by people with different aims, leading to sub-optimisation within the organisation.

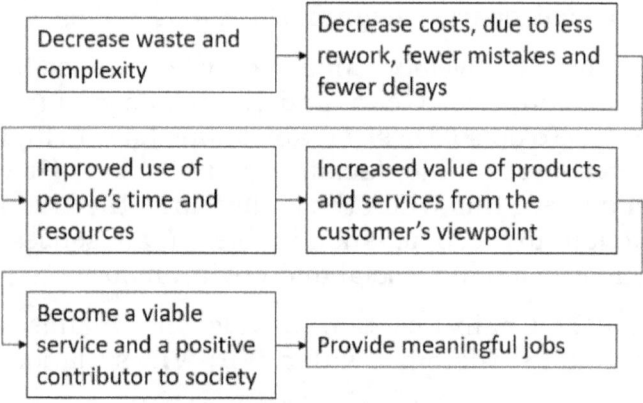

Figure 22: Service Quality Chain

Clarity of Purpose and Constancy of Purpose are essential if progress is to be made with identifying and taking the first vital step in the chain.

In public service operations, political and financial influences can be institutionalised, resulting in higher complexity. The need for clarity and constancy of purpose is paramount if the organisation is to achieve more than a muddled existence providing mediocre results. On the other hand, a sustainable organisation provides a **WIN-WIN-WIN** society where large numbers of people gain.

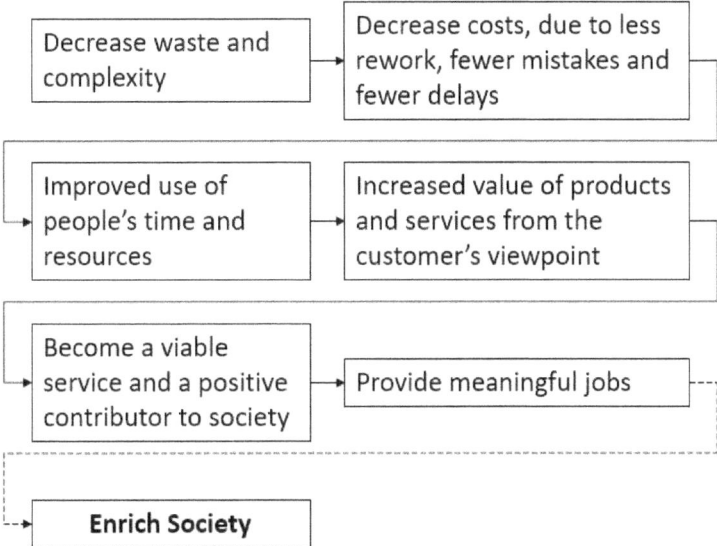

Figure 23: Enlarged Service Quality Chain

Start In The Right Place

Starting with the first box is what setting up a Sustainable Organisation using this MoSO approach is about. The leadership of an organisation should show clarity and constancy of purpose, aided by an understanding of the system of profound knowledge[13].

---

[13] See A System of Profound Knowledge, page 10

Without this clarity and constancy, an organisation runs several risks, such as those listed hereunder.

- Misled by numbers, management might not know whether they are looking at an average or extreme value, therefore, not knowing whether they can predict the future.
- It will not get the massive leverage in beneficial effects achieved by removing complexity.
- Suboptimisation will prevent the organisation from achieving its aims efficiently.
- It will find that good people are beaten by bad systems.
- It will generate unnecessary work, such as referrals of dubious output, overproduction of information, and delay or avoid decisions at the appropriate time; it will demotivate its people.
- Its people will not have the time or the knowledge to improve the organisation.
- They may not even be able to keep it viable.

For details and examples of how to become a sustainable organisation, go to the other elements of the model. Good starting points can be found elsewhere in this document. Consider starting by analysing your Voice of the Customer and identifying areas of Transformation. Your Operating System can give you a good outline, while the other elements can fill in the details. Management and Environment sections will provide the wider setting.

Self Examination Questions

1. Does your organisation understand the difference between "Cutting Costs" and "Removing the Causes of Costs", and does it know where the causes of costs are to be found?
2. What is the result of your constructing the Chain Reaction for your organisation?
3. How will you tackle the essential first step of the chain reaction? Without it, the remainder is just a wish list.
4. How does WIN-WIN help your organisation?
5. In what way can WIN-WIN-WIN emerge from your organisation's activities?

References

- Out of the Crisis, W Edwards Deming, 1984.
  The early position (page 3) of the chain reaction in this book shows what we would now call a 'sustainable organisation' can achieve in society.
- Fourth Generation Management, Brain L Joiner, 1994.
  The account in Chapter 2 highlights the improvements to the organisation's physical and human parts.

- The Improvement Guide, Second Edition, Gerald J Langley, Ronald D Moen, Kevin M Nolan, Thomas W Nolan, Clifford L Norman, Lloyd P Provost, 2009.
  The chain reaction in Chapter 13 is a crucial part of improving a business strategy's value.

Customers

Author   Alan Clark

Reviewers Terry Peterson, Alan Hodges

Overview

Customers are the fundamental element of every business or public sector organisation. They are the reason it exists. Meeting or exceeding the needs and expectations of customers is essential for sustained success and, consequently, for jobs, profits and dividends.

Customers are the only ones with a vote on quality, and it is whatever they think it is. Their expectations always rise over time, with the exciting becoming the norm and the norm becoming taken for granted. Therefore, this evolution gives rise to the need to continually improve and innovate.

Customers are a distinct element in MoSO since they provide the unique focus for the Operating System. They provide alignment for everyone within all organisations. Customers are a particular subset of society and, in turn, of the external environment in which businesses or public sector organisations operate.

Rightly, in recent times the needs and expectations of other stakeholders have become more fully recognised. This recognition must in no way diminish the pre-eminence of the customer.

Executive Summary

- Customers define quality since it is whatever they think it is. They decide whether to buy.

- Customer primacy in sustaining business success should be beyond doubt. The leaders of any organisation must not merely pay lip-service to the importance of the customer; their behaviour should set a consistent example. Customers are the focus of the organisational system, aligning everybody's activity.

- There are both internal and external customers for organisations. Internal customers do not usually have a choice of supplier.

- The aim should, at the very least, be customer satisfaction. Beyond that, it should be to achieve customer delight, excitement even insistence. Thus the outmoded practice of making to specification must be left far behind when seeking sustainable success.

- The spoken needs of the customer regarding quality only partly represent the situation, which Professor Noriaki Kano named as Normal, One-Dimensional or 'More is Better' quality. He proposed two more advanced types of quality: 'Must-be' and 'Exciting'. The latter is sometimes called Attractive quality. Both of these meet the unspoken needs of the customer. To satisfy customers, *normal* and *must-be* needs should be met. Going beyond *normal* to *delight, excitement,* or *insistence* requires exciting quality. Rising customer expectations drive perceptions down from excitement to normal and eventually to must-be. Failing to meet must-be needs is tantamount to giving business away.

- Innovations or breakthroughs are the responsibility of the supplier or provider. This exciting quality meets the unspoken or latent needs of the customer. The customer cannot say in advance how their needs can be met, explicitly describing a product or service. However, they are the primary source of information about their needs. They may have difficulty articulating their needs.

- Customer relationship management (CRM) should be firstly about building trusting relationships and only secondly about using IT. The primary activity of any sales person is building these trusting relationships. Too often, companies destroy trust through their actions, such as delivery failures or an unreasonable price rise, destroying the credibility and motivation of sales people. Although CRM primarily relates to sales activities, it covers marketing, customer service, and technical support.

- Listen to the 'Voice of the Customer' (see separate chapter). As mentioned above, customers' needs can be spoken about and unspoken. Many methods exist for capturing it. One important principle is that it should be recorded/taken down verbatim in their own words at the point of use.

- Design capable delivery systems and processes. The Quality Function Deployment (QFD) technique provides a method for translating the verbatim voice of the customer into customer requirements, prioritising these and deriving critical quality characteristics required of delivery processes. These critical quality characteristics provide the standards against which process capability can be measured.
- 'Moments of Truth' occur when the customer interacts with the organisation. Management's job is to support staff in all those moments of truth. Perhaps more important in service industries than in manufacturing or the automotive industry. Jan Carlson's classic book of the same title estimated that the moment of truth is as short as fifteen seconds, which was the average time customers were in contact with an employee of his airline, SAS.
- After-sales service is as critical to the overall customer perception of quality. In some service industries or industries where transactions of consumable products are ongoing, it can be more financially significant than the original purchase. Handling complaints effectively is an essential part of after-sales service. The

challenge always is to receive feedback without denial.

- Markets are where customers can allegedly choose from a range of suppliers. Unfortunately, they do not work as perfectly as economists would like to think. Perfect information is not available to all. It is tempting to be distracted by the activities of competitors. Ultimately it is what the customers perceive and whether they buy or not that is the acid test.

Main Article

Four of the main elements of MoSO 'from the outside in' are

- Environment,
- Society and Learning,
- People, Culture, Management and Leadership,
- Operating System (Your Operations).

The fifth major element is the Customer (or consumer) of the outcomes from Your Operations. How the operating system serves the customer is critical to the sustainable success of the business or public sector organisation. The following comments are illustrative of views supporting the idea of the primacy of the customer.

- "The consumer is the most important part of the production line. Quality should be aimed at the needs of the consumer, present and future." (Deming 1986, p. 5)

- "The consumer is more important than raw material. It is usually easier to replace the raw material supplier with another one than to find a new consumer. And a non-consumer who has not yet tried your product is still more important to you because he represents a possible additional user for your product." (Transcript of Deming's lectures in Japan 1950)
- "It will not suffice to have customers that are merely satisfied. An unhappy customer will switch. Unfortunately, a satisfied customer may also switch on the theory that he could not lose much and might gain. Profit in business comes from repeat customers that boast about your product and service and that bring friends with them." (Deming 1986, p. 141)
- "Deming also speaks frequently on the need for *staying ahead* of the customer. The customer does not know what he will need in one, three, five years from now. If you, as just one of his potential suppliers, wait until then to find out, you will hardly be ready to serve him." (Henry Neave 1990, p. 31)
- "Deming then spoke at length on consumer research, which he took care to illustrate in terms of two-way communication between manufacturer and both actual and potential customers. And this was still in the *Introduction* to his series of lectures!" (Henry Neave 1990, pp. 135-136)

Deming was unambiguous about the overriding importance of the customer:

> *"Who determines quality? The customer does: he can decide what he buys."*

Deming further talks about quality being that which "entices" and "appetises" the customer. And the same sentiments hold in our extended notion of what we mean by "customer". The situation is, of course, somewhat different internally: our internal customer may not have the choice as to whether or not he deals with what we supply, but if the quality of what we deliver is enticing and appetising to him, he will probably have greater pride in what he can in turn supply to his internal customer, while the whole quality of our own work is similarly affected by what is supplied to us:

> *People on a job are often handicapped by inherited defects and mistakes.*

- "Quality Guideline 1: Quality Begins with Delighting the Customer Customers must get what they want, when they want it, and how they want it. An organisation must strive not only to satisfy the customers' expectations. This is the least one should do. A company should also strive to delight their customers, giving them even more than they imagined possible. Your bosses may be ecstatic, the Board of Directors blissful, and your company may be considered a legend on Wall Street. But if your customers are not delighted, you have not begun to achieve quality." (Peter Scholtes, Heero Hacquebord, Joiner Associates Inc., 1987, pp. 202-222)

When talking about trust Steven Covey first introduced the author of this article to the concept of "customer insistence". He gave the example of a clam chowder restaurant in Boston. The clam chowder was outstanding, and customer insistence was apparent for all to see a queue that would form from about 11 a.m. and grow around the block by lunchtime. The restaurant was sold, and the new management thought they saw the opportunity to cut costs by thinning down the clam chowder. Customer insistence declined through delight, preference, to satisfaction, and the queue disappeared. The new owners realised what they had done and returned to the old recipe, but it was too late; trust had been destroyed.

> *"Customer delight is what you should aim for – they are paying to be satisfied."*
> *Hal Mather as heard by the author at an IMechE seminar on Manufacturing Logistics 1990*

The consensus is clear; the aim is to exceed customer expectations. Loyal customers defect. Strategy guru Michael E Porter says that strategy should be directed towards ensuring the offering is distinctive. What better indicator of being exceptional and successful than customer delight or insistence?

Kano Diagram – Three Types Of Quality

Professor Noriaki Kano and colleagues laid the foundation for a new approach to studying customer satisfaction in the late 1970s and early 1980s.

Seeking to go deeper into customer motivation, Kano augmented the 'normal' quality that customers spoke about by drawing on the earlier work of Frederick Herzberg on staff motivation.

Herzberg's Motivation-Hygiene Theory (or Two-Factor Theory) is based on his research into staff satisfaction. The theory states that some factors in the workplace cause job satisfaction, while different factors cause job dissatisfaction.

Kano proposed that certain factors in products or customer service cause satisfaction, while different factors cause dissatisfaction. These are summarised in Figure 24.

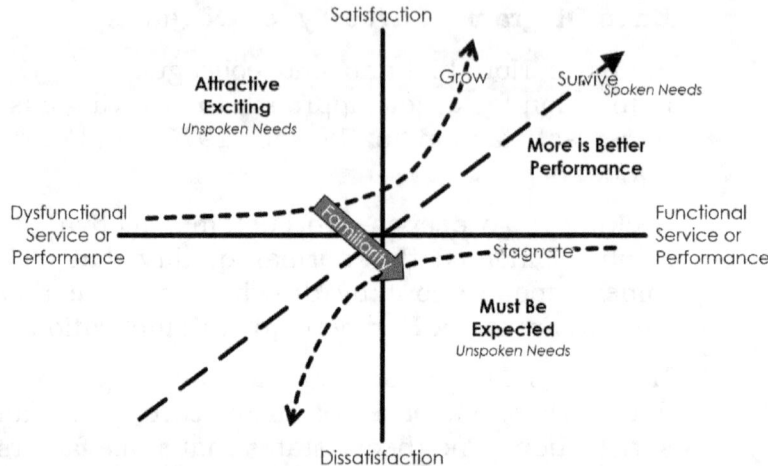

Figure 24: Kano Model Diagram adapted from Noriaki Kano

As can be seen, the spoken needs of the customer on quality only partly represent the situation, which Kano called Normal, One-Dimensional or 'More-is-better' quality.

Adapting Herzberg's hygiene factors, the dissatisfiers, he proposed that there are factors that customers would be dissatisfied with if they were not present. These he names 'Must-be' or Expected quality.

The satisfiers, Herzberg's motivation factors, Kano labelled Attractive or Exciting quality. Must-be and Exciting quality meet the unspoken needs of the customer. The former is because they expect or assume these requirements (e.g. safely functioning brakes on a car) will be there. The latter is because they do not know what solution will meet their needs, often unspoken or latent. Before they were invented, nobody could

146

ask for electric lights, pneumatic tyres or Walkman miniature tape cassette players.

The three types of quality can also be compared as

Dissatisfier	Must be / Expected	Cost of Entry
Satisfier	More is better / Performance	Competitive
Delighter	Exciting / Attractive	Differentiator

"Normal" and "must-be" needs should be met to satisfy customers. Going beyond to delight, excitement, or insistence necessitates exciting quality; this means innovation, which Deming states is the responsibility of the supplier.

Rising customer expectations drive perceptions down from excitement to normal and eventually to must-be; this implies that innovation needs to be deeply embedded to achieve a sustainable organisation. Failing to meet must-be needs is equivalent to giving business away.

Losing customers is more expensive than you might think. In his book The Loyalty Effect, Frederick Reichheld shows that loyal customers are more profitable. A range of industry sectors as varied as credit cards, car servicing, and industrial launderers confirmed the same. In the credit card industry, it might cost a net $80 to acquire each new customer against annual profits of $40, $66, $72, $79 and $87 if retained for the following five years.

Kano and his associates developed a unique paired-question format for customer surveys to categorise customer requirements into Exciting, More-is-better or Must-be quality. This question format can also yield ratings of Indifferent, Reverse and Questionable to a particular requirement, which should lead to a review of that requirement or the wording of the questions.

Customer or service user research for maximum effect is best carried out through point-of-use observation and recording verbatim what the customers' says.

Other sources of information are as follows:

- **Must Be's** – Focus Groups, Lawsuits and Regulations, Buzz on Internet
- **More is Better** – Competitive Analysis, Interviews, Surveys, Search Logs, Usability Testing, Customer Forums
- **Exciting** – Marketing/Branding Vision, Industrial Design, Packaging, Call Centre Data, Site Logs

The Voice of the Customer article provides further information on customer research. Customer comments, compliments, and complaints would, of course, form part of this. And also remember that 'Mistakes are treasures' *providing that you learn from them and do something about them!*

The Kano model can be used in Quality Function Deployment (QFD) to create the matrices that ultimately lead to the critical quality characteristics required of the delivery processes.

148

Professor Noriaki Kano is an emeritus at the Tokyo University of Science and formerly became a full professor and head of the Department of Management Science.

Moments Of Truth

The emphasis in any organisation must be on the customer. Each customer contact with a member of the organisation is a Moment Of Truth.

The business purpose should be defined as customer satisfaction; it is 'outside in'. In other words, it reflects a deep understanding of the value a customer wants in every transaction with the organisation.

It is expressed in terms of providing ever-improving value to customers and not just about perfectly meeting today's customer needs.

In a dynamic market, organisations must innovate products, services and processes to meet customers' future needs in an ever-enlarging market.

The system, processes and procedures should be organised to reflect this.

Management's job is to support staff in all those moments of truth. Perhaps these are more important in service industries than in manufacturing or automotive industries. Jan Carlzon's classic book *Moments of Truth* highlighted how brief these moments of truth can be:

> *"Last year each of our ten million customers came in contact with approximately five SAS employees, and this contact lasted an average of 15 seconds each time. The SAS is 'created' 50 million times a year, 15 seconds at a time. These 50 million 'moments of truth' are the moments that ultimately determine whether SAS will succeed or fail as a company. They are the moments when we must prove to our customers that SAS is their best alternative."*
>
> *Jan Carlzon 1987, p. 3*

Jan Carlzon became President and CEO of SAS Group (Scandinavian Airlines System) in 1981. At the time, it was losing $17 million per annum and had a terrible reputation for punctuality. The airline's punctuality and profitability were dramatically improved through a radical decentralization, moving decision making to the front line. In 1982 it turned in a profit of $54 million. And this was accomplished in the face of a global airline recession.

A central part of Carlzon's strategy was an ongoing training program called *Putting People First*. It focused on delegating responsibility to the front line, allowing customer-facing staff to make decisions to resolve any issues on the spot. He said, *"Problems are solved on the spot as soon as they arise. No front-line employee has to wait for a supervisor's permission."* In other words, they can decide to take action themselves during those moments of truth.

Disney is an example of another company where customer-facing staff are allowed to make decisions to resolve issues on the spot.

Responsibilities in such highly customer-focused organisations appear radically different. The organisation is top-down and bottom-up. In many ways, this has much in common with autonomous working. Typically they might have the following characteristics:

- **Associates** are empowered to respond to customer's requirements on the spot
- **Middle** Management is there to support the moments of truth. A manager's role includes:
  - supporting, mentoring, facilitating;
  - coaching and counselling, not judging;
  - creating trust;
  - creating an environment that encourages freedom and innovation;
  - listening and learning without passing judgement on those to whom they listen;
  - understanding that people are different from each other;
  - trying to create for everybody interest and challenge, and joy in work;

- trying to optimise the experience, education, skills, hopes, and abilities; this is not ranking people but recognising differences between people and attempting to put everybody in a position for development.
- **Top Management** provides leadership, strategy, vision, clarity, showmanship, and emphasis and designs the overall system.

Customer Relationship Management

Customer relationship management (CRM) should be firstly about building trusting relationships and only secondly about using IT. The primary activity of any salesperson is building these trusting relationships.

Too often, companies destroy trust through their actions, such as delivery failures or an unreasonable price rise, destroying the credibility and motivation of salespeople. Although CRM primarily relates to sales activities, it also covers marketing, customer service, and technical support.

The Market

Markets are where customers can allegedly choose from a range of suppliers.

Unfortunately, they do not work as perfectly as economists would like to think:

- Perfect information is not available to all.

- It is tempting to be distracted by the activities of competitors.
- Ultimately it is what the customers perceive and whether they buy or not that is the acid test.
- Markets don't buy products/services; customers do.
- Customers don't buy from organisations; they buy from people.

Summary

Customers provide a unique focus when viewing any business or public sector organisation as a system within its social and environmental context. Customers define quality and demonstrate this by deciding whether to buy.

To sustain success, a business or organisation requires loyal customers who return time and again and bring their friends! This need means that customer satisfaction must (at least) be maintained, which means providing Normal or More-is-better quality that meets needs. The unspoken, expected aspects of customer requirements must also be met because failing to deliver on Must-be quality will cause customers to leave.

They can leave even when satisfied, making it essential for the sustainable organisation to make working towards customer delight or even customer insistence a necessary part of an overall strategy. Accordingly, unspoken, latent customer needs must be divined, understood and turned into offerings that customers view as Exciting or Attractive quality. Whether through familiarity or rising expectations, initial customer perceptions will inevitably decline over time to a level taken for granted. The implication here is ongoing innovation in the offerings or how it is supplied to the customer.

The interface with the customer is a critical point. Management must take action to support staff during those "moments of truth", equipping them to take immediate action to resolve customer issues. People buy from people, so the relationship with the customer must generate high trust. Destroying trust will increase loyalty costs by having to find new customers, just like failing on Must-be quality.

There was a time, after the second world war, when demand exceeded supply, that product could be "pushed" out of the door without regard to customers or quality. Those that still hold that view will not achieve sustained success. Savvy customers and global competition mean customers are in the driving seat, and the "customer pull" of products and services is the only sustainable strategy.

Self Examination Questions

1. To what extent is the primacy of the customer recognised within our organisation?
2. What evidence do you have that you use your customers to align people and policy?
3. What evidence is there that you are really striving to achieve customer delight?

4. Where are customer perceptions of your products or services relative to the three types of quality: Attractive, More-is-better and Must-be? Be honest!
5. How much support does management provide front-line staff in moments of truth?
6. Give examples of ways customer-facing staff can resolve issues on the spot.
7. What active steps are you taking to build trust within your organisation and with your customers?

Your Operations

Author	Derek Richings
Reviewers	Tony Brown, Terry Rose, Tony Korychi

Overview

The **Your Operations** element of MoSO is used to map the end-to-end flow of work done by an organisation to **transform** Customer Needs into Customer Satisfaction or even Customer Delight.

This transformation needs to be performed with optimal efficiency and speed of response - creating a seamless, uninterrupted flow of work and information throughout the organisation.

The arrow reminds us that all work starts and finishes with the customer. Customers need to

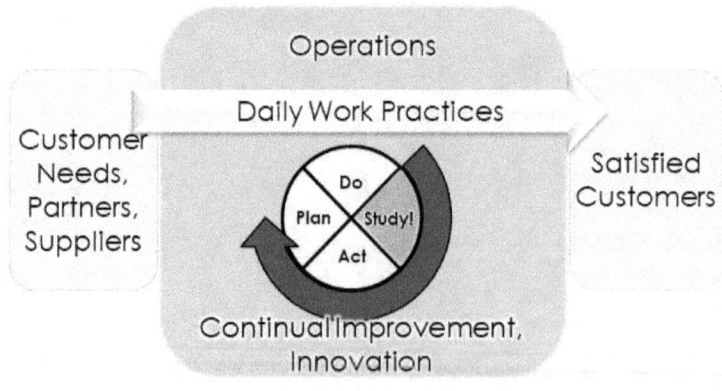

Figure 25: Your Operations

be *satisfied* for the organisation to continue to exist and prosper. *Customer Needs*, as expressed overtly through orders, specifications and contracts (or less tangibly through verbal feedback and even body language), drive you to supply your product, service or both. There will always be *Suppliers* on whom you have varying levels of dependency and sometimes *Partners* without whom you could not function successfully.

MoSO shows that to be sustainable, **Your Operations** comprise two distinct interlinked jobs:

- **Daily Work Processes:** viewed as an end-to-end flow of work from customer needs through to customer satisfaction;
- **Continual Improvement & Innovation:** the work done by everyone involved to systematically move the business forward and keep pace with ever-changing customer/market needs and expectations. The Plan, Do, Study, Act (PDSA) wheel represents the generic processes used by everyone to bring about improvements.

Daily Work Processes

Daily Work Processes vary enormously depending on the type and size of the organisation, the nature of the 'business' performed, and the processes by which they have evolved. Each organisation's Daily Work Processes are unique, helping to differentiate themselves in their 'marketplace'.

Organisations arrange or design their operations to achieve what they believe to be the best possible outcomes – or that's what you'd expect. In reality, many operational work processes (systems) are built in a topsy-turvy fashion over time, with many changes of direction along the way. Different departments or functions do their own thing – sometimes at the expense of other departments – irrespective or oblivious to the needs and expectations of customers.

To be sustainable, *Your Operations* need to be performed with the minimum of waste (in terms of materials, people's efforts, and environmental considerations), optimal efficiency, and speed of response - creating a seamless, uninterrupted flow of work and information through the organisation. Some might say 'Lean' or 'Lean & Green'.

In MoSO, the Daily Work Processes arrow represents this thought about rapid, seamless flow – as opposed to getting bogged down in departmental or functional silos.

Continual Improvement & Innovation (PDSA)

The PDSA cycle is a fundamental means of systematically driving renewal and improvement. In this cycle, data/information is reviewed, improvements planned, and changes tested and analysed.

The process is repeated until the required improvements are obtained. Many organisations have processes of this type, but often their use is limited to problems perceived as significant and is not rigorous or systematically applied. Sometimes this process is only initiated when issues emerge, and individuals are tasked to make changes or 'find solutions' but have no structured approach to follow. Embedding a PDSA cycle into your operations (the way you work) will significantly enhance the organisation. It does not have to be defined precisely in this way; the culture of driving improvement and innovation by thinking and acting in line with these principles is essential. Everybody can and should want to do it.

Are you comfortable with this picture? Why is *Study* coloured differently? Let's develop this basic model further.

The Enhanced MoSO Operating System

Daily Work Processes contain processes that construct a product or service and earn money (or funding or financial support) directly or indirectly! The more value they add, the better because that's where making a difference comes into play.

Sometimes non-value-adding processes must be conducted without which the organisation cannot function. They can be termed *Support activities* and typically include Finance, Human Resources, staff positions, etc.

Depending upon the sector, varying amounts of resources are consumed to meet sector-specific requirements imposed by governments or international bodies, particularly where public health and safety can be impacted. The model refers to these as *Regulatory Activities.*

The *Study* element of the PDSA cycle is that it is fed from inputs from at least three areas – we can call them voices or sensors.

The importance of the *Study* element of the PDSA cycle is that it is fed from inputs from at least three areas – we can call them voices or sensors.

The **Voice of the Customer (VoC)** is the most obvious input into what has to be captured and studied. The VoC can be gained by classic collection techniques such as Market Surveys and Customer Satisfaction Studies.

Sometimes there is no numeric data, but it is how your customer talks about you, whether in print or spoken, that you have to analyse; this is known as Language data. Whatever techniques are used, good quality data (both numeric and language) which reflects customer expectations is essential and should never be ignored.

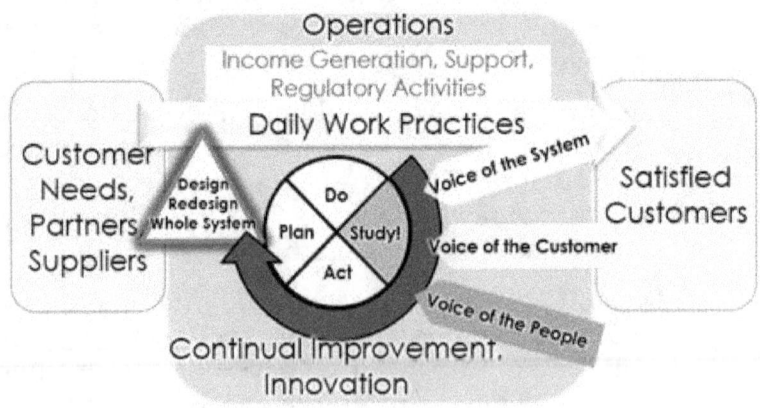

Figure 26: Study

The **Voice of the System (VoS)** is essential to understanding whether your value-adding processes are appropriately developed, robust and tuned to minimise variation, i.e. they are capable.

Without high levels of system capability, your customer's expectations will not be met, and your costs will rise. Process Behaviour Charts are typically used to determine capability. You may know them as Control Charts. The manufacturing sector and automotive manufacturing, in particular, have pioneered the use of Control Charts to understand and control variation in their products.

Process Behaviour Charts can be used for all products and services and by everyone in the organisation – from the boardroom to the backroom. A culture that uses them to drive continual improvement and innovation will significantly benefit your organisation. Choosing what to measure and monitor is vital. Getting performance data this way is hearing the Voice of the System (sometimes called the Voice of the Process).

The **Voice of the People (VoP)** may not be a familiar term, but it is how an organisation should understand its workforce's health (mental and physical) and capability.

Organisations have evolved their preferred ways of talking to and, more importantly, listening to their people. One-on-one discussions are common and represent a 'private, structured voice.' In contrast, large staff meetings are a conduit for unstructured and very public feedback. Any type of event which seeks to understand the work-force's feelings and issues is beneficial.

Design and Redesign of the System effectively happen during the Planning Stage of PDSA. Data from experimentation at the 'Do' stage is reviewed and acted upon, leading to either standardisation of the changes or another cycle of experimentation.

Hence it's at this stage of the cycle that the organisation works on and improves pieces of its structure – like processes, controls, measures, resourcing, and organisational structures. It's worth noting, however, that individual changes to any of these may emerge and modify how an organisation works at any time using various deployment methods.

What Do Your Operations Look Like?

The MoSO graphic for the Basic and Enhanced models does not show 'operations' in detail for three reasons:

1. The operating processes/systems for your organisation are unique. No matter how generic or detailed the model is, it cannot possibly map your system's setup. There may be suitable models you can use as a basis for your operating model or that act as mandated high-level frameworks, e.g., TOM for the communications industry. However, no organisation will ever be simply a clone of a standard model.

2. When mapping any operations, the tendency is to start at a high level and then systematically come down through levels of abstraction until the required level of detail has been reached.
3. The intent is for you / your team to do the work to map Your Operations and then ask questions about its suitability for the purposes defined, compatibility with the organisation's culture/identity, and viability.

To help you along the way, a generic example – at the next level down – has been developed.

This model may look more familiar because it has a well-defined Product/Service flow from Design through Customer Use and Support.

Customer Feedback driving improvement (or would it have been change?) is not new, but PDSA, VoS and VoP are now embedded.

Many organisations have invested considerable time and effort in improving departments and/or functions by developing skills in individuals and teams. Lean and Six Sigma techniques will typically be launched in Design and Manufacturing and, as their benefits are proven, will cascade through support activities. The complete Value Chain is often well understood through Value Stream Mapping.

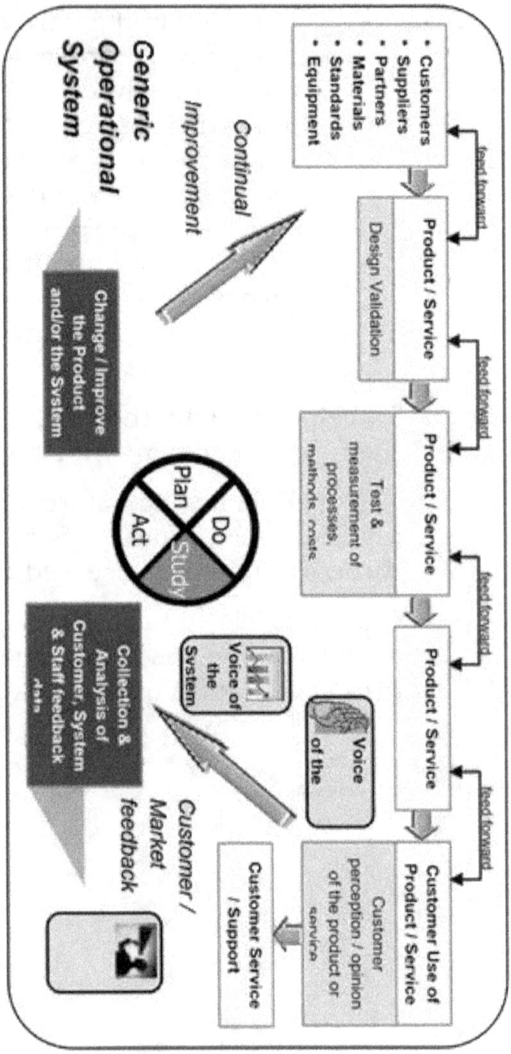

The value of a model of this kind, whether at a high or lower level, is that it shows the big picture and asks big questions, such as:

Figure 27: Value Chain

- Can you view your organisation in this way?

164

- Is it helpful to do so?
- Are the feed-forward and feedback loops institutionalised and robust?
- Do organisational chimneys still exist?

Some Self-Examining Questions

1. To what extent are you ready for this journey? What help or support do you need?
2. To what extent is your organisation ready for change – who will be the change champions who will work for you?
3. What constraints have to be overcome to gain initial momentum versus continued momentum?
4. How does the big picture of your organisation align with the MoSO model?
   a. Are the differences significant in terms of sustainable performance?
   b. If the differences are real, what can be done to introduce the missing elements or improve ineffective areas?
5. To what extent are the three voices to renew and sustain the organisation (VoC, VoS, VoP) used systematically and continually improved?
6. Looking at the MoSO model, what important influences are affecting, or likely to affect, your operations, and how are you recognising and managing these influences?

Plan Do Study Act (PDSA)

Author   Terry Peterson

Reviewers   Tony Brown, Alan Clark

Overview

PDSA is shown at the heart of MoSO: it applies equally to all model elements.

PDSA ("Plan-Do-Study-Act") is a cyclical, four-stage improvement process.   Experience has shown that applying a methodical sequence of stages to any problem-solving, experimenting, or design activity contributes to achieving the best

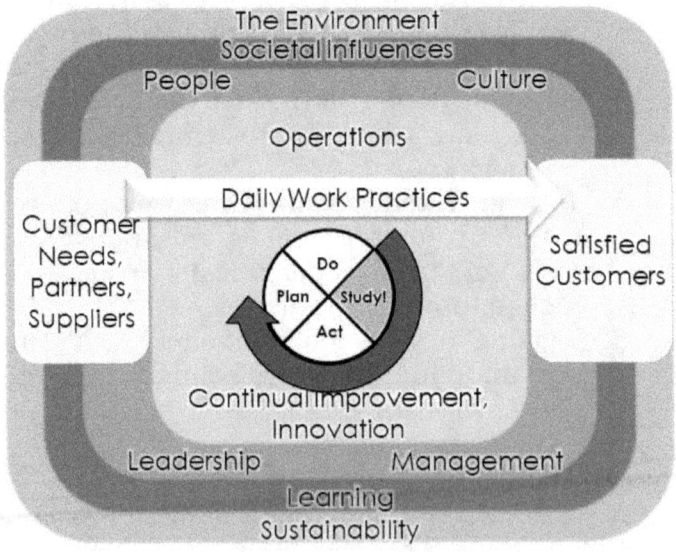

Figure 28: PDSA in MoSO

result. People naturally rush to action, which leads to frustrating and costly solutions. Careful planning is essential.

Many methods have been developed to aid this process, including the scientific method and engineering thinking. PDSA is simply a version of this process that has been proven beneficial.

- **Plan.** Recognize an opportunity and plan a change.
- **Do.** Test the change. Carry out a small-scale study.
- **Study.** Review the test, analyse the results and identify what you've learned.
- **Act.** Take action based on what you learned in the study stage.
    - o If the change does not work, repeat the cycle with a different plan.
    - o If you were successful, incorporate what you learned from the test into broader changes.
- Use what you learned to plan new improvements, beginning the cycle again.

PDSA is typically used in organisations for continual improvement. It is also known as the Deming Cycle, Shewhart Cycle, or the Deming Wheel.

You may also find value in reading about PDSA in other MoSO Supporting Information articles.

Main Content

The PDSA Learning and Improvement Cycle concept was initially developed by Walter Shewhart, the pioneering statistician who developed statistical process control in the Bell Laboratories in the US during the 1930s. It is often referred to as 'the Shewhart Cycle'. It was taken up and promoted very effectively from the 1950s on by Dr W. Edwards Deming and is consequently known by many as 'the Deming Wheel'.

The PDSA Cycle is used to coordinate continuous improvement efforts. It both emphasises and demonstrates that improvement programs that start with careful planning will typically result in effective action and move on again to careful planning in a continuous cycle.

The PDSA Cycle diagram can be used in team meetings to take stock of the improvement initiatives' stage and choose the appropriate tools to see each stage through to successful completion.

Guideline Stages/Steps For Using PDSA As A Continual Improvement Problem-Solving Methodology

Plan

- Stage 1: Identify The Problem

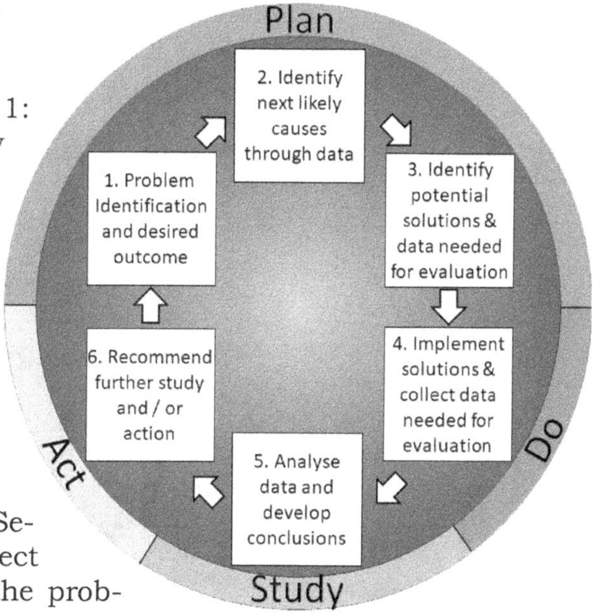

Figure 29: Plan, Do, Study, Act

  - Select the problem to be analysed
  - Clearly define the problem and establish a precise problem statement
  - Set a measurable goal for the problem-solving effort
  - Establish a process for coordinating with and gaining approval from the leadership
- Stage 2: Analyse The Problem
  - Identify the processes that impact the problem and select one
  - List the stages in the process as it currently exists

- o Map the Process
- o Validate the map of the process
- o Identify the potential cause of the problem
- o Collect and analyse data related to the problem
- o Verify or revise the original problem statement
- o Identify the root causes of the problem
- o Collect additional data if needed to verify root causes:
  - **WHO** does this plan impact (specifically, with what presumed or required characteristics or qualifications)?
  - **WHAT** is the purpose of the interface/relationship? What are we trying to accomplish? What change can we make that will result in improvement? (Whichever question is appropriate).
  - **WHY** does this support the end purpose of the system (i.e. 'vision')?
  - **WHERE** will this take place (addressing all characteristics of the intended location from parking to power to how many inches from the wall)?
  - **WHEN** is it to occur (i.e. earliest start/end, latest start/end, sequence/timing of stages/sub-processes)?

- **HOW** - a stage-by-stage procedure to convert any/all system/process inputs to all system outputs. How will we know that the change is an improvement?'
- Stage 3: Develop Solutions
    - Establish criteria for selecting a solution
    - Generate potential solutions that will address the root causes of the problem
    - Select a solution
    - Gain approval and support for the chosen solution
    - Plan the solution

Do

- Stage 4: Implement the Solution
    - Implement the chosen solution on a trial or pilot basis
    - If the Problem-Solving Process is being used in conjunction with the Continuous Improvement Process, return to stage 6 of the Continuous Improvement Process
    - If the Problem Solving Process is being used as a standalone, continue to stage 5

Study

- Stage 5: Evaluate The Results
    - Gather data on the solution
    - Analyse the data on the solution

o Has the Desired Goal been achieved?
  - If YES, go to stage 6
  - If NO, go back to Stage 1

Act

- Stage 6: Standardize The Solution (and Capitalize on New Opportunities)
  o Identify systemic changes and training needs for full implementation
  o Adopt the solution
  o Plan ongoing monitoring of the solution
  o Continue to look for incremental improvements to refine the solution
  o Look for another improvement opportunity

Reflection

After each cycle (spin), capture the lessons learned concerning how the PDSA process was used and what improvements can be made for the next cycle.

The PDSA Cycle is repeated continually - no ending point - and thus is the basis of genuine 'Continual Improvement.' This repetition can be applied in basic and nested cycles or "wheel-within-a-wheel" cycles.

When To Use Plan-Do-Study-Act:

- As a model for continuous improvement
- When starting a new improvement project

- When developing a new or improved design of a process, product or service
- When defining a repetitive work process
- When planning data collection and analysis to verify and prioritize problems or root causes
- When implementing any change.

The starting point of PDSA depends on where you are in the improvement process.

If a process already exists, you would probably start incremental improvement at the STUDY stage, where you observe the need for further change (SAPD).

Breakthrough improvement might start at the ACT stage, where some unexpected event acts on the process and causes us to plan to either eliminate the event if undesirable or institutionalise the event if it proves desirable.

> *Where you start in the cycle is not as important as the cycle itself. Nevertheless, the Planning stage is undoubtedly the most crucial step.*

Standardisation: Study current practices
- Adopt the best-known method
- Plan for the implementation of standard
- Do: implement standardised practices
- Study results,
  - then Act, Plan, Do, and back to Study, etc.

Problem-solving: Study the known data

- Analyse for the root cause(s)
- Plan tests to verify the theory of cause
- Do: experiment or run tests
- Study results,
    - then Act, Plan, Do, Study, etc.

Process improvement: Study current state (IS map)

- Analyse opportunities and benchmarks
- Plan changes (TO-BE map)
- Do: implement changes
- Study results,
    - then Act, Plan, Do, Study, etc.

Strategic planning: Study prior performance and environment

- Analyse strengths & opportunities
- Plan actions and deployment
- Do: deploy and implement
- Study to monitor progress,
    - then Act, Plan, Do, Study, etc.

Focusing cycle: Study opportunities & priorities

Before beginning any of the above SAP-Do cycles, there is usually a Focusing stage in which a decision is made to improve something, boundaries are established, a team is formed, decisions are made. One can even think of this as a SAP-Do cycle that precedes all the others.

- Act: decide upon one, establish boundaries, form a team
- Plan the improvement project
- Do: execute one of the cycles above
- Study results of this and other projects

174

o   then Act, Plan, Do, Study, etc.

Strengths Of The PDSA Approach

#1. It tests changes on a small scale

It allows you to see if the change strategies in your action plan will achieve their desired objectives; it is essential to test them on a small scale - in effect, implementing a change temporarily. Testing on a small scale has several advantages:

- **Big learning pay-off at a small expense:** Testing changes on a small scale can be accomplished quickly with a minimal expenditure of resources. At the same time, small-scale tests provide a good indication of problems and/or successes to expect from full-scale implementation.
- **Allows for early and effective changes to the action plan:** The experience and feedback gained from small-scale tests can be used to modify and improve the original Implementation Action Plan.
- **Improves staff buy-in:** Staff are more likely to buy into guideline implementation if change strategies are tested on a small scale. Staff members resistant to large-scale changes will be more receptive if they can provide input during a small trial run of the change strategy. Tailoring the approach to the needs and concerns of the implementing staff will increase staff acceptance of guideline implementation.

#2. It focuses on Process Improvement

Since the PDSA cycle is specifically designed to improve organisational processes, using this approach encourages your team to conceptualize the action items in the implementation plan as changes in processes. This orientation will increase the likelihood of effective process change.

#3. It allows for the testing of multiple changes through multiple cycles

Another advantage of the PDSA cycle is that it allows you to take multiple change strategies through

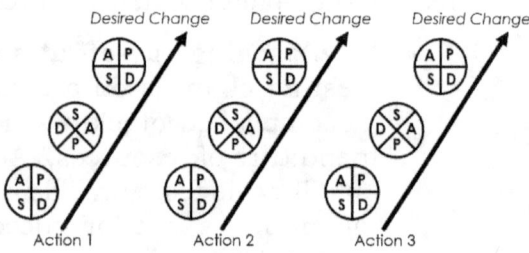

Figure 30: Multiple Iterations of PDSA

multiple improvement cycles, as illustrated in Figure 30. Each of the arrows represents an action item from your Action Plan. Each item is tested on a small scale and moves through successive cycles until the desired change is achieved. Not all action items will require more than one PDSA cycle, but testing every item with at least one PDSA cycle is advisable.

#4. Tried and proven changes can be extended and adapted

With evidence from the small-scale tests that your planned actions have the potential to create the desired improvements, it is time to move forward with broader implementation of those actions. Responsibilities for implementing each action should be clearly defined and compatible with each individual's organisational skills and functions. As with the approach for the small-scale tests, work incrementally in cooperation with staff involved or affected by the changes. Be alert to positive and negative feedback, which can improve your strategies. To extend and adapt small-scale changes, consider the following actions:

- Extend the change to other areas in the organisation
- Adapt the change to each area
- Make the change routine in each area
- Share the adaptations among all areas

#5. PDSA links with other areas of MoSO

Involving everyone in improvement harnesses the intrinsic motivation of people.

It is necessary to drive out fear so that the negative consequences of proposed changes can be freely explored.

Self-Examining Questions

1. To what extent is the PDSA Learning and Improvement Cycle understood in your organisation?
2. To what extent do you use a PDSA cycle in strategy and plan deployment?
3. Do you have a consistent process to improve your core operating processes to

achieve better performance, reduce variability, and keep the processes current with business needs and directions?

4. Do improvement teams have a consistent method based on PDSA?
5. Do you have a consistent process to improve your support processes?
6. How do you translate data from organisational performance reviews into priorities for continuous and breakthrough improvement and opportunities for innovation?
7. How are these priorities and opportunities deployed to workgroup and functional-level operations throughout your organisation?
8. How are improvements shared with other organisational units and processes?
9. When appropriate, how are the priorities and opportunities deployed to your suppliers, partners, and collaborators to ensure organisational alignment?

Appendix - History & Philosophy

The concept of PDSA comes out of the Scientific Method, as developed from the work of Francis Bacon (*Novum Organum*, 1620). The scientific method can be written as

$$\textit{"Hypothesis" - "Experiment" - "Evaluation"},$$

or Plan, Do, and Study.

Some of the first thinking on Plan-Do-Study may have originated with Dewey at the turn of the century in America. Baron & Sternberg (1986) describe a process of scientific inquiry that bridges everyday problem-solving and the scientific method, and they credit this thought process to Dewey (1933).

The stages of the process are:

1. feeling difficulty,
2. doubting what one has taken for granted,
3. defining the problem,
4. forming a hypothesis,
5. inferring possible consequences,
6. discovering a counter instance,
7. revising and broadening the hypothesis to explain the counter stance, and
8. applying the revised hypothesis to a life situation.

In Mind and the World Order, C I Lewis writes,

"The application of concept must be verifiable over time. We develop a hypothesis based on momentarily presented experience, which involves a prediction that can be proved/disproved by further experience, [...] Empirical truth (knowledge of objects) comes from the conceptual interpretation of the given. To ascribe objective qualities to a thing means that I can make predictions about further activity; *"if I do this . . . , then that . . . ."* this is the whole content of our knowledge of reality. The truth of such propositions is independent of the observer. The *"if"* depends on the active mind; the *"then"* is totally determined by outside reality. However, I start with *"if"*, the *"then"* is independent of my attitude/purposes."

Dr Walter A. Shewhart expanded

"if....then..." hypotheticals to a three-stage process; "make a hypothesis, carry out an experiment, test the hypothesis" (with a parallel in the 'state of control' as a cycle of specification, production, inspection). In *Statistical Method from the Viewpoint of Quality Control*, Shewhart described the old view of Specification, Production, and Inspection. These three stages must go in a circle instead of in a straight line, as shown [...] It may be helpful to think of the three stages in the mass production process as stages in the scientific method. In this sense, specification, production, and inspection correspond respectively to making a hypothesis, carrying out an experiment, and testing the hypothesis. The three stages constitute a dynamic scientific process of acquiring knowledge.

Shewhart described manufacture under "control" - under statistical control - as a three-stage process of specification, production,

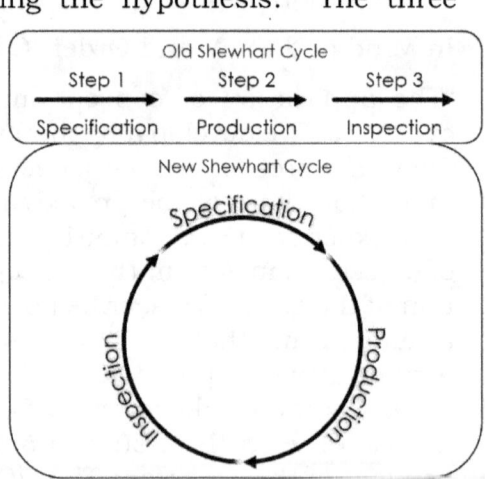

Figure 31: Shewhart Cycle

and inspection. He also specifically related this to the Scientific Method of hypothesis, experiment and evaluation. Shewhart says that the statistician *"must help to change the demand [for goods] by showing how to close up the tolerance range and to improve the quality of goods."* Clearly, Shewhart intended the analyst to take action based on the evaluation's conclusions.

Deming further refined this concept in his work with the Japanese in 1950. He proposed a cycle of:

1. plan a change,
2. carry out the change, preferably on a small scale,
3. Observe the effects of the change,
4. Study the results - what did we learn and what can we predict?
5. Repeat step 1 with accumulated knowledge,
6. Repeat step 2.

Initially, he termed this the Shewhart Cycle. In later work, he further modified this cycle to:

1. P. Plan a change
2. D. Carry out the change, preferably on a small scale
3. S. Study the results - what did we learn and what went wrong?
4. A. Adopt the change or Abandon it, or run through the cycle again.

He termed this updated version "the Shewhart Cycle for Learning and Improvement - the P-D-S-A Cycle".

181

Deming said that knowledge is built on 'theory'; without 'theory', there is no way to use all these data or this information. He points out that knowledge is built through systematic proposing, testing and extending/revising 'theories'.

Deming always credited Shewhart for the idea of the cycle, but Deming fostered the concept's expansion to all areas of learning and improvement. The Shewhart Cycle was introduced to the Japanese in 1950. It was taught along with Dr Deming's "*Production Viewed as a System*" model:

1. Design the product (with appropriate tests).
2. Make it; test it in the production line and the laboratory.
3. Put it on the market.
4. Test it in service through market research, find out what the user thinks of it, and why the non-user has not bought it.
5. Re-design the product in light of consumer reactions to quality and price.
6. Continue around and around the cycle.

Deming (1984) advised that any manager's job is to put everybody on a team to improve some activity. Each team will go through the Shewhart Cycle over and over. A team will be reconstituted for another task when one is brought to a satisfactory conclusion, ready for action.

Deming is clearly advocating the use of the cycle for everyone in the organisation. During 1988, the cycle evolved into what we know today as the *Plan-Do-Study-Act* cycle. Dr Deming documented this version of the "*Shewhart Cycle for Learning and Improvement*" in 1992 in *New Economics*. The letters P-D-S-A are now part of the cycle in this version. The cycle is now clearly aimed at all types of learning and improvement and can be utilized at any level for an entire organisation or for minor improvements or changes.

A fundamental principle of the scientific method and PDSA is iteration - once a hypothesis is confirmed (or negated), executing the cycle again will extend the knowledge further. Repeating the PDSA cycle can bring us closer to the goal, usually a perfect operation and output.

Improvement is a critical competitive factor in today's world. PDSA allows for significant 'jumps' in performance ('breakthroughs' often desired in a Western approach) and Kaizen (frequent minor improvements associated with an Eastern approach). In the United States, a PDSA approach is usually associated with a sizable project involving numerous people's time. Thus managers want to see significant 'breakthrough' improvements to justify the effort expended. However, the Scientific Method and PDSA apply to all types of projects and improvement activities.

The power of Deming's concept lies in its apparent simplicity. However, Deming warned that the effect of this view of how knowledge is increased means that empirical evidence is never complete. We are always at the mercy of newly discovered facts. He also advised us to be sure that our hypothesis is clearly based on linked cause and effect and not on co-incidence. He makes specific reference to p.195 of *Mind and the World Order*, where Lewis writes:

> *There is no knowledge of external reality without anticipation of future experience, [...] there is no knowledge without interpretation, the fact that it reflects the character of past experience will not save its validity.*

This idea is the basis of Deming's - often misunderstood - saying that experience and/or examples alone teach nothing without 'theory'. Experience can only be used rationally by applying analysis and mathematical/statistical techniques leading to understanding/knowledge.

In other words, management requires prediction based on a hypothesis, or 'theory' about how the organisation - as a system - works. Rational management planning involves a simple thought pattern; "*If our organisation, as a system in a known environment, works in the following way..., then if we do..., the following results will accrue*". This prediction can be tested with appropriate metrics and statistical techniques. Analysis of the results should lead to action to improve the system.

The fact that another organisation achieved a given set of results in a similar situation will not help unless you understand how they did it and how that might help your procedures. Deming warns that "*to copy an example of success, without understanding it with the aid of a 'theory', may lead to disaster*".

Nolan, Provost, et al. of API have extended this even further to demonstrate that PDSA brings the power of the scientific method into all our work activities.

Bibliography

1. Economic Control of Quality of Manufactured Product, Shewhart
2. Statistical Method from the Viewpoint of Quality Control, Shewhart
3. Out of the Crisis, Deming
4. The New Economics, Deming
5. The Foundation of Improvement, Langley, Nolan & Nolan – API
6. Bringing the PDSA Cycle to Life, Provost – API
7. Understanding Variation, Nolan & Provost, Quality Progress, May 1990

People, Culture, Leadership & Management

Authors	Antony Aitken & Ray Charlton
Reviewers	Derek Richings, Terry Rose

Overview

This article covers the four major components of MoSO:

- People and change
- Culture
- Leadership
- Management

People and Change

In any organisation:

- The customers for products or services are people,
- People provide the vision,
- People do the work – and improve things,
- People need to be engaged – they have a need, as does the organisation!

Understanding what goes on in any organisation – or outside it – requires an understanding of every aspect of the way people do and don't work together.

Culture

"The way we do things around here" is a simple description of culture – yet we need to look below the surface to work with culture instead of being frustrated by its seeming intransigence!

Organisation culture has been described as the emergent result of the continuing negotiations about values, meanings and proprieties between the organisation's members and its environment. (*Culture and Complexity: New Insights on Organisational Change*, Richard Seel - Organisations & People vol.7, no.2.)

Hofstede describes Culture as "the collective programming of the mind which distinguishes one human group from another" (Hofstede 1980).

Leadership

> *"Leadership is the capacity to release the collective intelligence and insight of groups and organisations. It is helping people to find their own answers. There are things that you as a leader need to know if you are to be credible but there are moments when you need to say 'I don't know' if others are to confront difficult issues and learn how to overcome them."*

(Living Leadership – a practical guide for ordinary heroes, Binney, Wilke & Williams 2005 Prentice Hall)

Leadership – by each individual or as a group – is responsible for creating the vision to see beyond today's difficulties – and a culture that will sustain the organisation for the longer term.

Management

Managers must understand, take responsibility for, and ensure the organisation's daily work is implemented.

Quality is determined by top management.

It cannot be delegated.

Make the work work.

Improved quality leads to increased productivity rather than quality comes at the expense of productivity. The need is to improve quality and reduce costs to meet today's customer requirements.

Develop a system of management that will ensure pride in achievement for everyone. Give people joy in work.

> *If you look after your people, your people will look after your customers*

Managers need to develop a correct understanding of data/information in a scientific context. Managers need to understand what they must learn from the things they measure and what these tell them about how the organisation is performing against its purpose. *Understand the wisdom of numbers.*

Managers should commit to continual improvement and innovation in design, product and process.

There should be a planned approach to improvement, innovation and learning.

Each of these four elements of the MoSO will now be covered in more detail, with more ideas on which to reflect and act – or join us in developing the MoSO model by engaging in the process with your comments and experience.

People And Change – More Ideas

Organisations change in response to their environment; if they don't, they die. The subject of **Organisational Development (O/D)** has been built over the last 40 years as leaders, managers, practitioners, and academics struggled with the theories and practicalities of helping 'organisations' to respond to changing demands – for that read 'helping people' to develop and change in response to the evolving needs.

And all this in place of judgement of people, ranking them, putting them into slots (outstanding, excellent, on down to unsatisfactory) - the aim should be to help people to optimize the system so that everybody will gain.

Dick Beckard of M.I.T. defines Organisation Development (OD) as "an effort, planned, organisation-wide, and managed from the top, to increase organisation effectiveness and health through planned interventions in the organisation's processes, using behavioural-science knowledge." In essence, OD is a planned system of change.

He also highlights the need to be aware of societal changes as we think about organisational changes.

Today's changing values include:

1. People should and are more independent and autonomous;
2. People have choices in work and leisure;
3. There is a need to meet higher-order needs;
4. People will choose to meet their needs instead of the organisation's if they are in conflict;
5. Organisations should arrange things so work is meaningful and stimulating;
6. The power of bosses is reduced.

What is OD?

- A planned change effort,
- Involvement of the whole system,
- Managed from the top - the top is involved,
- Designed to increase organisational effectiveness and health,
- Achieving its goals through planned interventions using Behavioural science knowledge.

Other definitions

"OD is a system-wide process of planned change aimed at improving overall effectiveness". (Bradford & Burke)

"OD is a long-range effort to improve an organisation's problem solving and renewal processes". (French & Bell)

"OD is poorly understood because it is a mixture of disciplines and transcends functional boundaries. OD is more of a scavenger discipline. It borrows from many areas, e.g. Systems-Thinking, behavioural science, psychology, sociology, anthropology, systems theory, organisational behaviour, etc.

"OD is crucial in today's fast-moving and changing environment. And yet even HR practitioners do not understand what is meant by OD, even the basic principles and practices that could make such a difference to organisational effectiveness.

"OD recognises that organisations are part of an open system. Environmental factors [inputs] influence what the organisation exists to create [outputs]. OD looks at the total systems and the linkages between the parts and how change in one part will affect another part." (Linda Holbeche in CIPD quarterly review)

What is involved in OD

- Theory in action
- Action Research

The OD practitioner is a helper/enabler using

- diagnostic data and
- then intervening within the system
- using structured interventions

Operational goals of OD

- Create a viable self-renewing organisation

- Optimise effectiveness - continuous improvement
- Achieve high collaboration and low competition between interdependent units within the system
- Create conditions where conflict is brought out and managed
- Reach a point where decisions are made based on information rather than power

Characteristics of an OD effort

- A planned programme involving the whole system
- The top of the organisation is aware of, committed to and involved in the effort
- It is long term
- Activities are action-oriented
- It focuses on changing attitudes and behaviours
- Usually relies on some form of experience-based training
- OD efforts work primarily in groups

Kinds of organisational conditions that call for an OD effort

- A change to managerial strategy
- Making the climate more consistent with individual needs and the changing needs of the environment
- A change in the cultural norms
- A change of structure and roles
- A need to improve intergroup collaboration
- The need to open up communication systems

- The need for better planning
- The need to cope with the problems of a merger
- The need for a change of motivation in the organisation
- The need for adaptation to a new environment

Skills and Abilities

The skills and abilities that individuals need to achieve success in an OD change

- Interpersonal competence
- Problem-solving knowledge and skills
- Goal setting skills
- Planning skills
- Understanding the process of change and changing
- Skills in System Diagnosis

How to develop your OD skills

Organisation development (OD) deals with managing dynamic and complex change, putting people at the heart of their organisation, determining mission, values and strategy, introducing new systems and processes, and restructuring and enhancing leadership.

OD is difficult to define, yet it sits at the heart of any planned, holistic approach to improving organisational performance, aligning strategy, people and processes. OD balances the need for organisational effectiveness and well-being with adapting to the external environment in which it operates. While the boundaries between OD expertise and other related fields are not clear-cut, the way the expertise is used makes OD what it is. More and more HR practitioners now have an OD function in their job, but many don't understand what it is or requires.

1. Start with process

The OD practitioner is crucial to the success or failure of an organisational development intervention. To succeed, OD practitioners must help organisations define their agenda rather than be reactive to needs. OD practitioners do what they do by working at a process level. They make a difference by enabling organisations to understand their processes.

2. Gathering and assessing data

Any OD intervention begins with gathering and assessing data to decide how to intervene and, crucially, ensure that the intervention will impact the root cause of the problem, not just the symptoms. One of the ways of doing this is using an action research process, whereby issues and concerns are highlighted through reflective practice and addressed. The diagnostics of this need to be done with the client and the OD practitioner – watch for deeper issues as the data is gathered, recognise what is relevant and understand how data from different parts of the system affect each other.

3. Feedback and decision

OD practitioners need to be able to communicate the outcomes in a comprehensible format. The

194

key is to create a non-threatening atmosphere and involve participants early, so they feel some ownership in the whole process. Process consultation is one way of dealing with feedback that enables the individual to take an active role rather than relying solely on the OD practitioner's expert opinion.

4. Form your plan

OD works better when it isn't a knee-jerk reaction to a crisis but a considered approach. Work with colleagues or departments in need to distil recommendations from the data. Focus on action that has high impact with minimum costs and implement a plan that is at the heart of the organisation.

5. Intervene

Make sure that your intervention is pitched at the appropriate emotional depth. Be clear about where the focus is – the individual, group or whole organisation – and choose the right type of intervention for your scenario. There are many examples of different interventions ranging from restructuring to coaching, transformational change journeys and learning and development.

6. Evaluate

Make sure you choose the correct evaluation method. One thing to consider would be using an action research approach: this is ideal for continually assessing the impact and results so that changes can be made as you go along rather than after the event. Remember to consider the cultural fit, why the information is required, how it will be used and budget constraints.

Key points

- Build OD into processes from the start.
- Data gathering (and feedback on those data) is essential before beginning any intervention.
- Work closely with other functions, focusing on actions that will have the most comprehensive benefit.
- Evaluate any process from start to finish, and don't be afraid to make changes as you go along.

References

Organisation development: Strategies and models. Beckhard, R (1969) Addison-Wesley

Organisation development: Its nature, origin and prospects. Bennis, W. (1969) Addison-Wesley

Organisation development: Behavioral science interventions for organisation improvement French, W., & Bell, C., Jr., (4th ed), (1990) Prentice-Hall

OD - what's in a name Linda Holbeche CIPD Director of Research and Policy and Mee-Yan Cheung- Judgein CIPD Impact no 26, February 2009

How to...in OD Sylvia Baumgartner principal consultant for organisational development, Roffey Park, People Management February 2009

Culture – More Ideas

We need to understand the culture: what it is, where it came from, and who is interested in retaining it - or changing it.

A further distinction Hofstede suggests (1991) helps think about the culture of an organisation – and of the surrounding society:

- **Individualism/Collectivism** - a range from communities where the ties between individuals are loose to communities where people from birth are integrated into strong, cohesive in-groups.
- **Power distance** - the extent to which the less powerful members of institutions and organisations within a country expect and accept that power is distributed unequally.
- **Uncertainty avoidance** - the extent to which the members of a culture feel threatened by uncertain or unknown situations.
- **Masculinity/Femininity** - a range from societies and organisations in which social gender roles are distinct to communities in which social gender roles overlap.
- **Confusion dynamism** - a range from long-term orientation to short-term focus.

And also:

- process-orientated versus results-orientated,
- job-orientated versus employee-orientated,

197

- professional versus parochial,
- open systems versus closed systems,
- tightly versus loosely controlled,
- pragmatic versus normative.

Yet more questions for each of us to consider about our work environment - on the journey to understanding how we do things around here - and what we might do about it.

- Do we connect culture with organisation structure or with something else? Like the beliefs and values of the founders or those of current leaders?
- Do leaders create a culture - or are they products of it? Do they know which condition applies to them? Do they recognise their own assumptions and preconditions, which can limit acceptable thought (of their own or others!) - and if so, do they restrict outcomes? Are they actively doing anything about it?
- What is the organisation's purpose – and on what does it rely? And does the current culture help or hinder that purpose?
- Should the responsibility of leaders and managers be to create an environment where people can perform to the best of their ability and ingenuity, then what responsibilities must those leaders and managers take for the culture? Are you one of those leaders or managers?
- What are we trying to do?
- Through what lens do we see the world?

And some more questions for you to consider:

- What is it like around here?
- What would you like to be different?
- For what are you responsible?
- What influence do you have?
- How might you begin to change that?
- How does this all start with you?

A Framework for Leadership

Here we propose a framework linking essential leadership ingredients - context, practices, styles - and self-awareness - in valuable ways. We encourage people in organisations, especially those with greater responsibility, to find ways to understand the complexity that is effective leadership and to recognise that there are no prescriptions. If there is no simple answer, then leadership is about continually reflecting on today's actions and consequences to improve tomorrow's performance.

This demand for Self-Awareness is then crucial to assess the competing needs of all the people in the organisation - and the contributions they can make, providing the leader can provide the appropriate environment to release their skills.

199

Figure 32: Self-Awareness

As a leader, how can I best balance the following? And how will I know how I'm doing?[14]

- Drivers for change
- Scale and speed of change
- Sticking with what we have now

Guiding Questions

- How would you describe the Leadership Style of the people within your organisation?
- How do you help them to provide the conditions for effective work?
- How do you help them communicate the organisation's vision and purpose?

---

[14] See "Leadership Matters – the power of self-awareness" Occasional Paper No 7 – Resources – www.transitionpartnerships.com

- Would you recognise any of these styles?

Leadership Models

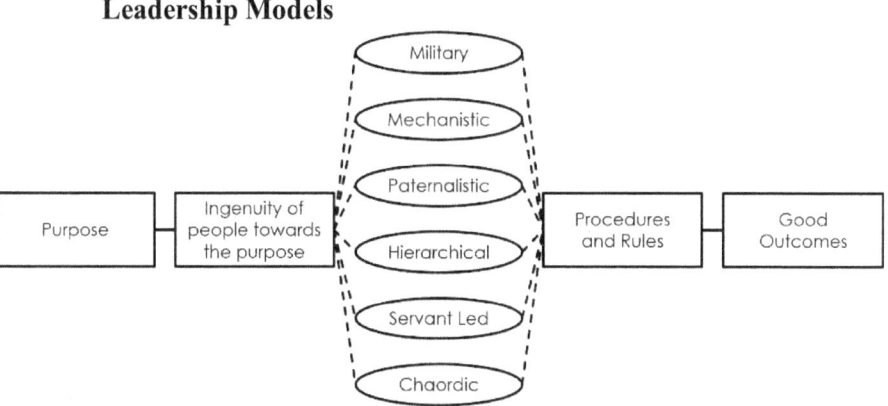

Figure 33: Leadership Models

(And the presumption here is that the Outcomes will be Good! They may equally be Bad! What impact does the culture have? And how effective is the System?)

And even now, we need to add another possibility – the Network – an animal connected for some to social networking groups, to anarchists – even to crime – yet increasingly, it is seen as a creative structure for 'wicked problems' which materialise in our complex, integrated, global world. Yet where does Leadership reside in such a model?

Using the model of the Critical-Tame-Wicked problem from Grint (2008), Mike Pedler argues that leaders will need to understand and conform to different needs within a Network which is challenged by a wicked problem:

In Grint's threefold model, the progression from 'critical' to 'tame' to 'wicked problems is marked

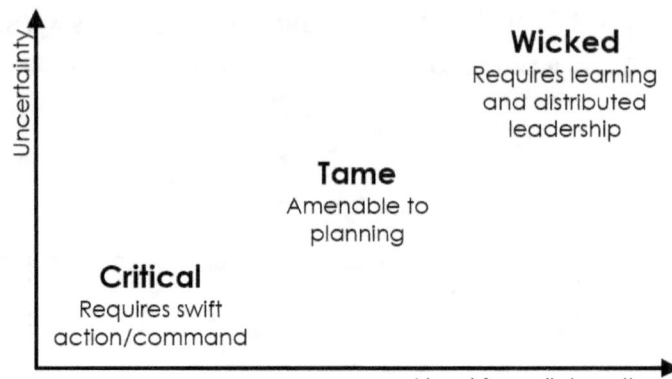

Figure 34: Types of Problems

by an increase both in uncertainty about solutions and the need for collaboration. 'Critical' problems are the domain of command: crisis situations such as heart attacks, train crashes or natural disasters demand swift action, leaving little time for procedure or uncertainty. 'Tame' problems, though they be very complex, such as timetabling a school, planning heart surgery or building a new hospital, are essentially amenable to rational tools and constitute the natural domain of management. "Wicked" problems defy rational analysis and are the domain of leadership.

Three Types of Problems[15]

Where past business issues, though complicated, could often be solved within hierarchies, Network Leadership is needed for real, system-pervading 'wicked' problems:

---

[15] Grint 2008

> *"A network is a grouping of individuals, organisations and agencies organised on a nonhierarchical basis around common issues or concerns, which are pursued proactively and systematically, based on commitment and trust." (WHO 1998)*

The idea is plastic and polymorphic: the highly controlled, commercial supply chain, proven effective with some complex "tame" problems, differs significantly from the professional network, and the informal networks are different again. It is also a powerful idea: claims that "networked companies" already outperform conventional ones[16], whilst others warn that the success of (unaccountable) informal networks may be undermining (accountable) bureaucracies[17]. The latter is a reminder that the network is the organisation of choice for terrorists and criminals. Crime syndicates, for example, now permeate many national cultures and governance systems, possibly contributing 20% of the global GDP[18].

However, the network's potential to resolve the legitimate problems of organisations and societies is yet to be realised. Currently, some seem to believe that the collaborative possibilities of the new

---

[16] Häcki & Lighton 2001
[17] Bradwell & Reeves 2008
[18] Castells: 169-211; Glenny: 8

technologies make unnecessary all other organisational forms: everyone can harness "the power
of organising without organisations"[19]. In the
neo-anarchist world of social networking, "you
are what you share", and power accrues to the
"connectors"[20]. However naive these visions are,
they attest to the power of ideas. The realisation
of this power is another matter.

...and Managed Networks

The attractiveness of networks is in their flat and
loosely coupled natures, flexible working and the
local freedom to act, with members pursuing
their own purposes in a common field. But in the
context of formal organisations, this looseness
and freedom create interesting problems: How is
a strategic direction to be determined? How is
leadership possible? How are resources allo-
cated? And critically, how are the actions of network members governed and made accountable?

Ideal-type networks are rarely found in formal organisations, where they are "managed" or "structured" to a greater or lesser degree. Where the
needs for control, predictability and external accountability are high, networks are likely to complement and exist alongside hierarchies. In the
NHS[21], for example, working with hierarchies and
networks is a hallmark of the "innovating organisation"[22]. Design primers can be found to create
"loosely coupled clusters of interacting units"

---

[19] Leadbeater 2008; Shirky 2008
[20] Gladwell 2005
[21] British National Health Service organisation
[22] Pettigrew & Fenton 2000

contributing to and being guided by a "strategic core"[23].

Distributed leadership

However, networks are enacted and co-created by their members' activities and cannot be overprescribed. Network organising works through local initiatives, via personal ties, links, and relationships, and too much ordering will repress these energies and reproduce a limited engagement. To enact the network in anything like its "ideal type" requires distributed rather than focused leadership. Described as "the collective capacity to create value"[24], this implies more rather than fewer people being engaged in decision and direction. Researchers also stress the critical importance of context and situational factors: "School leadership is best understood as a distributed practice *stretched over* the school's social and situational context"[25].

Building and sustaining the network relies on this distribution of effort. The principle of voluntary engagement means that if the network does not generate enough energy or deliver enough benefits, members will soon drop away. Developing network leadership, governance, and accountability processes also requires collective attention. The problematics of leadership, governance and accountability make for good action learning questions:

---

[23] Campbell & Goold 2002
[24] Senge 1990
[25] Spillane et al 2001

- Who is eligible to join the network, and what are their rights and obligations?
- What are the rules of engagement?
- How is behaviour regulated in the network, and conflicts resolved?
- How will we hold ourselves accountable?
- Can we develop user-centred accountability?

And so on. Skilful designers cannot resolve these questions in advance but must be enacted through experiments and lived experience.

Contributing as a manager to the "managed network" may also require much new learning for those reared in hierarchical institutions. There are many tensions to manage in reconciling free association for mutual interest with the accomplishment of collective tasks. This tension requires sensitivity and creativity around the sorts of systems that can encourage this way of working, together with the skills of animation that generate participation and engagement[26].

Some more definitions – and you will have your own

Military   Structured around a clear chain of command, with well-proved processes and training, so that individuals know how they will be expected to act in most situations – and when

---

[26] All in a Knot of One Another's Labours: Learning, Self-determination and Organising; Mike Pedler (2009) Inaugural Lecture – Henley Management College

they do not, they have sound models of behaviour and action on which to fall back.

Mechanistic Following the product, where people are tools in the process.

PaternalisticThe organisation will look after you in all respects – and expects undying loyalty in return.

HierarchicalThe people at the top know best – and can and do give instructions to those lower down by the authority of their position. People lower down are not expected to use their initiative – they are instruments of someone else's power and agendas.

Behaviour is compelled – it rarely emerges out of a shared community.

Servant Led Leaders and managers respect the skills of their people and expect them to deal with the situations they know and understand best within a strategic vision and framework in which they feel engaged. Can be described as 'upside down' when compared to Hierarchical – where the leaders support the led with what they need to do their job, having the humility to know that they, the leaders, cannot do the work, that interference can stifle ingenuity and that it takes determination to stick to the plan!

Chaordic	Created or emerging, where individuals, parts or groups reflect a natural survival process within their local environment – where chaos and order meet.
Purpose	The purpose is the unambiguous expression of what people wish to become. Principles, People and Concept then define Structure and Practice in an iterative, living process.

Some quotes

"Organisational learning, development, and planned change cannot be understood without considering culture as the primary source of resistance to change."

"This ability to perceive the limitations of one's own culture and to develop the culture adaptively is the essence and ultimate challenge of leadership."

"The bottom line for leaders is that if they do not become conscious of the cultures in which they are embedded, those cultures will manage them. Cultural understanding is desirable for all of us, but it is essential to leaders if they are to lead."

So, what is the culture in your patch?

What language might we use to describe it? And does it help or hinder? And can we change it – if only in our bit of the organisation?

What 'control beliefs' do we hold?

What route might we take to self-efficacy?

- Primary control – I can change my world
- Secondary control – I can change my needs to conform to my world

"So.... when might I start?"

References

- **Organisational Culture and Leadership**. Edgar Schein , Professor of Management at M.I.T. 2nd Edition, Jossey-Bass 1992 ISBN 1-55542-487-2
- **Birth of the Chaordic Age** . Dee Hock, Founder and CEO Emeritus, VISA for the concepts around a Chaordic organisation Berrett Koehler 1999 ISBN 1-576-75074-4
- **Servant Leadership** – a journey into the Nature of Legitimate Power and greatness – Robert K Greenleaf (1977) Paulist Press
- **Stewardship** – Choosing Service over Self-Interest – Peter Block (1993) Berrett Koelher
- **Living Leadership** – A practical guide for Ordinary Heroes – G Binney, G Wilke & C Williams (2005) FT Prentice Hall
  - **Leadership, Limits and Possibilities** Basingstoke: Grint K (2005) Palgrave
  - Leadership, Management and Command – Rethinking D-day Grint K (2008)
- All in a Knot of One Another's Labours: Learning, Self-determination and Organising Mike Pedler (2009) Inaugural Lecture – Henley Management College

The Role Of Management – And Others

> *Leadership is doing the right things ..... whereas Management is doing things right.*

Also[27]:

- The proper role of management is to lead people to understand the business as a system that links everyone's efforts to best serve **customer** needs.
- A business's goal is to continually nurture team members' creative talents (including employees, suppliers and partners) to understand, meet, and exceed customer expectations (both present and future).
- By focusing on **what** people do and **how** they do it, the manager will improve the system's capability to serve customers.
- Management's main job is to help each employee realise their potential, and therefore it is to learn what people do in their jobs and how what they do serves customers.
- Such learning is difficult, if not impossible, in organisations that manage solely by results (i.e., without regard for or knowledge of system capability).

---

[27] Adapted from Johnson & Broms, 2000

> *"Leadership is of the spirit,*
> *compounded of personality and*
> *vision: its practice is an art.*
> *Management is of the mind, more*
> *a matter of accurate calculation,*
> *statistics, methods, timetables*
> *and routine; its practice is a*
> *science. Managers are*
> *necessary; leaders are*
> *essential."*[28]

While people may believe that they are all acting purposefully, they need to be aware that accommodations will be necessary between conflicting points of view, which enable action to be taken. Individuals see the same concept from multiple perspectives – hence the complexity of perceived reality. System/model is not the world – it is a device to structure debate/dialogue between individuals.

Change comes through conversation – a model can be 'oppressive', and participation means the willing submission of the 'good self' ...to the wisdom of a collective tuned to a transcendent wisdom – and in the free flow of dialogue, people find themselves speaking what they did not realise they thought.

---

[28] Address to the Australian Institute of Management 1957 by Field Marshall Sir William Slim

> *Leadership is one-third sensing the outside world and the whole business environment, one-third understanding how the organisation is performing to deliver its purpose, and one-third developing more good leaders[29].*

"Management by results creates 'needs', goals that we feel we must achieve for our survival or personal gain. Management by means nurtures aspirations and aims that we pursue because they matter to us. The difference is subtle yet profound [...] it is a tragedy when we lose the ability to distinguish needs from aspirations."[30]

"Management:

1. Manage self,
2. Manage the bosses,
3. Manage peers and all others around you,
4. Hire good people to do the same!"[31]

> *Anyone can be a leader – first, they need to lead themselves.*
> *(Jim Collins in Level 5 Leadership)*

How much better can we do?

---

[29] How I spend my time - A senior leader of a global defence business 2007
[30] Peter Senge in the Foreword to "Profit Beyond Measure" by H Thomas Johnson and Anders Broms
[31] Dee Hock, Founder and CEO Emeritus, VISA

> *"If you have a stable system, then there is no use to specify a goal. You will get whatever the system will deliver. A goal beyond the capability of the system will not be reached. If you do not have a stable system, then there is no point in setting a goal. There is no way to know what the system will produce: it has no capability." (W Edwards Deming)*

Management   Leadership

Dealing   with   theCreating the culture.
known.

Recognising the risks. Accepting the 'unknown'.

Having the courage toRespecting the skills of
act.   others.

The Role of a Manager of People

The new role of a manager of people after transformation:

1) A manager understands and conveys to his people the meaning of a system. He explains the aims of the system. He teaches his people to understand how the group's work supports these aims.
2) He helps his people see themselves as components in a system, to cooperate with preceding and following stages to optimise all stages' efforts toward achieving the aim.

3) A manager of people understands that people are different from each other. He tries to create for everybody interest and challenge, and joy in work. He tries to optimize the family background, education, skills, hopes, and abilities of everyone.

    Management is not ranking people. It is, instead, a recognition of differences between people and an attempt to put everybody in a position for development.

4) The manager is an unceasing learner who encourages the team members to study. When possible and feasible, the manager provides seminars and courses for the advancement of learning. The manager encourages continued education in college or university for people that are so inclined.

5) The manager coaches and counsels but does not judge.

6) The manager understands a stable system and the interaction between people and their work circumstances. They understand that the performance of anyone who can learn a skill will be stable—upon which further lessons will not improve performance. A manager of people knows that telling the worker about a mistake is distracting in this stable state.

7) The manager has three sources of power:
    a) Authority of office
    b) Knowledge
    c) Personality and persuasive power; tact.

    A successful people manager develops (b) and (c) and does not rely on (a). They are obliged to use (a), as this source of power enables them to change the process - equipment, materials, methods - to bring improvement, such as reducing variation in output[32].

They who are in authority but lack knowledge (b) or personality (c) must depend on their formal power (a). They unconsciously fill a void in qualifications by making it clear to everybody that they are in a position of authority. My will be done.

8) They will study results to improve their performance as a manager of people.

9) They will try to discover who, if anybody, is outside the system and needs special help. This discovery can be accomplished with simple calculations if there are individual figures on production or failures. Special help may be only a simple rearrangement of work. It might be more complicated. Those needing special help are not in the bottom 5 per cent of the distribution of others: they are clean outside that distribution.

10) The People Manager creates trust and an environment that encourages freedom and innovation.

11) They do not expect perfection.

12) They listen and learn without passing judgement on the person to whom they listen.

13) They hold an informal, unhurried conversation with every one of his people at least once a year, not for judgement, merely to listen.

---

[32] Dr Robert Klekamp

The purpose would be to develop an understanding of the people, their aims, hopes, and fears. The meeting will be spontaneous rather than planned.

14) They understand the benefits of cooperation and the losses from competition between people and groups.

References

Beyond Selfishness; Mintzberg, H., Simons, R, & Basu, K. (2002.) MIT Sloan Management Review Fall

"Servant Leadership - asking questions and delivering good outcomes" – Occasional Paper No 13 – Resources – www.transitionpartnerships.com

Some Roles – for Leaders and Managers

Figure 35: Leadership Roles

Noise →Data →Information →Knowledge →Understanding →Wisdom

What informs the sequence above?

Trust, Logic, Emotion: all in proper measure.

Some Self Examining Questions

1) What else would you add?
2) On reflection, what more might you do?
3) How could you engage and encourage others to do likewise?
4) What responsibility can you take for designing the system?
5) How capable are the processes?
6) How will you avoid 'tampering'?
7) Where does PDSA apply?
8) How do you lead by example?
9)

Societal Influences & Learning

Author   Fabian Hiscock

Reviewers   Tony Korychi & Terry Rose

Overview

The society in which we live and work has a profound and ever-changing effect on our lifestyles and, therefore, on our expectations of the products and services we purchase and the types of jobs available to us.

In this technological age, change comes in waves that hit hard and fast – at an ever-increasing frequency.

No company or organisation exists in a vacuum – at least, not for long. Product life-cycles are often measured in months rather than years (or even decades, as for previous generations). Skills, both individual and organisational that have been acquired over many years can become redundant over night. Working methods, including management methods, need to adapt to new realities. Rapid societal learning requires a revolution in management thinking – from 'Secrets' to 'Sharing' – from 'We don't do it that way' to 'Openness to learn and change', including learning outside the present business sector.

Societal learning can be thought of as learning from the network of companies, customers, suppliers, and others trying to improve how their companies function. Such mutual learning is necessary because organisational change and improvement methods are not a theory a company can learn and follow easily. Companies develop their internal practices through trial and error.

Possible Other Topics

Societal Infrastructure Elements that Support a Vibrant Business Community

- Venture capital firms/investors
- Business networks (formal and informal)
- A well-developed IPO market
- Use of tax system to support business activities
- Government-backed 'infrastructure' schemes (e.g. Skills development)
- Education (schools and Higher education)
- Professional Bodies (e.g. CQI)

Infrastructure for Networking

- National Promotion
- Training schemes
- Sector Knowledge Dissemination
- Societal promotion
- National Standards
- Development of new methods (sponsored by CQI?)

Background

Enterprises seeking to sustain their businesses interact routinely and naturally with the society in which they operate. Large enterprises often express this interaction through their Corporate

Social Responsibility activity, but much smaller undertakings still need to consider their societal influences.

The CQI[33]'s Body of Quality Knowledge points to several key features in considering Societal Influences on the sustainable organisation:

- The need for organisational values and codes of conduct, professional principles and business ethics,
- The influence of global cultural differences,
- The effects of technology on people and the environment,
- The impact of different legal frameworks, including consumer protection, enforcement agencies, employment directives, product liability and business governance,
- The importance of maintaining compliance with appropriate standards for societal interactions,
- The role of corporate governance: arrangements and accountability, ethics, audits, management reviews, communication and reporting structures, corporate citizenship.

These are expanded below.

---

[33] Chartered Quality Institute

Purpose Of This Article

This short essay is intended to highlight some of the ways in which the sustainable enterprise influences (and is influenced by) the society (or societies) in which it exists and suggest how the enterprise can use or meet them to ensure that it is indeed "sustainable". This effort might or might not require "transformation"; it will undoubtedly require a constant and well-managed change to keep abreast of the developments generated by its existence.

The Influenced Society – and its Influence

In many societies, there are strong Regulatory frameworks. Even where there are none, the sustainable organisation still lays down and adheres to a framework within which it will work. At a minimum, this will consider financial dealings and the requirement to avoid killing or injuring its stakeholders. Failure to do this is fatal to sustainability. The more mature organisation does more and goes on to consider also its impact on the physical environment and on the community within which it works.

The management frameworks which result from compliance with these regulatory constraints are considered in the sections 'Company/Organisation Culture' and the 'Operational System'.

Societal influences on sustainable organisations also include:

- The educational history and framework of the society

An enterprise depending on high-quality engineering skills will find it difficult to maintain itself in an agrarian society, or indeed in a more advanced one in which the value placed on science and engineering is decreasing;

- The religious and cultural features and history, including the openness to change An enterprise which expects to change, as is likely for long-term sustainability, will not find it easy in a profoundly conservative society;

- The ethical framework Society may or may not reward behaviours crucial to long-term sustainability;

- The Nature and History of the labour market The availability and flexibility of human resources will affect the enterprise.

It is also necessary to consider and adjust, where necessary, the impact on society of the enterprise's own operations. Even very small companies purchasing goods overseas can have a significant local impact where the cottage industry is the model. On the other hand, large undertakings can be relatively insignificant in a heavily industrialised area. Factors to be considered by a sustainable enterprise include:

- The effect of economic dominance, if achieved, and the social responsibilities this might bring – a decision to ignore these is a conscious one;

- The impact of a large industrial operation in a rural area;
- The availability of transportation and the consequences of providing it: the social history of the inter-relationship of the canals of England and the industrial revolution is a largescale example. For well-regulated societies, 'development planning' frameworks often offer societal control, but this is not always present;
- The impact of day-to-day activities that might not be illegal but may affect people living nearby – for example, noise pollution.

Considering the macro-societal influences, the sustainable enterprise will consider its own operations.

These include:

- The fitness of the working environment for the workers;
- The fitness of the industrial process for the surrounding environment and society;
- How the enterprise's output meets the needs of the society where the customer lives and works.

It will also seek to ensure that society (including the workers) observes that what is promised occurs. The building and maintenance of trust are vital to a sustainable organisation.

The modern or developed 'customer society' is interested in the whole lifecycle of its consumption. Those supplying the UK Ministry of Defence will be familiar with the CADMID cycle, which runs from Concept through Assessment [of the options] and Development to Manufacture and the In-service phase, which is usually the longest. But it finishes with the Disposal phase, and the supply chain is invited to consider at the start how the product is to be dealt with (and indeed replaced) at the end of its useful life.

By extension, a well-considered 'Through life' approach for any project would recognise the possibility of innovation or investment in solutions and allow problems later in the cycle to be anticipated (at the time of writing, the cost tends to be a key driver, which may discourage this). But when equipment lifetimes get extended (for example, for airliners), this will be increasingly important as the regulatory framework, and the issues associated with climate change alter the agenda during the life of the equipment.

While this may appear to apply to large enterprises, the principles are relevant to all 'sustainment' considerations. Unless adequately managed, the modern trend towards 'planned obsolescence' is highly prejudicial to the sustained environment. Economic modelling is also being developed to show its effect on financial sustainability.

Assurance

The developing principle of Accountability seeks to ensure that high standards of stewardship, sustainability and transparency are maintained by organisations which seek to be sustainable, and the Accountability Assurance Standard AA1000 aims to ensure this. In the UK, BS8900 (Managing Sustainable Development) addresses many of these issues, and ISO 26000 (Social Responsibility), develop the theme further. In the USA, applying the Sarbanes Oxley Act imposed many of these principles on businesses, and this trend is likely to increase worldwide.

Summary

Sustainable commercial and industrial enterprises are required in many countries to consider a much more comprehensive range of their interactions with the society in which they operate than has been traditional. If they fail to do so, their true long-term sustainability is under threat.

These considerations include the physical environment, which should not be damaged, and the hosting society's economic, cultural and educational components, all of which should be enhanced.

An enterprise that works with all its stakeholders (from staff and customers to environmental groups and the wider society) to take positive environmental, workforce, community and marketplace initiatives will ensure a sustainable organisation.

The Environment – A Deming-Centric View

Author	Mike Upstone
Reviewers	Alan Clark, Tony Korycki

Overview

> *"The environment is everything that isn't me."*
> (Albert Einstein)

Dr Deming's philosophy uses very different approaches to those of many prevailing business paradigms. As a philosophy geared toward optimising complex systems, it is entirely consistent with managing environmental sustainability. Deming's principles provide profound insights into an organisation's external environment and internal environment, emphasising system optimisation, stability, logic, understanding of the process (particularly the factors involved in process variation), psychology and measurement.

Summary

A variation on an old joke:

>   "How do I get to ecological sustainability?"

>   "If I were you, I wouldn't be starting from here."

Einstein said: *"insanity is doing the same thing over and over and expecting different results."*

Dr Deming grew up on a small holding in Wyoming, where the settlers' survival depended on climate and management of the soil. Environment and climate change are now a top priority for modern society and, therefore, a critical issue for every enterprise. A key implication of Deming regarding environmental policy is that decisions based on the premise that (a) nothing changes or (b) political self-interest come back and bite us: the environment, including society, is a dynamic system that constantly changes and will eventually hold us to account for our actions (or inactions), based on invalid or outmoded assumptions.

Deming's background gave him a direct experience of the interdependence of the environment and humanity within a philosophical yet profoundly practical approach to understanding 'a system'. Systemic approaches cater to reality and not to artificial constructs; they produce a deeper understanding of processes, enabling practical outcomes to be created and subsequently measured. Therefore, this approach treats strategic change in a deeper, broader and longer-term context than a strictly departmental or short-term exercise.

Deming philosophy is the polar opposite of some practices used by successful organisations, which would be far more successful over the longer term if they followed Deming principles. This philosophy's core is not about focusing on fads, financial management or costs but about creating enduring, sustainable, balanced systems that develop in an organic way to eliminate

227

waste naturally. To do this, we do things differently: the key is to continually strive to do everything better through a holistic understanding of organic systems and working with a constancy of purpose.

Most of us are socially programmed to focus on maxima (sales, profits) and minima (costs, workforce); in doing so, we can entirely miss the point of understanding the system/process itself and optimising it organically and sustainably; the weakness in our thinking can be ascribed to our level of understanding and the assumptions we use to interpret our data.

It is essential to remove any idea that organisations and the environment, both internal and external, are dissociated. Such thinking explains why some organisations fail to reach anything like optimal performance and are driven by politics, fads and short-termism. To see the whole picture, we need to look at the entire system and understand interrelationships in an entirely new way. The constancy of purpose underpins this drive to innovative thinking. The primary purpose of any company is to go beyond just satisfying: it must aim to delight its customers because without them there are no sales, profits or shareholder values. We need to keep our priorities in order.

Deming principles provide a platform for action that accurately reflects an organisation's internal environment and recognises its interdependency with its external environment. Whilst this may

228

sound complex, the practical application of Deming principles shows that it helps to simplify how we deal with the complexity of life, business, public service and government, making it balanced, manageable and sustainable.

Main Content

> *Any defects within a process*
> *contribute to poor environmental*
> *performance for a company.*
> *(Deming)*

Richly fertile American farmlands turned into dust bowls in the early twentieth century through farming mismanagement and short-term policies. Deming, who witnessed these events as a young man, appreciated the importance of the environment concerning any system.

It is an academic convenience to view an organisation, even an artificial, manufactured construct such as a corporation, as being unaffected by or detached from its environment. Yet such is the accepted thinking of some prominent corporations and political leaders, who rationalise it as practical or pragmatic, especially in the face of complexity. Such a thought process provides convenient assumptions for an increasingly complex world; however, it is artificial: assumptions are often incorrect in the first place, and those that do work can rapidly become outmoded.

This kind of assumption (or paradigm) means even helpful ideas become defunct, often causing bad decisions in a world where change is increasingly dynamic. Assuming that an organisation is detached from its environment is particularly alien to any farmer who deals with the world's most complex and unpredictable environment: the natural world. It is also foreign to a psychological definition of a Rational: one who recognises patterns and pictures (therefore causes and effects), is less concerned with details than outputs, and makes decisions based on principles based on those patterns. Deming was both a Rational and a farmer's son.

Deming's contribution to management thinking is much deeper than a prescribed set of tactical tools for implementing quality. The principles he created form a holistic philosophy, which has often been misunderstood and sometimes misapplied, especially in the West. These principles encompass psychology, economics and social well-being and contradict some prevailing corporate and political paradigms. Deming's principles form a practical, robust and sustainable philosophy which covers much more than ISO exercises or fads such as Total Quality Management (TQM).

The Theory of Profound Knowledge

Deming proposed the "Theory of Profound Knowledge" in his book *The New Economics*. He described this theory as a lens or a way of seeing that can be used as a practical mechanism for understanding systems and, thus, for implementing systemic improvement and creating bal-

230

ance, thereby making an organisation sustainable in the longer term. This concept is a more practical way of viewing systems than (for example) simply picking groups of successful companies and analysing common factors: such things have been done in the past, and many of the shining examples of corporate success ended up in companies that rapidly declined and fell. The lesson is that companies can and do encompass damaging behaviours within strategies that can be successful over the short-term, but failing to understand how and why things really work within a system is liable to cause destructive behaviours to become the norm and consequently get entrenched and copied, but that does not make them any less damaging.

The system Deming explained in the Theory of Profound Knowledge covers four elements and their interactions:

- Appreciation for a system,
- Psychology,
- Knowledge of variation,
- Theory of knowledge.

This methodology offers distinctly practical ways of understanding complex systems, enabling us to improve the 'quality of management, quality of life and quality of interactions with one another and our environment'.

Appreciation for a system

Attempts to optimise the sub-units of a system without appreciation for the system as a whole typically transfer costs, destabilise and ultimately create sub-optimal output. Such exercises often manifest themselves as maxima and minima projects – sales pushes or cost reduction exercises – which ultimately increase costs, reduce margins and increase waste. The root of this problem is a lack of understanding about how a system's components, processes and sub-processes work together and are interdependent. In manufactured systems, it is, therefore, imperative that the system's aim is considered, defined and clearly explained. This definition is crucial to optimising the system: without clear logical goals and values, based on collaboration and co-operation, you are very unlikely to achieve them.

Focusing on system elements without catering to the system whole leads to decreased efficiency and effectiveness.

Deming advocated 'constancy of purpose' as a counterpoint to short-term, confusing and contradictory management fads, which waste resources, undermine workers' morale and shake faith in leadership's direction, quality and effectiveness. In the case of the climate and the environment, the goals of our economic system are clearly in contradiction if they are focused on a mentality of "profit maximisation and cost minimisation". While this makes superficial sense, it falls apart as a functional theory when introducing systemic complexity.

> *It is unwise to pay too much, but it is unwise to pay too little. When you pay too much, you lose a little money; that is all.*
>
> *When you pay too little you sometimes lose everything.*
>
> *Because the thing you bought was incapable of doing the thing you bought it to do. The common law of business balance prohibits paying a little and getting a lot.*
>
> *It cannot be done.*
>
> *If you deal with the lowest bidder, it is well to add something for the risk you run and if you do that, you will have enough to pay for something better."*
>
> *(John Ruskin in the "Common Law of Business Balance")*

Deming said:

"Co-operate on common problems, then compete" and *"Every example of co-operation is to the benefit of them that choose to co-operate".*

We all understand the kind of problems that politics introduces, especially when it comes to tackling climate change. Recognition of a common problem does not always lead to common solutions. The debate is widely seen to be politicised; nevertheless, what has been termed 'coopetition' can and does work – it enables companies to share costs in developing solutions for common problems while relying on companies recognising that short-term and divisive approaches are unsustainable.

Regulation is being put forward as a solution to the world's climate problems, but the danger is that this will enforce short-term, politically driven solutions and exacerbate the issues. While regulating light bulb standards aims to improve energy efficiency, it has led to increased investment and technological developments. Will "carbon caps" marry with a nation's short-term or strategic interests intent on low fuel prices or generating short-term competitive advantage? What will carbon 'offset' deals do, if anything, to address the root cause of excessive CO_2 production from major industries?

The main problem with regulatory approaches is that they are, by nature, political and divisive, based on assumptions about the world and our place within it – and are hierarchical. On this basis, they fundamentally contradict a Deming approach. Deming stated that he viewed good stewardship as leaving a better world behind for our children than the one we inherited, and, in his intellectual approach, he subscribed to Einstein's view that "Problems cannot be solved by the same level of thinking that created them".

Instead, can carbon gases promote faster crop growth within contained environments? Can animal or vegetable 'filter feeders' be used to help sustainably remove pollution from the environment? For example, thinking within the existing power production system is unlikely to yield such solutions. A corporate entity is systematically a difficult one for ideas people and inventors to engage with due to a commercial propensity for self-protection ("What if we had the idea first?") and for thinking within corporate paradigms ("We have the best brains in the business, how could anyone else come up with a better solution?").

The danger of hierarchical, politically driven solutions is that they can make all the right noises (which they are certainly designed to) but ultimately fail to deal directly with root causes. By adding bureaucracy and waste, they consume even more resources, leading to more entrenched paradigms. The objective can be muddied or misplaced entirely by compromising on goals due to political imperatives. So, instead of empowering, they disempower, undermine grassroots support and lead to individuals and organisations finding ways of getting around the system instead of contributing to sustainable solutions because they don't 'own' those solutions. In the USA, support for global warming hypotheses fell by 20% between 2006 and 2008.) You are unlikely to arrive at the correct answer if you don't ask the right question.

> *The greater the interdependence within a system, the more important the need for clarity of and alignment with the system's aim, and the more critical the role of management.*

Thus if the key issue is the reduction of carbon emissions, why not use the price mechanism? Why not fine or tax polluters relative to the cost and the amount of cleanup associated with the waste of their production process? And why not provide tax breaks for those that can demonstrably prove they leave a zero cost to the environment with their 'carbon footprint'? Isn't one of the dangers of a regulatory approach that only large companies can comply with, in which case what is the predictable outcome for millions of small businesses that employ over half the American workforce, for example?

Representing organisations through charts showing systems or process flows rather than organisational charts makes sense when describing how an organisation functions and where each individual, as well as each department or subsidiary, fits within it – they represent the system, its relationships, its functions and the interdependency of its constituents. Such tools can provide a more profound understanding of the system than an organisation chart in explaining how a system works; this is particularly important when delayed reactions separate causes from effects.

236

Many leading economists, including the chief economist of the World Bank, widely predicted the current economic situation. The unsustainability of the situation was not only predictable, it was an inevitable consequence of policy, given an understanding of the monetary system. The fact that causes do not necessarily beget outcomes immediately does not mean the outcomes are unrelated. The problem of appointing specialists instead of making environmental responsibility a concern of all management means that the policy is less likely to be effective.

We need to account for tomorrow's costs today and to do it realistically: to do it effectively, the entire organisation needs to think systemically and get involved directly.

Such engagement needs leadership from the very top. However, unless a systems approach is built into the decision-making process at every level of an organisation as a philosophical/core value, it will likely be treated as simply more theory and PR by 'initiative fatigued' employees and management. Should such leadership and organisational thinking be developed, it is proven that employees engage deeply with concerns that are not immediately associated with self-interest or the more commonly perceived corporate goals (such as profit). Deming had a distinctly different view of work and the psychology of labour from the prevailing paradigms of control, hierarchy, competition and bonuses – he believed that most individuals want to do a good job, take responsibility and be recognised for it, to be fulfilled and take joy in their work.

Information is the key to applying the Deming philosophy, and it is via appropriate and timely information that efficiency is optimised and costs can be reduced to an optimal level. According to Deming, reviewing and rewarding systems or using numbers as targets contribute to systemic inefficiency: they replace cooperative activity aimed at a joint goal with internal competition. Consequently, instead of finding better methods, the organisation gets stuck on the old method but tightens the screw harder.

In the finance sector, the argument has been made that bonuses are essential in recruiting and retaining the best staff; this hypothesis is based on the premise that the best staff are already in place and are always driven by gambling linked to enormous personal rewards. This concept is potentially part of why the banking system was not viable long-term. Did such people need to earn millions a year when they pursued other careers before or after working in finance? Were they any less capable individuals before or after they worked in banks? Are the most expensive individuals necessarily the best ones for this kind of work in any case? Even if we accept a hypothesis that the greediest gamblers are essential for ensuring bank competitiveness, how do we account for the fact that, in 2008, the banking sector lost more money than they made in profits in the previous 25 years combined? Furthermore, can we justify assertions that banks are 'too big to fail' when the cost to the rest of the economy of their gambling is ruinous?

238

What about the cost of this failure to the rest of the system? The other 95% or more of economic activity?

Psychology

Humans tend to think in paradigms, self-limiting boxes of assumptions usually based on the language of 'Us and Them' or 'everyone thinks/does that'. They do not, and such an assumption is dangerous: it is an excuse for non-thinking, as is any tendency to put something into a box, such as 'conspiracy theory' or 'terrorism'. Usually, the connotations are deeply emotive, a key indicator that there is more than rationality at play.

Theories are the key to all our most important scientific achievements. Ideas become hypotheses; these develop into theories based on inductive or deductive logic, underpinned by facts, measurement and experimentation. Only when theories are tested and evaluated against expected outcomes can we prove their validity and practicality, allowing them to become helpful in accurate forward prediction, not just in explaining the past. Failure to question our assumptions is common, but it can lead to massive waste and inefficiency in an organisational context where assumptions are leveraged to form policy.

Those who question or challenge assumptions are often put into boxes themselves, usually pejoratively, providing an excuse to disregard them. Often such independent thinkers are investigators, researchers, social watchdogs, emerging leaders, scientists and our most creative members of society. Ways to improve the system are often reframed as criticism within an organisation that views itself as the best or the leader. Most opportunities to change are lost because the questions either come with attached solutions or lead to a train of enquiry that can produce a technical or otherwise breakthrough.

> *The discovery of truth is prevented more effectively not by the false appearance of things present and which mislead into error, not directly by weakness of the reasoning powers, but by preconceived opinion, by prejudice.*
> (Arthur Schopenhauer)

Social views are currently even more narrowly defined than ever, primarily due to the impact of mass media, which we would initially expect to lead to a diversity of views and information. Neuro-Linguistic Programming is used to slip messages laden with assumptions 'under our radar' continuously. The news is framed in simplistic paradigms; these are reinforced by the relatively narrow spread of resources most of us use for gathering information and forming our views of the world; this means they get repeated, and repetition itself frames the debate, reinforces views and closes minds. This communication bubble explains why some individuals may consider people from another country 'strange' – but are all foreigners 'the same'? If not, how does such thinking account for the variation involved in any population?

Organisational culture works similarly: within a framework of social conditioning, we tend to disregard our assumptions quickly once we have accepted them, and at this stage, they become dangerous by dropping off our radar, and we thoughtlessly use those assumptions to make policy and strategic decisions.

> *He that will not apply new*
> *remedies must expect new evils,*
> *for time is the greatest innovator.*
> (Francis Bacon)

Thus many organisations systemically and unconsciously discourage innovation and new ideas; they are often framed first and foremost as a problem (i.e. negative and counterproductive) instead of golden opportunities for improvement. Such environments sap the energy and the talent of those driven to learn and improve, wasting their most important resource, creativity and new thinking.

> *A mind is like a parachute. It*
> *doesn't work if it's not open.*
> (Frank Zappa)

Theory-X vs Theory Y

Most organisations use Theory X management, as defined by Professor Douglas McGregor, which he called the "traditional view of direction and control". This model is predicated on the assumption that the average human dislikes work and responsibility and will avoid it if they can. However, Professor McGregor also put forward

Theory Y, which was fully supported by Deming, who also had a favourable view of people.

Interestingly most of us would prefer to see ourselves in an organisation run along the lines of Theory Y.

Deming stated that the most productive managers: "*create an environment that encourages freedom and innovation*", and they do this by understanding "*that people are different from each other*" and "*the interaction between people and the circumstances they work in*". Nevertheless, it is surprising how many managers still use Theory X as a preferred method of handling others when they simultaneously assert that they would respond more positively to positive workplace treatment.

Fair treatment is one of the most important points covered in this theory, and it relates directly to Deming's assertion that target-based planning and the use of reviews and bonuses to underpin performance have a definite effect: division and destruction. Theory X underpins many management policies: the rules used to govern an organisation speak for themselves in communicating secrecy, lack of trust, lack of respect and lack of fairness. In this respect, as in all others, policies beget outcomes, but not necessarily the ones expected when formulated.

Driving out fear is essential if trust is to be built, which is a cornerstone of Deming's philosophy. For this to happen, the organisation has to change; for that to happen, there needs to be a complete commitment from the leadership, who often appreciate that change always comes at a cost. Optimisation will be the outcome if the change is from a static set of outmoded assumptions to a dynamic system-based organic growth. For this to happen, we also need knowledge of the process variation.

Knowledge of variation

It is inherent within Deming philosophy that waste, in all its forms, be eliminated from the production process as far as possible as an ongoing effort. Underlying this principle is the notion that all waste represents cost, and residual waste driven outside a company and discharged into the environment is still a cost; that cost has to be accounted for, directly or indirectly, now or in the future. So how do we locate this waste? Deming used the theories of Walter Shewhart relating to process variation to show how and where the system can be optimised.

Every system or process generates fluctuations over time, which can be plotted as a graph. Most process fluctuations come under the category of 'noise', what Deming called 'common causes' and was defined by Shewhart as 'chance causes'. These causes are not statistically significant as they appear random, although they occur within defined limits. Fluctuations that operate outside the normal process range are not a product of chance and are attributable to what Deming called 'special causes' (Shewhart called them 'assignable causes').

The principle underlying this concept is that if no other changes are made to the system over time, the level of variation associated will remain stable. A Process Behaviour Chart can identify when process variation is outside the normal fluctuation range and is, therefore, attributable to special causes. This information can be used to interpret process data, enabling management to identify causes, take appropriate action, improve processes, and reduce waste and inefficiency. The messages in variation provide a guide for action, policy and planning.

> *"Setting numerical goals or targets outside the boundaries of the system's capabilities and expecting people who work in the system to reach those targets without any changes to the system will generally not produce sustainable improvement."*
> (McKeon and Ramney)

Another potential problem is what Deming called 'tampering' –when normal fluctuations in the process are incorrectly ascribed to special causes, something we frequently see in the media and to which politicians tend to react. By translating specific circumstances into general responses, reactions are usually counterproductive, often taken against the firm views of their internal specialist advisors.

Management decisions in reaction to events can therefore be erroneous if the context is not taken into account – it can mean that the policy introduced produces the opposite effect of the desired one. If this occurs, it can lead to escalating costs, administrative burden, errors and reduced production and profitability.

Theory of knowledge

> *Management is prediction*
> *(Deming)*

A factory that discharges toxic waste into waterways and onto the land devalues that land for the future, creates a requirement for clean-up, or in a worst-case scenario, if left unchecked, it may lead to irrevocable damage, poisoning, ill health, or even death. Historically, the actual cost involved may or may not come back to damage the entity at the root cause. In a world increasingly well-connected, better informed and alarmed about the impact of pollution and extinction events, the trend is for such damage to have an impact more directly, quickly and expensively than ever. Even abstract damage such as that to the image of a company can and does have a direct impact in terms of consumer preferences (sales boycotts), investor decision-making, share value, or even fines and imprisonment; such a legacy is increasingly costly and more directly connected in terms of cause and effect than ever.

Thus the cost of waste or systemic damage never disappears. However, like many other cost considerations driven by short-term self-interested thinking, it can be shifted within a system, generating a rising cost and not one that tends to fall. So, it is better to do things correctly the first time around. Such thinking underpins the Deming philosophy, which emphasises that we all live within interconnected systems and that sweeping things under the carpet makes a clean-up harder at a later date. Deming represents the opposite of 'Us and Them' thinking; he outlined the 'Shewhart Cycle' – the PDSA (Plan, Do, Study, Act) cycle as the scientific methodology for systemic change. Underpinning this is a series of questions aimed at dispelling assumptions and focusing on the basics.

The question is: "Is what we are doing having the effect we desired and intended?" Underpinning this is a requirement for observation, measurement and prediction.

Internal environment

An environmental and systemic focus within Deming's work also reflects the logic that strategy, leadership and organisation combine to create an internal environment that shapes attitudes and creates predictable outcomes: a liberation of creativity and cooperation (or of division and fear, which inhibits change and progress). Critical thinking is necessary in order to improve. A politicised environment usually leads to such striving being categorised as trouble-making instead of an opportunity to identify problems that have solutions, leading to better process efficiency. Politics is created by systems that a nation, government or organisation creates and sustains, not vice versa; hence, changing the system will change the politics.

Political environments replace discussion and negotiation with discord and conflict. Nothing is more damaging to an organisation than the self-perception of perfection or simply being 'the best' to discourage an active culture of continual improvement. More damagingly, the debate might never take place at all.

Deming's organic, environmental, systemic approach of Deming has often been fundamentally misunderstood, especially within the world of Quality and reduced to a series of short-term tactical policies based upon box-ticking, thereby losing the bigger strategic picture. Unfortunately, the true power of Deming's philosophical approach can only be unleashed by abandoning a narrowly defined focus. Without a holistic, long term and stable set of objectives, short-term initiatives will only create a short-term impetus.

The inherent power of such a rational and measurement-based approach is its focus on long-term optimisation and stable systems that develop organically. It is important to emphasise that Deming is about taking a broad view over the longer term, and although the application of his principles to any organisation can have a powerfully positive short-term impact, such tactical approaches often fade away unless the underlying strategic philosophy focuses on the system itself and relates all factors in a drive for waste reduction and the achievement of optimal efficiency. Deming is not about picking a process, reducing it to a procedure and then sticking to it, nor does it aim at a collection of quality badges.

Deming's approach is about

- creating an organic, self-sustaining mechanism
- focused on continually improving the process,
- one which incorporates feedback mechanisms as outlined by the Shewhart Cycle,
- one which devolves responsibilities, empowers, and removes bureaucracy.

This is why Deming referred to 'rational prediction': prediction based on theory and systemic modelling, as is all scientific knowledge. This approach is relevant when dealing with any system, whether social, political, economic, technological or environmental, and has implications for banking, manufacturing, or selling groceries.

As many industries have demonstrated, the cost of environmental clean-up regarding toxic waste is far higher than that of instituting proper processes beforehand. The price of radioactive pollution manifests itself in increasing rates of illness, death and disability – which represents a real cost on an almost endless basis; it is massively expensive to remove afterwards. We have not yet faced the true costs due to the political nature of the organisations involved; according to the EU, some 60 million people died up to 1990 alone from environmental radiation poisoning.

Nuclear considerations may have influenced Deming after he visited Japan, where he could not fail to notice the profound and extended effect of the bombs at Hiroshima and Nagasaki.

Equally, his environmental concerns would have resonated with his Japanese audience, who recognise the vital truth of a philosophy to leave the world in a better condition than we find it. This sustainable approach to nature is reflected by virtually all ancient civilisations, from the American Indians to the Buddhists, yet seems curiously neglected in modern Western philosophy.

Deming's philosophy can provide a powerful and incisive insight into climate change. The debate is highly contentious, especially in the USA, where policy has been mauled on the grounds of biased data, political agendas and stealth taxation. Moreover, environmentalists have harmed their cause on the grounds that carbon taxing introduces a global tax, offsets the problem from the first to the developing world, and, worst of all, avoids tackling root causes directly. Deming philosophy encourages dialogue and listening to incorporate alternative views and open up new outcomes.

It is inescapable to conclude that Deming's long-term outlook would have avoided environmental problems altogether - his goal of leaving the world in a better state than the one we inherited would have wholly nullified divisions in policy by removing the emphasis on short-term, narrowly defined self-interest, by basing it on test and measurement: most of all upon improving the system and the process, supported by an understanding of the nature of variation.

So, Deming's environmental philosophy reflects a reality that is often overlooked: we are all products of our environment, and our workers are shaped and constrained by their education, health and other factors that derive from our surroundings. It also caters to the universal truth that we reap what we sow and that actions and inactions both leave a logical, predictable legacy. It is a serious counterpoint to self-interested thinking associated with prevailing political, social or corporate paradigms. It encourages us all to engage and focus on measurement and the long term, knowing that policy of all kinds always begets outcomes.

The global climate debate is highly politicised, and there is strong evidence, presented in 2009 in New Scientist, that the 'official line' (including the J-curve/hockey-stick hypothesis) uses selective data, deliberately skewed. It seems part of a broader agenda that focuses on producing outcomes of global governance, hierarchical control and taxation; it uses deceit and deception to pursue that agenda but fails to address the underlying causes directly. The media subtly pushes the official agenda and undermines the causes for concern raised by those who challenge it; it is cause for concern to any subscriber of Deming's philosophy whenever debate, facts, figures or science are being suppressed. Deming represents a very human philosophy, but, being logically based, it is the opposite of self-interest or politics.

Some groups in the USA have picked up on climate data manipulation and further politicised it to challenge all environmental efforts, but a Deming approach based on the fundamental premise to leave the earth in a better condition for our future is juxtaposed to conclusions that 'carry on regardless' justifies deliberate waste or negligent pollution. These groups especially point to cyclical fluctuations in climate linked to solar emissions, and, whether this is accepted or not within the context of a highly political debate, the conclusion seems to be unavoidable that genuine scientific climate data is being manipulated, misrepresented and even suppressed; this approach demonstrates that things than other the environment underlie the political agenda.

While the cyclical solar emissions seem to be a factor underpinning current climate change data, it is a different matter to use that information to justify more significant pollution - the fact is that we do not know the precise extent of our impact on our environment, what (if any) destructive limits or tipping points exist, nor how capable our planetary system is at countering human-made imbalances.

Are global extinction events linked purely to climate or environmental toxins, chemicals, radiation, pesticides, or even genetically modified crops? There is substantial information relating to data suppression and policy manipulation by some corporations, supporting a stated agenda to develop global dominance in specific economic and political areas.

The point is that if we followed Deming principles, we would have a vastly improved environment, and this would all be a non-issue; in this respect, Deming is essentially anti-political. Notably, the carbon offset 'solution' is being used to establish an uneven economic playing field for the third world, taxation and, worst of all, it is being used to provide polluters with reasons not to address the underlying issues causing environmental damage (which seems to be what an 'offset' actually means in practice).

The UK sits in the worst category, routinely dumping nuclear waste into the air, seas, rivers, drains and landfills. The UK's radiation pollution is equal to, or greater than, that of every other nuclear country combined, according to *Britain's Nuclear Nightmare* (Cutler and Edwards). Recent wars in Iraq and Afghanistan have also left a devastating legacy of congenital disabilities and deaths, which have been directly related to the use of depleted Uranium munitions, the irony being that such discharge was subsequently blown around the planet, trailing across North Africa and subsequently over Europe and the UK, as was the fallout from every nuclear test. Radiation is a pollutant for which there is no viable, safe minimum: the tiniest speck of radiation within the body can lead to illness and death.

In conclusion, we can draw from Deming's philosophy regarding the natural environment that, if our theory of how the planet is run does not appear to be supported by the evidence, perhaps we should be looking for a new theory and questioning our assumptions, no matter how dearly we hold on to them? One thing seems to be sure: climate data and the use of science appear to have been subsumed into the political agenda in this case.

> *Without theory, there is no way to use the information that comes to us.*
>
> *New knowledge comes from the innately curious individual responsible to no one.*
> *(Deming)*

Deming's profound knowledge summarises nine principles of systemic organisation that juxtapose prevailing, politicised views. He advocated:

- Co-opetition over competition
- Interdependence over compartmentalisation
- Interdependence over disparate self-interest
- Information intensity over energy intensity
- Transformational opportunity over the cost of change
- Human adjustment to the environment over attempts to engineer the climate
- Value-based change over the appointment of an individual to push sustainability (or quality) - to manage the unquantifiable over managing what you measure
- That profit is a consequence of good management, not a goal.

Within the working environment, we should consider that many of these principles apply first and foremost to the environmental limits that exist within our own minds: we need to recognise the limits of our belief systems and seek to question our own fundamental and cherished assumptions if we are to optimise outputs and implement a regime of continual and organic improvement.

Deming principles have a great deal to contribute to the current debates on our environments (both internal and external) in terms of identifying problems, offering solutions and explaining the intricacies of complex systems with no artificial boundaries. The principles are eminently practical, offering genuine options for scientifically dealing with current and future problems. While some principles may seem counter-intuitive, there are many examples to prove they have endured over the long term to nurture excellence: the British Army uses a philosophy of servant leadership enshrined in the Sandhurst motto, 'Serve to Lead' and the UK Special Forces regularly use 'Chinese Parliaments[34]' to discuss and plan missions with all members participating equally. Above all, Deming's powerful principles provide a structure and framework for identifying and challenging the theories and assumptions we all carry within our heads, enabling them to be

---

[34] The term "Chinese Parliament" is used by the SAS andothers to reflect the idea that all voices are heard and considered equally, similar to the way that (theoretically) all members of the Chinese parliament have the opportunity to express their opinions and concerns.

replaced by ones that are measurable, capable of modification and proven to work...

> *Insanity: doing the same thing over and over again and expecting different results.*
> (Albert Einstein)

"Self-appraisal questions:

1. Does our management structure empower all levels of our organisation to eliminate waste? Does our theory/self-image fit the facts?
2. What are we doing to introduce 'co-opetition' to share approaches and reduce costs with competitors to address common environmental concerns?
3. What are we doing to change from a focus on maxima or minima to one where we continually improve the system/process in order to eliminate waste?
4. Does our system encourage or discourage innovation and the adoption of new ideas?
5. Are we driving out fear to encourage heart-felt feedback from every level of our organisation? What is this feedback's quality and frequency, and how do we measure it?
6. Are our targets self-interested and short-term, or are they sustainable and stable over time, outside management initiatives and fads? What exactly are we measuring, and why?
7. Do we genuinely encourage our creative thinkers and recognise that their new

ideas may solve tomorrow's problems? How do we do that? How can this be improved?

8. Do we have a cooperative relationship with our community, or do we view them as an obstruction and a nuisance we would rather ignore? If so, how do we change this relationship for the common good and mutual benefit?

9. Do we have a separate environmental function within our organisation - or is our view of the environment and sustainability something every single member of our organisation participates in and takes pride in, from the very top to the very bottom?

10. Are we running an organisation that will make the world a better place for our communities and children? If not, what should we do now and on an ongoing basis to address the issues?

11. Do politics and self-image obstruct our attainment of a genuinely sustainable, efficient and environmentally friendly organisation? Are we being faithful to these goals? Does our aspiration in this area equal our self-image in other areas of organisational performance? If we view ourselves as a world leader, are we also a world leader in our environmental policy?)

12. Are we really a zero-waste organisation? How do we continually move towards this goal by creating a sustainable, organic system - and what exactly are we measuring when we make our policy?"

13.

Voice of the Customer

Author   Terry Rose

Review-   Tony Brown, Tony Korychi
ers

Introduction

The expression Voice of the Customer, or VoC, is typically used in two ways:

1. We refer to the Voice of the Customer as the **data** that defines or describes customer needs and expectations. This data can be in numbers, language, or both. In other words, VOC defines what is wanted.

2. An organisation may also have Voice of the Customer **processes** used to systematically capture and analyse the voice of the customer data and drive improvements in products, services and processes.

Voice Of the Customer (VOC)	
We typically use the expression *'VOC '* in two ways:	
• We refer to 'capturing' the Voice of the Customer, which means fully understanding customer needs and environment.	**Data**

• It is a well-defined process used to capture the voice of the customer systematically.	**Process**

VoC is shown on the Enhanced MoSO - as one of the three inputs or voices into the PDSA cycle at the very heart of the model.

Why Listen to The Voice Of The Customer?

Because all work starts and finishes with the customer. In other words, the customer defines and determines the quality of our work.

Ask someone, "What is your job?" and you will hear "sales assistant", "nurse", "doctor", "MD", "PA", "software engineer", etc.

If someone works in a truly customer-focused organisation, they will add the caveat, "My real job is to do whatever I can to satisfy the needs of my customers (clients, patients, etc.)".

These words express their determination not only to 'do their work', but to achieve the best possible outcomes for their 'customers'.

Prof Shoji Shiba, in his book *Four Practical Revolutions in Management*, makes the distinction between '**Product-Out**' (doing work according to the established process – an internal focus) and '**Market-In**' (a focus on customer satisfaction). He says that Product-Out is good but not good enough – you also need Market-In.

To achieve this, you have to know who your customers are (internal and external customers) and what their expectations are now and will be in the future. How many of us can say, hand on heart, that we have this information to hand?

Listening to and being able to interpret the voice of the customer is essential to achieving **customer satisfaction** which is the best and only lasting means to organisational sustainability.

What are the Consequences of not listening to the Voice of the Customer?

If an organisation does not **systematically** listen to the Voice of the Customer, it is guilty of being "unknowingly indifferent to customer needs and expectations."

This consequence is most likely brought about by a failure in **organisational capability** – both in terms of a lack of skills and poor or non-existent VoC processes.

One often hears front-line customer-facing staff (Sales, Customer Service, nurses, etc.) bemoaning that their first-hand knowledge of customers is not listened to or headed by 'management'. 'Management' is often frustrated because the inputs they receive are not in a form that is actionable or factual. Emotional language clouds the real issues; it is a consequence of an organisation not having the capability to listen to the voice of the customer.

The Importance of the Internal Customer Concept

When discussing customers, we intuitively think of the 'external' or end customer, so it is worth considering 'internal' customers and their role in continual improvement. Perhaps a simple example may help to show the importance of internal customers.

Phillip worked as a Financial Analyst. He prided himself on producing error-free financial reports – on time, every time. He had an efficient, well-defined process to capture the data and format it into reports for department heads.

Phillip was, therefore, surprised that his manager thought there was scope for improvement in his work. His manager suggested that he discuss this with his 'customers' (users of his information).

A little put-out, Phillip went to see one of the department heads. Susan confirmed that the reports she received every month were indeed accurate and timely. However, it turned out that on receipt of Phillip's reports, Susan had to spend a substantial amount of time reformatting the data to produce the figures she needed to manage her department. Other managers that Phillip subsequently interviewed were also having the same problem.

Phillip had inadvertently got into a **Product-Out** mentality – his process was working well, and he made sure that he met the requirements. Nevertheless, by fully understanding the needs of his internal customers, Phillip rapidly changed his process to produce a superior product, satisfy his customers, and play his part in improving the company's overall efficiency.

Language Skills

Voice of the Customer heavily emphasises collecting, analysing, and understanding **data**. When we think of data, we typically think of numbers. Nevertheless, we predominantly use language data when interacting with internal or external customers (and colleagues).

Skilful collection and analysis of language data require a basic knowledge of the tools & techniques of semantics - such as distinguishing between Language of Affection and Language of Report and skilful use of the Ladder of Abstraction. The book *Language in Thought and Action* by S.I. Hayakawa is a seminal work on this subject.

Listening and questioning skills (such as those based on Jiro Kawakita's 5 Principles for collecting quantitative or language data) are also very important for VoC work. When coupled with semantic skills, we can exchange information & ideas and come to a common understanding of a situation – including customer expectations.

Our language skills impact our capability to manage by facts.

VoC Processes

The aim of VoC processes is not just to capture the customer's written or explicitly stated requirements but to gain a deeper understanding of the issues and problems with which the customer has to deal.

By having this deeper understanding, we may be able to help our customers be more successful in doing their job.

There are numerous processes or practices associated with VoC. Implementing a process changes what is often considered an ad-hoc or by-chance activity into an agreed way of working; this process can then be systematically repeated and improved, building essential skills and organisational capability.

Four generic processes are outlined here – covering the scale from relatively simple (able to be carried out by all employees if given the basic language skills) to very complex (typically carried out by experts, internal or external to the organisation)

1) **Customer Discussion / Interview**: Typically internal to the organisation. Discussions are held with staff from a 'customer' department. Basic language and listening skills are used to discover present and future needs – and possibly to get the facts associated with adverse performance (errors, defects, tardy response, etc.)

2) **Customer Visitation (VoC) Process**: A well-documented step-by-step process for carrying out customer visitations with a specific aim in mind (e.g. understanding the customer's current environment and challenges, discovering new product requirements, reviewing service level agreements and performance, and problem resolution). **This is definitely not a sales-related process.**

Typical steps could be:
a) Describe the Purpose for the VOC Activity;
b) Prepare for the Customer Visit (select customers; develop interview script);
c) Conduct the Customer Interview (ideally Face-to-Face, but alternatively by telephone/Internet where customer contacts are distant or geographically dispersed);
d) Analyze the VOC Data (e.g. using a Language Processing diagram and numerically, where appropriate);
e) Develop, Implement, and Monitor an Action Plan (check with the customer);
f) Reflect on the Process (STUDY the process and ACT to improve it based on actual experience);

3) **Kano Method:** A method to investigate the characteristics of customer requirements developed by Professor Noriaki Kano of Tokyo Rika University. This method differentiates between Must-be, One-dimensional, and Attractive customer requirements. This type of differentiation, based on the responses to a questionnaire, is useful when defining what customers really need and are willing to pay for – as opposed to 'would be nice' but will not pay for[35].

4) **QFD**: Quality Function Deployment process. Often a complex process typically used for

---

[35] An alternative is the "MoSCoW" approach to identify what Must, Should, Could or Would be included. Reinforcing this with penalties for change requests dependent on the stated importance of the requirement allows to ensure that all the 'Must' items are finalised early in the lifecycle.

translating the voice of the customer into high-quality products. Key customer product requirements are identified and operationally defined. This is used extensively in the motor car industry.

A Word about Customer Surveys

Voice of the Customer data can be collected through a questionnaire (survey) or interview – the preferred process discussed in this article (excluding the specially formulated Kano Questionnaire). Surveys can be a very valuable tool in search for the Voice of the Customer, but in the view of the author, they have significant limitations.

Some organisations use an initial survey to highlight possible areas of concern and then use interviews – often in the customers' work environment – to get the underlying facts/data.

Breakthrough Management - When Not to Listen to Your Customers

Dr Ishikawa is quoted as saying, 'The customer is king but sometimes blind' (perhaps to other possibilities or future needs of *your* organisation).

Organisations may need to explore entirely new products, a completely different strategic direction, or new ways of working to survive. Current customers (internal and external) may see these' breakthroughs' as being contrary to their best interests and have been known to try to prevent them from being implemented.

Self Examining Questions

It is hoped that the following open questions will stimulate and assist reflection on the use of the Voice of the Customer:

1. Do I/we know who our customers are (both internal and external)?
2. Do I/we truly know the needs and expectations of our customers – both now and in the future
3. What is the predominant culture in my/our organisation – Product-Out or Market-In?
4. Do I/we have the basic language skills to capture the Voice of the Customer accurately?
5. Do I/we have the appropriate Voice of the Customer processes in place?
6. Do I/we understand that to deliver excellent performance, it is necessary to align the Voice of the System with the Voice of the Customer? (See Voice Of The System, page 281)

Bibliography

- S.I. Hayakawa and Alan R. Hayakawa. Language in Thought and Action. Harcourt Brace & Company.
- Shoji Sheba, David Walden. Four Practical Revolutions in Management – Systems for Creating Unique Organisational Capability. Productivity Press. Specifically: Chapters 4 and 5 relating to Customer Focus and Proactive Improvement Chapter 27 for more information about Breakthrough Management

Glossary of Terms:

- **Voice of the System** defines what you will get from a process/system
- **Voice of the Customer** defines what you want
- **Semantics** is the study of how people use language to communicate
- **An 'Internal' customer** refers to the people or processes that receive or use the result of our work, product or service
- **Breakthrough Management** refers to a systemic approach to exploring significantly new directions or horizons needed to sustain the organisation. Breakthroughs could be in processes, technologies, how a business operates or a new business area.
-

Voice Of The People

Author Tony Korycki

Introduction

Voice of the People is a crucial approach for assessing the health and capability of any organisation. Leaders need to recognise the difference between what people can do and will do; however, too many organisations allow their people to be transient and uncommitted.

The contribution of people to organisational performance is vital as it generates aspects of products and services that are often of critical value to customers. People are commonly the primary way customers experience an organisation; failing to listen to the voice of people can lead to leaders misunderstanding the nature of how their people interact with customers at critical moments of truth.

Questions to ask about the Organisation

How well does the organisation:

- Structure an approach to capturing feedback from its people?
- Actively deploy that approach, seeking out and acting upon feedback?
- Capture data and knowledge about its people's morale, attitude and capability?
- Communicate key issues, progress, success and learning from failures?

Definition and Place in the System of Profound Knowledge

The Voice of the People is a critical element of the mechanisms for assessing the health and capability of any organisation, alongside and complimentary to the Voice of the Customer (see page 257) and the Voice of the System (page 281).

Historically, the voice of the people can be traced back to the communication of Alcuin of York to Charlemagne in A.D.798. Whilst initially interpreted as having a religious interpretation, the VoP is now commonly taken to mean the derivation of various answers and opinions on any given subject.

Why is the 'Voice of the People' Important?

Structure is everything[36]. Nearly all organisations contain multiple structures, for example, physical spaces, processes, equipment, systems, market/societal stakeholders and how people are organised to meet the organisation's mission.

The contribution of people to organisational performance is vital as it produces key aspects of products and services that are of critical value to its customers. Almost every organisation holds valuable knowledge that is tacit, subtle, elusive and embedded in its peoples' talents; this knowledge is, therefore, not easily transmitted or imitated, or 'owned' by organisations. No organisations arc 100% automated; customer service

---

[36] Schwarz, 2005

relies on people, yet this dimension of health is neglected in many organisations.

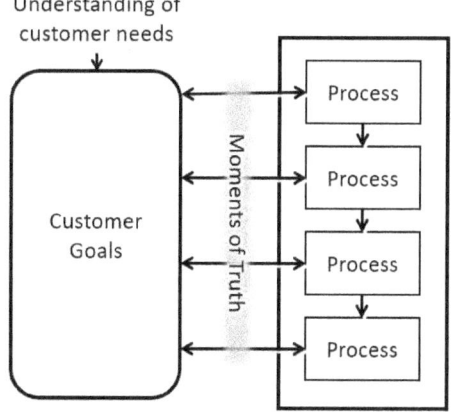

Figure 36: Moments of Truth

Pressures are placed upon an organisation's people to prove value through their capability to create, judge, imagine and build relationships. Leveraging knowledge and collaboration requires

- the creation, articulation and sustained alignment of peoples' shared values,
- a focus on building relationships, not structures that impede cooperation.

Leaders need to value their people's knowledge, education, experience and creativity while recognising that accurate measurement of peoples' qualities and contributions is elusive. The real value is the difference between what people can do and what they will do; too many organisations allow their people to be transient and uncommitted.

Employees and volunteers only commit when they feel a mutual bond. People are commonly the key behind how customers perceive an organisation; failing to listen to the voice of people can lead to leaders misunderstanding the nature of how their people interact with customers at critical moments of truth. Considering investing time in people as something to do after leaders have finished running their organisation is wrong! People are at the heart of organisations, and leaders who want organisations to survive encourage constant experimentation, hire people who think outside norms and protect them. All of these benefits to organisations can only be accrued if leaders have in place approaches for listening to the voice of their people.

Approaches to Capturing the Voice of the People

All organisations, large or small, public or private, can and should understand how their people feel and perceive the organisation, its environment and its processes. There are many different ways this can take place, some of which require administration and technology, but, unsurprisingly, many do not. There are structured and unstructured approaches and public or private ways of capturing people's views, which can be used in almost any combination, depending on the spread of an organisation, how fragmented it is by nature, and the variety of people employed.

In addition, depending on the organisation's circumstances, there are rules and protocols for how an organisation can listen to its people, all of which are built on the trust between the people within an organisation and its leaders.

Some mechanisms to capture VoP

	Structured	Unstructured
Public	Focus Groups Rich Pictures & Brown Paper fairs Back to the floor Suggestion scheme	Town hall meetings Management and team meetings Management by walking about Discussion groups
Private	Survey One-to-Ones	Peer to Peer Knowledge sharing Informal networks

Public Structured voices

Focus Groups

The approach consists of a structured approach to gathering groups of people, whether a narrow or wide range of people. They are typically selected based on a topic chosen by leadership for which specific feedback is sought. This approach has the advantage of allowing the organisation's spokespersons to self-select into the group (choosing the group is not necessarily recommended), but has the disadvantage of not necessarily providing an outlet from junior people or those with a valid opinion, but who do not step forward first when volunteers are sought.

Rich Pictures & Brown Paper fairs

These approaches are primarily designed to explore aspects of processes and 'organisational systems'; they constitute a valuable source of intelligence about current and emerging issues from the people within any organisation. Since these methods specifically invite people to give feedback about what does or does not work about processes and organisational and relationship issues, analysis from workshops and products of these exercises can capture valuable insights.

Back to the Floor (Point of Use)

This approach is similar to Management by Walking About, as it represents a public form of management engagement with the organisation's people but tends towards a formal, programme-driven and scheduled set of activities. Whilst it is possible to mandate involvement and 'hosting' by operational teams, the best schemes integrate back to the floor within strategic, operational or quality/business improvement programmes, with management and hosts volunteering to engage.

Such engagements represent a valuable opportunity for management to engage with individuals and teams, with learning and listening being essential skills, so that hosts feel that interactions are valuable in sharing key issues, as well as being non-judgmental.

Suggestion (New Ideas) Scheme

This approach is used very effectively in many organisations, and, as such, there is a wealth of in-depth guidance and best practices available on capturing new ideas. However, there are some fundamental principles for how new ideas schemes are managed:

- Input should be open to anyone operating the organisation's processes, including contractors and key suppliers;
- New Ideas may be periodically themed or a general free-for-all, all-comers, all-topics input; no subject should be off-limits (i.e. the scheme should capture more than just technological ideas);
- Timely assessment of new ideas is essential, with the mechanism for assessment involving relevant and openly declared subject matter experts to give credibility to assessments;
- The organisation should measure engagement and value derived from its peoples' ideas, e.g. numbers captured, assessment timeliness, ideas implemented, financial and other benefits derived, recognition/reward to people/teams, so that people understand how their ideas are used.
- Recognition and reward may be in some way proportional to the benefits derived from ideas they should, wherever possible, be nominal to avoid the risk of ideas and suggestions becoming a way for the organisation's people to perceive the scheme as an informal 'bonus'.

Public Unstructured voices

Town Hall meetings

These tend to be large meetings, often used for communications at critical points of change for an organisation or where an organisation chooses to consult about critical developments in the life-cycle of change programmes or strategy formation. As such, they can be used to garner feedback, either ad-hoc or pre-submitted questions or issues for discussion. The possibilities for engagement to capture feedback depend on many factors, including the culture of trust and openness, what the organisation seeks to understand and at what level of depth feedback is sought. There is a risk that such meetings can raise expectations about follow-up action that managers may be unwilling to endorse, so attendees must be explicitly informed about the purpose of information captured via such meetings.

Management & Team meetings

While management meetings are often an instrument for communications in operational environments, decision-making and planning, it is entirely possible to use such meetings to capture 'feedback'. Such VoP feedback sessions need to be scheduled into meetings, so that attendees are aware of the opportunity to provide input, as well as an environment of trust and openness, to allow a dialogue of value to all parties.

Management by Walking About

MBWA is a fundamental learning technique about how quality companies operate and is referenced in various texts. This approach may be combined with Back to the Floor engagement but represents something more formal. It may consist of relevant managers taking time out every day or week to invest with their operational people. As with Back to the Floor, an open-learning, listening and non-judgmental mindset are crucial to foster trust and dialogue during MBWA time.

Discussion groups

These usually are online and allow any participants to raise a discussion thread and for anyone else to share their views. While good groups can be moderated, they can be challenging to use to provide data for analysis and action and can degenerate into gripes and whinges. However, these are valuable safety valves and places for rapid knowledge sharing across locations, especially if fragmented teams exist.

Private Structured voices

Exchanges here tend to be scheduled and periodic, planned and designed to fulfil particular management purposes, but the two examples are very different.

Management One-to-Ones

One-to-one meetings are designed to create an environment for a two-way exchange between leaders/managers and individuals within their teams; they allow performance assessment, coaching, development planning and reviews to take place. Any feedback obtained here should only be included in analyses and actions with the consent of both parties in the One-to-One. Otherwise, the information gathered destroys trust rather than engendering a dialogue within the organisation.

Survey

Surveys are commonly used globally across many organisations, large or small, public or private.

The features of organisations using this mechanism are listed below in no particular order of importance.

- Scoring relevant factors: most organisations will have critical objectives they are pursuing and against which they need to gauge peoples' willingness, commitment and capability to achieve. Engaging with people to score their feelings and feedback about critical objectives requires that the factors are relevant to the survey audience and that they can visualise how leadership can take action based on their feedback. If done well, survey scoring can act as a valuable 'weather-vane' for organisations, identifying areas where people are unhappy or lack confidence or capability to perform, helping to set priorities for organisational development, training or investment.
- Determining importance: individuals or groups often list things they need to do, buy, or about which they are concerned.

However, it is rarely true that all items on a list are equally important. Voice of the people surveys, therefore, need to allow employees to rank in some way the importance they assign to the relevant factors since this can allow organisations to understand variations between perceptions relating to different locations, professional disciplines, process stages or functional structures (this list is not exhaustive).

- Verbatim feedback: having a score against a critical factor is only of limited value if an organisation is blind to the rationale behind feedback, so organisations may seek a narrative in support of scoring, particularly at the extreme of scoring ranges, or to identify additional information, for example, 'top three issues to resolve' or 'top five successes to celebrate'. Arguably this is the most valuable aspect but requires considerable analysis to fully extract patterns and shared issues (especially if an organisation is large), so it may demand analysis within a structure (an operating division or location).
- Confidentiality: people can provide feedback in the knowledge that they cannot be identified, and neither will the organisation seek to investigate originators of adverse feedback.

Private Unstructured voices

The exchanges here are essentially continuous and One-to-One or within small groups, occurring face-to-face, online or by telephone. Because such exchanges are essentially private and not part of structured activity, organisations do not have a right to information generated. They can badly damage trust if they gather or act on them. Whilst an organisation can ask an informal network for feedback, this effectively becomes a structured activity, and even then, any Voice of the People information gathered here needs to be carefully treated and may be subject to peoples' cautiousness about opening up what may previously be a private discussion to scrutiny.

Acting on the Voice of the People

Successful organisations only derive real value from listening to their people if they act on what they hear and communicate openly and honestly about the issues raised and how they intend to do to address them.

Avoiding the 'I hear what you say' trap

People in an organisation will only honestly share their feelings, concerns, frustrations, knowledge and ideas if they genuinely believe that the organisation is willing and able to act on them. When the same questions appear every month, quarter or year, but nothing changes in the policies, practices and behaviours within an organisation, it not only tarnishes the subject being explored but potentially the whole feedback mechanism itself.

Communicate the Findings & Conclusions

- Analyse, plan, and assign ownership: all data and information gathered from the organisation's people should be analysed and matched to previous data to identify ongoing and new patterns, issues and priorities for action. The people volunteering their input will expect nothing less. Analysis should allow leadership to agree on actions at relevant points and assign ownership with clearly defined scope and time scales.

- Communicate what will happen next: VoP feedback is seriously devalued when there is no response, admission of issues, or commitment to action on identified priorities. This communication needs to be fit for purpose, for all roles and locations, avoid slogans and exhortation, focussed on what leadership has agreed to do, driving improvement, and how people can become involved or support.

- Be Candid about constraints: any and all mechanisms to capture feedback set up expectations about what management and leadership will do based on the feedback. Organisations need to prepare if the feedback generates a demand for some investment, facility or service simply not possible in economic circumstances, to say "thank you, but sorry we cannot" and offer evidence and reasons; otherwise, people may feel that subjects they consider as important have been ignored or 'dumped' by leadership.

Share Progress & Successes

- Celebrate positive shifts: study the organisation as it transitions through changes generated through feedback analysis. Then communicate to people volunteering their views the news about successes, ensuring that they are 'real' and can be experienced daily in the workplace.
- Be Honest about Failures: not every attempt to improve following the peoples' feedback will be successful; organisations that pretend otherwise risk discrediting their VoP mechanisms. Leadership or management needs to admit when aspects of their improvement agenda do not result in the benefits expected, plus what they have learned from the initiative attempted.
-

Voice Of The System

Author   Terry Rose

Review-   Tony Brown, Tony Korychi
ers

Introduction

Voice of the System, or VoS, is the terminology used to describe the use of a simple Process Behaviour Chart (a form of Control Chart) to characterise the performance of a process or system over time.

VoS is present in the Enhanced MoSO as one of the three inputs or voices into the PDSA cycle at the very heart of the model[37].

By interpreting the Process Behaviour Chart, it is possible to define, with a high degree of certainty, what level of performance the process or system can achieve and to determine what type of action can best be taken to improve its performance.

Do not be deceived: VoS is much more than a simple yet powerful technique; it is a way of thinking that can drive continual performance improvement instead of only 'fire fighting', taking what is often inappropriate action when a target or expectation has not been met.

---

[37] See Figure 15: The Enhanced MoSO, page 66.

What is the Origin of the Voice Of The System Terminology?

The term Voice of the System (sometimes called Voice of the Process) was used in the Ford Motor Company during the early 1990s; Donald J. Wheeler popularised it in his excellent book <u>Understanding Variation – the Key to Managing Chaos</u>, which is possibly the only book one needs to understand the importance of listening to the VoS.

The book title gives a clue to using VoS: a basic understanding of variation. Whilst all data contain noise (natural or routine variation), some data contain signals (exceptional variation), the cause of which should be investigated and removed as soon as possible. A Process Behaviour Chart filters out the noise to detect signals.

> *The distinction between signals and noise is the foundation for every meaningful data analysis.*
> *(Deming)*

Why Is It Necessary To Use The Voice Of The System?

Despite living in the 'Information Age', where in everyday life and at work we are bombarded with numbers for one thing or another, most of us find it challenging to digest numeric data and extract knowledge that may be locked within the figures. Not because we are uneducated or not very bright but because most of us have not been taught how to use elementary arithmetic tools to understand data. Without a 'formal' way of analysing data, we are forced to use 'informal' ways – such as eye-balling the data presented in a table or relying on Bill because he can spot a suspect number in a spreadsheet from fifty paces.

What Are The Consequences Of Not Understanding Data?

Consider a typical news or current affairs program.

- A set of figures relating to (say) the economy, hospitals, schools or business has just been announced;
- Politicians and experts are brought in to analyse the figures. Almost invariably, different conclusions are reached based on the same set of numbers;
- If the numbers went down compared to last month, last quarter, or the same quarter last year, then drastic action must be taken – it is obvious the government or management is incompetent;
  - The system has to be changed.
  - Heads must roll;
  - Hold an inquiry!
  - Write a report!
  - The more corrective actions or recommendations for improvement generated, the better.
- If the figures have gone up, we are on track – a sure sign that the last set of actions taken is working. We can rest easy. Or can we?

What do the numbers mean? Probably all we can say for sure is that the figures will have changed next week, month or quarter, and the politicians and experts will yet again be telling us that the change is significant. Action must be taken!

While we have come to expect politicians to take adversarial stances, we would want and expect the organisations for which we work to have the know-how to correctly interpret important data (often referred to as Key Performance Indicators or KPIs). The consequences for an organisation or department could be dire. Inappropriate actions only exacerbate the situation – or perhaps even worse, no action is taken when correcting a situation or preventing re-occurrence would be necessary.

Failing to understand data and the natural process variation can disrupt any organisation. A board or senior management team that attempts solely to manage by instinct or a table of figures will often fail to recognise the natural variation in their performance. Actions will be issued for relevant managers to investigate, quite often, minor variations upwards or downwards within the normal behaviour of a process or system, resulting in a cascade of actions all the way to first-line management or supervisory level. This disruption takes people away from the search for improvement since the management behaviour generates fear, defence mechanisms and behaviours that encourage people to seek blame and 'cover themselves' rather than work together. Imagine if this happens every month, week, or day; how can an organisation function effectively under such circumstances?

What Does A Process Behaviour Chart Look Like?

A Process Behaviour Chart is simply a Run Chart (or Time Series Chart) generated from a data table or spreadsheet - with three lines plotted on the chart:

- An Average line (known as X bar for the mathematically minded), plus
- Two lines equidistant of the Average line, known as the Upper & Lower Natural Process Limits (UNPL & LNPL). These lines are calculated from the data points using a simple equation (and <u>not</u> a Standard Deviation calculation as some folks believe – there is a difference).

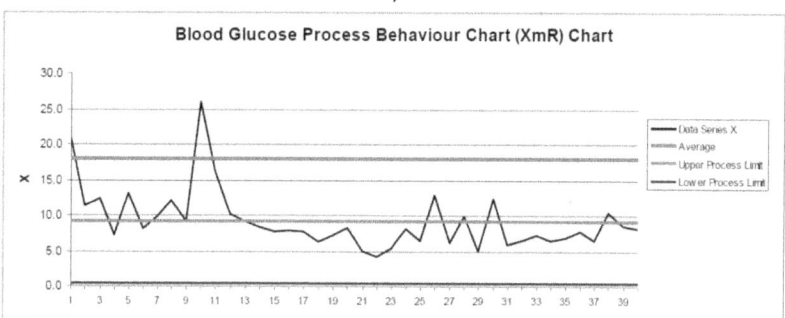

Figure 37: Process Behaviour Chart

Note: A common misunderstanding is that UNPLs & LNPLs are specification or target lines.

Nothing could be further from the truth. Specifications/targets are often called the Voice of the Customer (VoC)[38].

Comparing VoS With VoC

By comparing the Voice of the System to the Voice of the Customer, it is possible to determine whether an established process/system can consistently meet customer requirements or expectations (a definition of excellent performance).

If you now realise that being in control is not the same as being on target, you are on your way to understanding the importance of the Voice of the System.

Self Examining Questions

It is hoped that the following open questions will stimulate and assist reflection on the use of Voice of the System:

1. When trying to make sense of numeric data, do I have a binary view of the world – always either "Doing OK" or "In trouble"?
2. Do my management reports simply compare two values (for example, where we are now compared with last week/month/quarter or compared to an average value) and use that comparison to drive actions?

---

[38] See page Voice of the Customer, page 204.

3. Are my management reports 'eye charts' of tabular data from which people are expected to extract vital trends and unexpected values?
4. To what extent do our current data reporting systems allow us to distinguish between normal behaviour of the process/system and identify exceptional (special) events and causes for investigation and improvement action?
5. Do I know the consequences of not understanding data?
6. What checks would I need to carry out to know whether our data is sufficient to assess System behaviour?
7. Have I progressed from reporting data in tabular or graph formats to using Process Behaviour Charts?
8. Do I know the difference between the Voice of the System and the Voice of the Customer?
9. Do I understand that to deliver excellent performance, it is necessary to align the Voice of the System with the Voice of the Customer?
10. Do I realise that setting goals does nothing to improve the system?
11. Is being in control the same as being on target? Discuss.
12. To what extent am I using Voice of the System thinking to drive continual improvements and innovation?

Bibliography

The following books are recommended:

Donald J. Wheeler. *Understanding Variation – The Key to Understanding Chaos.* SPC Press

Donald J. Wheeler, David S. Chambers. *Understanding Statistical Process Control.* SPC Press.

Shoji Sheba, David Walden. *Four Practical Revolutions in Management – Systems for Creating Unique Organisational Capability.* Productivity Press (Chapter 8, *Process Control and Variation*, puts Voice of the System into a broader context).

Frank Price. *Right First Time, Using Quality Control for Profit*, Gower Publishing (nicely written, accessible and 'fun' guide to using process charts of various types).

Glossary

Voice of the System defines what you will get from a process/system

Voice of the Customer defines what you want

Innovation

Author   Malcolm Gall

Review-   Derek Richings, Alan Hodges
ers

What is Innovation?

For a sustainable organisation, proper engagement with innovation is inescapable.

Innovation is not invention; neither is it just improvement or novelty. Effective innovation creates value, either social or economic.

Improvement	Doing existing things better
Invention	Finding or creating a new thing
Innovation	Doing or using new things to change for the better

Some definitions.

Unplanned Discovery	Serendipity — Finding a use for something you have found.
Planned Discovery	Having a use in mind for something you are looking for.
Invention	Making a model or prototype that works.

Innovation	Introducing a new good or service to customers.
Entrepreneurship	Making a business out of new goods and services. Perhaps starting a new venture.
Serial Entrepreneurship	Bringing new goods and services to the market, one after another.
Breakthrough	Completely new "out of the box" thinking (eg. Shiba).

Innovation is essential for survival.

Every organisation today is pressured to be efficient in pursuing its aims and do more with less. Without innovation, an organisation will see its customers or stakeholders drift away.

When addressing the role of management's responsibility in securing its organisation's future by pursuing innovation, Deming used to say:

> *Improvement is essential but relatively unimportant*

Deming gave Four Prongs of Quality, starting with the most important:

- Innovation in product and service
- Innovation in process
- Improvement of existing product and service
- Improvement of existing process

Innovation is necessary, but not sufficient, for survival

Some innovation comes from <u>continuous improvement</u> activities. Removing confusing signals, by separating special and common causes of variation, for example, enables processes to be understood. The effect of a special cause may be highly desirable (they are not all bad!), but it has to be understood if it is to be produced as a consistent new feature.

For some organisations, it is necessary to install improvement before self-generating innovation so that innovation can be carried through reliably.

Conditions for Innovation

These can only be set by the senior members of an organisation. It is their responsibility. They must understand why innovation is vital to the long-term survival of their enterprise so that the nurturing conditions are in place.

How to innovate

A purposeful approach to Innovation: Innovation follows a path:

- Create (idea generation)
- Judge and evaluate
- Develop
- Implement

Every organisation has its own aims, systems processes and self-awareness. This affects how innovation happens within it. Every organisation also has its own degenerative tendencies, which can stifle innovation.

The following steps show ways of making innovation a way of life for an organisation:

Step 1. Decide to do it;

Step 2. Set up strategies, policies and plans appropriate to the organisation;

Step 3. If improvement is already formalised, include innovation;

Step 4. Give Permission;

Step 5. Study opportunities for innovation;

Step 6. Identify the most promising opportunities and assess them by trials;

Step 7. Implement, but learn from what you are doing;

Step 8. Make sure that innovation is an established part of your organisation.

The order of steps 2, 3, and 4 may vary or not even be applicable in some organisations.

Step 1. Decide to do it.

Like it or not, you are now engaged in managing change. Your current organisation has its own history and culture, which make it what it is. You may have values you do not want to lose (e.g., of public service and justice). You may also have practices and a culture that stand in the way of progress or survival. You must decide how to change these. Even the vocabulary you use may be troublesome. You may not want to formally be "a *learning organisation*" or "a *knowledge organisation*", although you will adopt some of these

292

characteristics. You may need external help (this is most usefully engaged at the start).

Viewing the organisation as a system has many benefits, not least recognising the elements of the enterprise and the connections between them, all potential areas for innovation. You also have the opportunity to recognise the future system, i.e. what you want the organisation to be and what it should be able to do, and therefore plan to create it and achieve new aims. You may recognise that you need external help in cooperation, creativity or Systems-Thinking. Again this is best employed from the start.

Step 2. Set up Strategies, policies, and plans appropriate to the organisation.

Reduce conflicts with existing practices, including reward policies.

Make constraints clear

Constraints include topics such as safety and confidentiality. Carte blanche experimentation by all and sundry cannot be allowed. For example, the safety engineers at Chernobyl were trying to find out how little retardation the core needed to run safely; they went into new territory, which proved irreversible.

Make clear when people can innovate

Innovation may be restricted to within their area of responsibility, when it does not adversely affect the overall process and when there is agreement from all affected stakeholders.

Step 3. If improvement is already formalised, include innovation.

Established programmes for improvement may already exist with or without formal management steering. Make sure that you tackle innovation appropriately in the organisation. Additional mechanisms may be needed to encourage creativity and bring forward innovative ideas.

Step 4. Give permission.

This is part of the psychology of change. Some people in an organisation are less likely to come forward with innovative suggestions unless they know they are allowed to. Some people may take pride and derive comfort in 'doing the same job' all the time. They have become experts. You have to show them that innovation is not a threat and is not just change for change's sake.

In some organisations, suggestion schemes encourage widespread participation; in others, schemes have petered out, mainly due to a lack of feedback. Compulsory suggestion schemes, where everyone (up to and including the chief executive) must submit at least one idea for improvement, do at least show commitment. They require much work to administer, and expectations are raised. The question of reward is nearly always raised and is always in everyone's mind.

Step 5. Study opportunities for innovation.

The most significant opportunities arise when observing customers using the product or service. One can see what they are trying to do, what frustrates them, and what bores them. One can even see if they really understand what their own aims are.

The opportunities to innovate have been classified into seven areas by Drucker. He sees these as windows – more than one window can offer a different view of the same innovation. The windows are not the same size – some are much bigger than others.

Technological changes are the most noticed by the superficial observer. Technical innovation can hide many management failures. This may come to light when the competition has also adopted the new technology as an industry standard and their management is better.

Step 6. Identify the most promising opportunities and assess them by trials.

The selection of potential innovations should be informed by knowledge. When making choices, understand the systems within your organisation's current and potential operations.

It is best to keep the innovation simple and focused, although you can still aim to be a leader. If your innovation is complex, ensure you have the resources to support it during difficult starting times. Do not stumble into diversification. If diversification is your strategy, do it knowingly, get the knowledge and resources, or you will flounder.

Pilots are useful; they can uncover unimagined faults. See the story of the Sinclair QL as an example of this.

Step 7. Implement, but learn from what you are doing.

Check that the innovation is doing what you intended and that it supports the aims of your organisation. It may give you the means to further your organisation's aims.

You must learn from failures, successes and delays in your organisation.

Example

"Working for a FTSE100 client to improve their accounts receivables from 98.7% to over 99%, our consultants encountered comments about a particular individual within the client receivables unit, perceived as a troublemaker and negative. While gathering facts, we decided to leave our interview of this individual until last in the department. When we spoke to this individual, it became clear that they concurred with our conclusion that the factor holding back improvements was a culture stating that the clients were so good that they could never be wrong! We concluded that most of their receivables delays were due to legitimate client queries, misdeliveries, etc. The failure of their department to take such queries seriously was their main stumbling block, creating client friction and further delaying payments. The individual involved was thus not only correct in identifying the problems, but his colleagues were overlooking that he was also offering a solution enabling their department to be even more successful in future.

Dealing with unexpected success is challenging. Everyone is very busy, and the management has misunderstood the customer or emerging customers. No alarm signals are going off and, unlike cases of unexpected failure or external changes, there is no recognised urgent need for investigation, just pressure on resources.

Huge success is an invitation for competitors or other providers to join in.

A large organisation may find running the innovation as a distinct activity advantageous, with different controls from established routine operations.

Step 8. Make sure that innovation is an established part of the organisation.

If innovation is an integral part of the organisation, one can adapt to changing environments and develop new aims.

Example:

During World War 2, the 617 RAF squadron was tasked with delivering bouncing bombs to attack German dams. They encountered a problem establishing and maintaining their height at precisely 50 feet at night, as was necessary for the innovative bomb to work reliably. This detail was resolved after crew members visited a theatre and got the idea to focus two spotlights overlapping at precisely 50 feet: a simple innovation that made the difference between success and failure.

Look ahead. Do not paint yourself into a corner.

Examples of innovation:

Innovations fall broadly into three categories:

297

1. Innovation in product or service (product innovation);
2. Innovation in skills and processes used to make the products or services and bring them to market (managerial innovation);
3. Innovation in the marketplace, customer behaviour, and values (social innovation) (for example, iPod, iTunes and iPhone, what about Xerox in Palo Alto, where they invented the PC, mouse, GUI interface, networks and more)

Product innovation

The Safety Razor

W King Gillette did not invent the safety razor. His razor was sold cheap. His business made money by selling replacement razor blades. His customers believed they were buying a safe shave rather than just a razor blade.

Safety Razor blades in the 1960s used stainless steel to replace carbon steel. The lower-stress corrosion gave a longer-lasting blade. The same manufacturing plant could be used.

Much work went into finding a material which gave thin, durable coatings on the blade tip. The best material was PTFE, an intractable polymer that melted but did not flow at 327°C, at which steel discolours in the air. Developing a reliable process that could coat millions of blades per week was long and arduous. The first company to succeed patented the coating and process. The product gave such superior comfort and lifetime performance over uncoated blades that all man-ufacturers had to provide such a product and had to pay royalties to the first company.

Cars

Manufacturers produce new models every few years.

Enter a market segment new to a manufacturer. Toyota entering the luxury market segment with the Lexus was an example of strategic innovation, as was their Prius petrol/electric hybrid.

Solar-powered miner's lamp

This concept came out of an R&D department's creative Forced Paradox session. Obviously, the sun does not shine underground.

In mines, there is a need for local meters and gauges. What is not wanted is kilometres of ca-bling or a stand-alone device with a battery that needs replacement. Mining engineers would not want to carry such devices or even the extra bat-teries to power them around. They do carry lamps or flashlights. A meter powered up from photocells charged up by a flashlight just to give the engineer a reading there and then, when he needed it, was a solution and gave rise to a range of products.

Process Innovation

Chemical Industry

In a continuous chemical process, there was a stage which involved a stream of product, a solid suspended in water, dropping under gravity over plates in a column while being exposed to a counter-current of vapour. Because the product got caught up in the column, the company had a programme of periodically cleaning the column by stopping the process, partially dismantling it, and cleaning it by hand, which resulted in the loss of one day's production plus downgraded material several times a year.

The company had a structured improvement programme which functioned primarily by facilitated projects. A shift supervisor proposed to his local steering group a proposal for investigating a procedure of stopping and bubbling the column for a few hours to keep the plant clean. The supervisor was given team leadership, his own shift, and technical help from process engineers. The team developed a procedure which resulted in a much lower loss of production time and downgraded material.

A process for training in new methods existed in the plant already, and qualified training staff were available so that shifts ended up following the same procedure within a few days. The innovation is put in across many plants within the company in several countries.

Farm Machinery Sales

In the nineteenth century, many American farmers were too poor to buy harvesting machinery. A manufacturer, Cyrus McCormack, introduced instalment buying so the farmers, or groups of local farmers, could use future earnings and past earnings (savings) to get the machines that increased their productivity.

300

Penny Post

Roland Hill did not invent the postal service in the UK.

The existing postal service required senders to take their letters and packets to a post office and get them costed according to weight and distance of the destination. They were then taken to the receiver, who would pay for them only if they wanted the letter or had the money. If not, the letters were taken back. The change to a charge pre-paid by the sender got the income. Using adhesive stamps made the use of pillar boxes for letter collection possible. Also, the charge was cheaper. One penny replaced possible charges of around a shilling (12 pence). Thus writing and posting letters became a much more popular activity.

Product & Process Innovation together

Innovation	Product Or Service	Skills And Processes	Market Place
Safety Razor	Product		Social
Stainless steel blades	Product		
PTFE coated blades	Product	Process	
Automobiles	Product		Social sometimes
Miner's equipment	Product		

Innovation	Product Or Service	Skills And Processes	Market Place
Chemical process		Process	
Farm Machinery Sales		Management (Financial) Process	Social
Penny Post		Management Process	Social

Innovation FAQ

What is the best way to have a good idea?

> "Have lots of ideas." Linus Pauling (Winner of two separate Nobel prizes).

Can people have ideas in your organisation?

> They will, but some structure is needed for the ideas to appear and be developed.

How can the ideas be turned into action?

> This is a clear responsibility of management.

How can your organisation recognize a 'good' idea?

> Examine the idea: can it be made into a product or service or improve a process?

How can you systematize innovation?

"You cannot." Steve Jobs (Apple and Pixar). Is he right? From where did Apple's innovation come? Do not confuse creativity with innovation.

Is there a hard and fast difference between improvement and innovation?

Not really. If you were to take an out-of-control process and remove the special causes of variation, you would have improved it. If you change the mean value and spread (stable variability), you are beginning to innovate. Innovation essentially involves putting ideas together that have not effectively been connected before. At the extreme of innovation is starting a new venture to bring users a brand new product or service.

Can pubic service organisations innovate?

A public service has legal duties, aims and a budget (rather than earnings). If it wants to extend, or even achieve, its aims concerning its budget, for example, it has got to innovate.

Is innovation essentially technological change?

No, scientific and technological changes are only one type of innovation. See Drucker's work to identify all the other types. Technological change is a relatively high risk, slow to deliver, and has many participants. You do not have to invent everything new. You can buy it in, license it, or outsource the need. Some organisations are in activities where they benefit from having research activities, skunk works etc., and having proprietary knowledge.

Can real innovation only be achieved by a genius inventor?

The flash of genius is like a miracle cure. It does happen, but very rarely. It cannot be taught or learned. Nevertheless, genius inventors are rarely one-idea people - their ability to identify potential problems and rationalise them into solutions can be used in many areas.

Innovation is more reliably (and much more commonly) achieved by hard work in a structured, purposeful way.

Just about every human being has had an experience where everything came together and can recall the exhilaration of that moment. They may call it "Finding the missing piece", "the electric light coming on", the "ah-ha moment", the "eureka" moment, or "epiphany".

Archimedes was given a problem by his local tyrant, who had been sold a crown claimed to be made of gold. The tyrant wanted to know whether the crown was truly made of gold so that he could pay the supplier or execute him as a cheat. Archimedes knew how to weigh things, and he understood about density – the same sized block of gold weighed more than one of silver, iron or copper - but he spent much thought on the problem of how to estimate the volume of an irregular-shaped, bumpy object (a crown, shaped like a laurel wreath). When he walked down into his bath, he saw that an irregular-shaped, bumpy object (Archimedes himself) displaced a volume of water, and the water level rose. He realized that the water would drop to its original level when he got out of the bath. At this moment, all his previous thoughts came together to give him his shout of "I have got it" – Eureka. Whether or not he ran through the streets naked shouting is irrelevant but typical of the human love of telling stories and trying to make them memorable.

> *Genius is 1% inspiration and*
> *99% perspiration.*
> *(Thomas Edison)*

From where would people in your organisation get their inspiration?

Try listening to your customers or users. See VOC.

Does the customer know what is needed?

Not necessarily, but he may think he knows what he wants. He will recognise what he really wants when someone shows it to him. He will be enthusiastic about acquiring it and tell his friends where he got it from (you).

What is the best type of innovation?

> The one where people say, "Why didn't we think of that?"

> In these circumstances, you must have put together familiar things in a novel way to get that sort of response. Well done. What can you learn from this?

> As time passes, you will look back at the innovation, and it will appear in increasing retrospect to have been more and more logical and almost inevitable. That is just human nature.

Should we copy Toyota (generally accepted to be best-in-class)?

> Not necessarily. Toyota has spent fifty years getting to where they are now. Their tools and techniques have a context. This context may differ significantly from yours, and their tools and techniques may not be relevant to you. Their guiding principles of Continuous Improvement and Respect for People will undoubtedly be. However, perceptive authors have written many books about the company, which may help you. Some of these are given in the reference section below.

What did Deming mean when he said innovation could only come from people who take joy in their work?

> It is said there are only two fundamental human emotions in essence; love and fear.

In an organisation that is dominated by fear or that has its attention consumed with meeting targets, a context of negativity or punishment is liable to stifle innovation (due to perceived individual risk); at the same time, it will reduce enthusiasm, erode individual input and focus practical and pragmatic individuals onto what it not possible, or what is not socially acceptable. Thus the culture itself encourages a limiting, negative outcome.

Want to know more?

There are hundreds of books, chapters, articles and websites covering Innovation.

The following resources look at innovation from a systems perspective *and* show an understanding of what makes people tick – you need both to support innovation and manage change effectively.

The Deming Dimension, HR Neave, 1990, SPC Press.	Particularly chapter 14
Innovation and Entrepreneurship, P Drucker, 1993, Collins, and 2007, Elsevier (BH)	A classic text with still much relevance today. It expounds on principles with many examples. A few of his exemplars of innovation have now been overtaken by new innovators using the

	principles that Drucker identified. In the second half of the book he gives a lot of insight into entrepreneurship and its impact on the USA economy in the late twentieth century.
The Myths of Innovation, S Berkun, 2007, O'Reilly.	A good corrective to over-reduced business school case histories, vigorously displaying the human factor present in all innovations. The author was on the Microsoft Explorer development team.
Harvard Business Review **On Innovation**, 2001, HBS Press	Eight interesting, detailed cases. Very instructive if read bearing Drucker's classifications in mind. Application of the elements of the System of Profound Knowledge enables the reader to envisage extensions in scope and duration of the innovations described.
The Toyota Way, J K Liker, 2004, McGraw Hill.	Chapter 5 covers a Strategic Innovation, the creation of a new brand,

	the Lexus, done in the Toyota way.
The Toyota Way Fieldbook, J K Liker and D Meier, 2006, McGraw Hill.	Chapter 11 includes an account of the Toyota Suggestion Scheme. Since Toyota is a somewhat individual firm, this should be read with an account of its culture, which supports improvement and innovation.
Toyota Culture – The Heart and Soul of the Toyota Way, J K Liker and M Hoseus, 2008, McGraw Hill.	Chapter 6 covers the engagement of people in continuous improvement and innovation.
Smart things to know about Innovation & Creativity, D Sherwood, 2001, Capstone.	A how-to-do-it book that covers the four basics of innovation: - Idea Generation - Evaluation - Development - Implementation
The Toyota Product Development System: Integrating People, Process and Technology by	All about the art and the science of innovation, with a good section on set-based innovation

James M. Morgan & Jeffrey Liker	
The Elegant Solution: Toyota's Formula for Mastering Innovation by Matthew May 2007, Simon & Schuster.	Another book on the principles, practices and protocols of the Toyota Product Development System
Product Development for the Lean Enterprise: Why Toyota's System Is Four Times More Productive and How You Can Implement It by Michael Kennedy	Another book on the Toyota Product Development System exploring some of the pre-requisites for innovation: Vision, system, engaged leaders, involvement
Competing on the Basis of Speed.mp4 by Mary Poppendieck http://video.google.com/videoplay?docid=51059104528642836 94.	Great thinking about innovation in software development with many applications elsewhere and an overview of set-based innovation
Breakthrough Management, Shoji Sheba & David Walden, 2006, CII	How to change your organisation fundamentally so that it operates entirely

	differently. It describes how to use image and language data as well as numerical data
Four Practical Revolutions in Management, Shoji Sheba & David Walden, 2001, Centre for Quality Management	This book describes four revolutions: Customer Focus, Continuous Improvement,Total Participation and Societal Networking. Chapter 14 covers Proactive improvement to Develop New Products.

Self-Examination Questions

1. Have senior management in your organisation shown leadership in innovation?
2. Is there a support infrastructure for innovation in your organisation?
3. What is the difference between innovation and improvement in your organisation's terminology?
4. Do you know where to start?

Glossary

Forced paradox is taking two different viable ideas and pushing them together to see whether the outcome is viable. An example would be the first time someone thought of putting a modern minicamera into a mobile phone.

Continual improvement is the sum of continuous improvement (e.g. Kai Zen) and discontinuous improvement, eg. breakthrough, such as would come from radical innovation.

Thoughts On Business Sustainability

Authors	Tony Brown, Alan Clark, Terry Rose

Overview

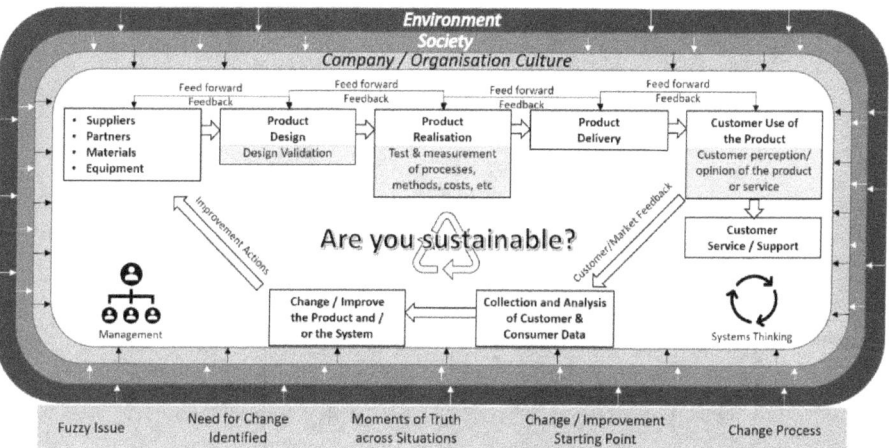

Figure 38: An Organisation viewed as a sustainable system (after Deming)

Never before has the rate of change in our society led to the demise of so many enterprises, whether in financial management, banking, automotive or other industries, the rate of decline, job loss and industrial infrastructure loss.

The rate of technological progress continues to speed up. Globalisation has seen governments helpless to prevent the flight of capital, industries or outsourcing to low-cost countries. The prospects for the future are grim.

Survival is management's number one task. Sustainability has to be the number one item on every CEO's agenda. Dr Deming's track record with companies that have stood the test of time is convincing. His legacy, philosophy, System of Profound Knowledge (SoPK) and other teachings provide a platform for survival and a bedrock for building a sustainable enterprise based on quality management principles.

Introduction and Executive Summary

> *If it is hard to make a success of something, it is an order of magnitude harder to sustain the success.*
> *(Andy Grove, former Chairman and CEO of Intel Corp.)*

Sustainable success is, indeed, hard to achieve. We seem to accept as the norm that organisations in the public, private and not-for-profit sectors will not last over the long term. Partly the difficulty is due to sustainable success being a balancing act of three elements: social, economic and ecological. Long-term success cannot be achieved in one area at the expense of the others.

Two quotes from Dr WE Deming: *"It is not necessary to change. Survival is not mandatory"* and *"Learning is not compulsory... neither is survival"*. These seem to sum up the essence of sustainable success, namely that it requires learning and change. The fundamentals of sustainable management are listed below and explored in greater depth elsewhere in this book. However, the core is the focus on the customer and what flows from that, quality. Quality is what the customers say it is, and this will continually change due to rising customer expectations and the complexity of the global operating environment.

Forces of destruction are continually at work, limiting the life of an organisation. Like ice melting in a glass in a warm room, organisations tend towards chaos or at least lose the vital spark essential for longevity. Top management becomes unwilling to experiment or try new solutions to problems, becomes inflexible, cannot learn from the present, and finally becomes submerged by tradition.

The three elements of enterprise sustainability are social, economic and environmental, also known as the "triple bottom line" (see page 328). Whilst economic considerations have traditionally been at the forefront when considering viability, a more balanced approach is taking hold. Human factors within organisations go back as far as Robert Owen at the beginning of the nineteenth century. In the twentieth century, the human relations movement led to the recognition of the importance of human factors in organisational performance and, in this century, in organisational longevity. More recently, the broader social impact of organisations has gained importance, as has the natural environment. Even in the unlikely event that it is shown that CO_2 emissions are not linked to human activity, there are the peak oil situation, pollution, and the impact of global population growth on water and food to consider.

The silent killers that stalk the corridors of enterprises link directly to the forces of destruction and result from the loss of that vital spark. Several of those forces listed below can be fatal, but the most serious is neglecting customers. It seems obvious, but it still happens even to the best companies (see the Toyota case study, page 324).

Deming was quite clear that top management is responsible for the fitness of the enterprise system. The elements of the system and its capabilities, as a whole and individually, determine long-term success. People can and do make a difference, but the system always wins if left unchecked.

At the end of this article is a list of enterprises that make worthwhile case studies. Many examples of long-lasting and, sadly, the majority who do not survive are out there.

Main Content

What Is Sustainability?
"Extend the socially useful life of an enterprise so that they contribute resources to achieve the enterprise's and society's environmental, social and economic goals."

Sustainability may be thought to have taken one step closer to the mainstream with the publication of ISO 9004:2009 *Managing for the Sustained*

316

Success of an Organisation - A Quality Management Approach. This standard defines **sustained success** as the 'result of the ability of an organisation to achieve and maintain its objectives in the long term'. It defines the **organisation's environment** as the 'combination of internal and external factors and conditions that can affect the achievement of an organisation's objectives and its behaviour towards its interested parties.'

Fundamentals for Sustainability

Sustainable organisations are characterised by the following

- Putting customer first
- Quality is job number 1
- Devolution of leadership
- Avoidance of the forces of destruction
- Good enough is never enough in the search for the competitive edge
- Keeping the culture agile and achieving constant renewal
- Maximising the enterprise's capabilities

Achieving these requires leadership throughout the organisation and particularly by top management. It also requires a management style transformed from the typical Western management style or at least the Anglo-American one.

The Forces of Destruction

Top management is usually responsible for unleashing the forces of destruction through misguided belief, the sins of omission or sometimes just greed. The following are some of the most obvious:

- Takeovers or 'buyouts' funded by large borrowings that laden companies with debt
- Asset stripping
- Inappropriate Mergers
- Bonus payments that are assumed to be the way to obtain performance
- McCollough's cycle:
    - emergence
    - full flower of growth
    - prestige
    - stagnation
    - death
- Obsession with direct labour costs
- Abandoning large businesses with low margins
- Creating a mismatch between the product and the marketplace
- Using resources to buy other companies
- Appraisal systems

Peter McColough, cited above, was one of the founders of Xerox. A creative thinker, he started their research facility, which invented most of the ideas that formed the basis of the success of Apple, Intel and Microsoft. Xerox had failed to develop any of its innovations. They also lost the battle with the Japanese for their copier market.

> *Is it inevitable that such organisations as Xerox should have their periods of emergence, full flower of growth and prestige and then later stagnation and death?*
> *(Peter McColough)*

Indeed, relying on the management dogma listed above is the opposite of the reflective and agile mindset required in a constantly changing operating environment. The inflexibility of top managers unprepared to challenge the perceived wisdom is at the heart of the problem, but then the status quo is easier.

Elements of Enterprise Sustainability[39] (see page Appendix 1)

- **Social sustainability** – human factors, internal and external
- **Economic sustainability** – producing returns and funds for reinvestment
- **Ecological sustainability** – husbanding the natural environment and resources
- **A culture built on efficiency**, effectiveness and involvement in the development, renewal regeneration of the enterprise and societies

The Silent Killers

Many silent killers are usually present in any organisational failure. Again it is the unwillingness

---

[39] See page 255

to try something different, inflexibility, unwillingness to learn and the straightjacket of tradition
that combine to nurture these issues:

- Customer neglect
- Unclear strategy or conflicting priorities
- An ineffective management team
- Command and control management style
- Poor vertical communication
- Poor coordination across functions
- Insufficient leadership skills from top to bottom

Enterprise fitness – enterprise elements

A healthy and, therefore, sustainable enterprise
will comprise many features, some unique. The
following list provides those common to all organisations:

- Systems-Thinking
- Leadership team
- Vision, values and mission that crucially feature quality and quality management
- Policy deployment
- Management systems and lean processes
- Reliable work system
- Human resource system
- Supply chain synergy
- And you may know of others.

Generic Model – Systems-Thinking

Figure 39 on page 321, developed by Terry Rose,
schematically brings together many of the ele-

ments in-
volved in
taking a
systems-
thinking
perspective
of a sus-
tainable or-
ganisation.
The sus-
tainable or-
ganisation
continually
tries some-
thing dif-
ferent, is
flexible,
even agile,
willing to
learn and
free of tra-
dition.

At every
level, cus-
tomer fo-
cus and the
engine of
the cease-
less learn-
ing cycles
of PlanDo-
Study-Act
rejuvenate
the whole enterprise. The knowledge that

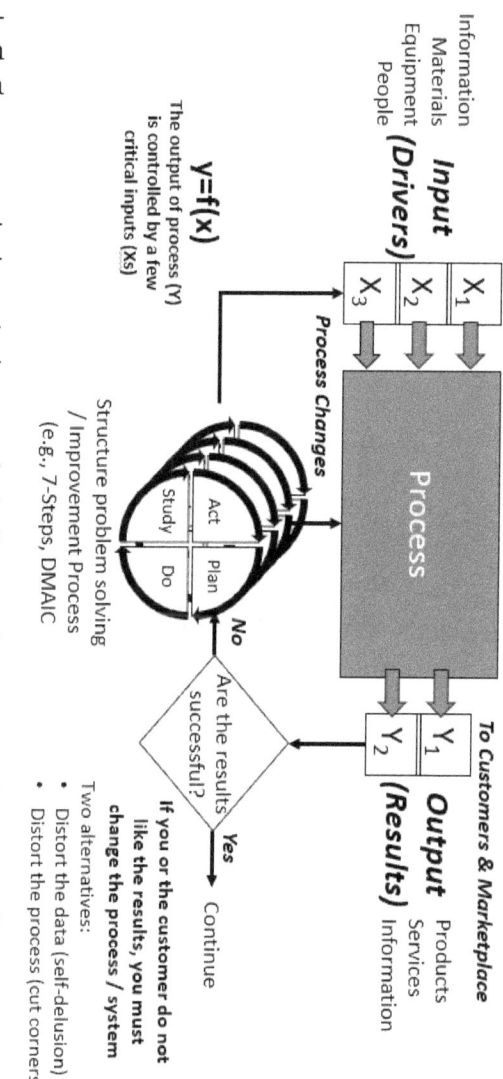

Figure 39: Systems-Thinking

emerges from this openness to learning feeds step-by-step improvement and innovation.

Enterprise Capabilities

Systems and processes must be in place to continually educate, train, research and renew these capabilities; otherwise, the enterprise will decline. Knowledge and new knowledge are critical success factors, even more so today. How capable is the organisation in all of the following areas?

- Coordination
- Human competencies
- Commitment brought about by inspirational leadership
- Innovation, continual improvement
- Capacity and delivery system
- Capable management processes
- Knowledge learning, transfer and management

In addition, the enterprise must integrate into a coherent strategy three management paradigms

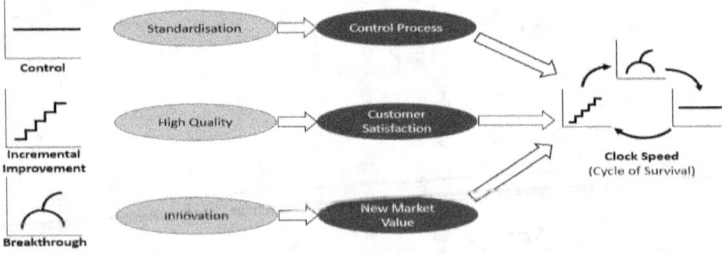

Figure 40: Business Logic of the Three Management Paradigms

322

of control, incremental improvement and innovation. Again any one of these on its own is not a survival strategy.

Figure 40 is a diagram provided by Terry Rose based on the original work by Prof Shoji Shiba on Breakthrough Management.

Case Studies

A health warning! While the following companies offer excellent examples, what is most important is the thinking behind the actions. Each organisation is unique, as are its people, time and place. When studying the following businesses as examples of sustainable organisations, look for the underlying thinking. How could it apply in your situation?

- WL Gore – autonomous management system
- John Lewis – not-for-profit enterprise
- Toyota – 50+ years of profit improvement and market share, Deming award winner in 1963
- Ford Motor Co. Deming transformation lost and regained. 1980-2009
- Dunn's Bakery – Crouch End London excellence since 1827!
- Lloyd's shipping over 250 years – still transforming itself

This article will only take as an example one of these: the Toyota Motor Corporation

Brief Case Study – Toyota

> *"Toyota has recorded annual losses in the last two years of global recession, after nearly 50 years of achieving unmatched financial results in its industry"* Shoichiro Toyoda, the 84-year-old family patriarch and honorary chairman of Toyota Motors, responded to this by announcing a stunning shake-up of top management. He chastised top managers for losing sight of the fundamentals that had made the company so outstanding and promised that the company would "return to basics."*
>
> *(Tom Johnson November 2009 Qualityworld)*

Toyota's expansion into an increasingly dispersed global network of plants and suppliers made it challenging to fill customer orders for the manufacturer's increasing variety of models in a reasonable lead time.

The loss of highly skilled, Toyota-trained people and the inability to fill the gaps with suitably trained replacements in the Toyota Way

Producing to customer orders – a condition relentlessly pursued in Toyota plants for decades – requires patient effort on the shop floor to increase the mix of models and decrease delivery lead times. However, after the late 1990s, Toyota often replaced its patient problem-solving techniques with quick compromises or workarounds, such as shipping units over long distances, compromising long-standing fundamentals such as flowing work continuously in lot sizes of one and addressing any abnormality with an immediate solution – Stop and Take Action.

- Toyota's management culture at its zenith was process-driven, not results-driven.
- Toyota eschewed the financial markets' absurdly impossible demand to produce higher results quarter by quarter.
- It rejected the idea espoused by lean authorities that a company can improve its overall performance by subtracting parts.
- It assumed that a properly orchestrated process would generate results sufficient to sustain the organisation's ongoing activities.
- Its pathway to higher results echoed Deming's advice, given many years ago, to improve the capability of the process, not to demand that people meet higher targets.
- The reversal of Toyota's fortunes at the beginning of the century suggests that many of its top managers lost the habit of thought that had previously shaped the company's policies and actions.
- They lost the habit of thought that caused the company, perhaps unconsciously, to act like a living system.

325

- Toyota adopted the finance-oriented mechanistic thinking that spawned the inferior management practices and the poor performance of most of its competitors after the 1970s.
- And, because it abandoned living-system thinking for mechanistic thinking, Toyota began to embrace a virtual world of finance, not a concrete world of humans in cooperative relationships.

What is interesting about the malaise of Toyota is that it confirms that it was the underlying principles that led to success. It is almost as if fate decided to conduct a scientific experiment to prove that it was the underlying principles that were responsible for success. By departing from these principles, performance and quality declined, resulting in poor financial results and vehicle recalls. By returning to the fundamentals, both financial and quality results will be regained.

Summary And Conclusions

'Predicting the future is a tough gig; history is bunk', said Henry Ford. What are the conclusions?

We have seen that even the best companies can stray from their successful principles, and when they do, performance declines. Sustaining success is hard, but the social, economic and environmental rewards are high. To achieve this success it is essential that the people, particularly top management, are prepared to try new things, be flexible, value knowledge, learn new knowledge and not be hidebound by tradition.

It is not required to do these things: as Deming once said, survival is optional.

Self Examination Questions

1. To what extent do you think your organisation is currently sustainable as a business?
2. How can you measure the vitality of your organisation? Do you dare?
3. Which of the silent killers stalk your corridors?
4. What is your enterprise fitness rating out of ten for each listed enterprise element?
5. How do you rate your organisation's capabilities against each of the items in the list above?

Bibliography

- *Out of the Crisis* by W Edwards Deming 1986
- *The New Economics* by W Edwards Deming 1993
- *ISO 9004:2009 Managing for the sustained success of an organisation — A quality management approach*
- *The Unnatural Environment* by Tom Johnson QW Qualityworld ISSN 13528769 November 2009 Vol. 35 issue 11, pp32-35

- *Profit Beyond Measure: Extraordinary Results through Attention to Process and People by H* Thomas Johnson and Anders Broms 2000
- *Toyota Production System: Beyond Large-Scale Production* by Taiichi Ohno 1988
- *Built to Last: Successful Habits of Visionary Companies* by James C Collins and Jerry I Porras 1994
- *Good to Great: Why Some Companies Make the Leap and Others Don't* by Jim Collins 2001
- *Breakthrough Management: Principles, Skills, and Patterns for Transformational Leadership* by Shoji Shiba and David Walden 2006
- *The Three Secrets of Green Business: Unlocking Competitive Advantage in a Low Carbon Economy* by Gareth Cane 2010

Appendix Some Models Associated with Sustainability

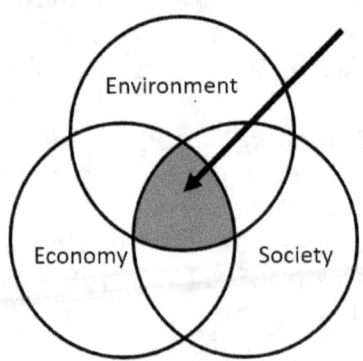

The most popular way of visualizing sustainability is that of three interlocking circles representing the economy, society, and the environment.

Figure 41: Traditional Sustainability

The nexus in the middle is regarded as sustaina-

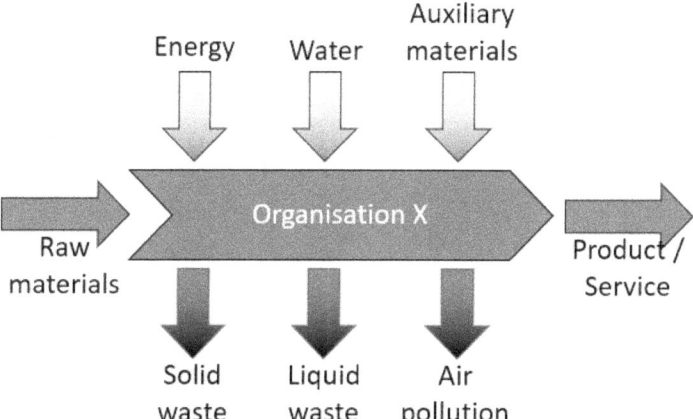

Figure 42: Organisational Impact on the Environment

bility, as illustrated in Figure 41.

The danger of this model is that it suggests that sustainability is a balance between the three and implies that not hitting the target is an option.

Finding a social, economic and environmental benefit to any enterprise is very easy, but this does not mean it is sustainable. True sustaina-
bility requires a para-
digm shift.

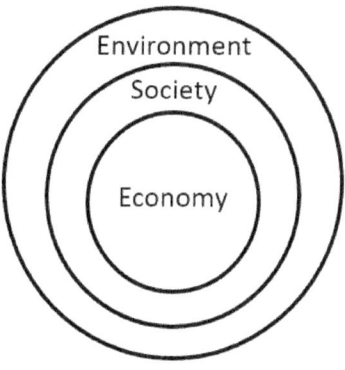

Perhaps a more mean-
ingful version is the 'fried egg' model, in which sus-
tainability is defined as the situation where the economy operates within limits set by society and

where society flourishes within the ecological limits placed on it by the natural world.

MoSO captures these imperatives from an organisational standpoint.

Figure 42 illustrates organisational inputs and outputs from an environmental perspective.

Transformation

Author	Terry Rose
Review-ers	Tony Brown, Antony Aitken, Alan Clark

Introduction

For MoSO, transformation is seen as a journey that an existing organisation may take to become ever more sustainable.

Transformation is the journey of change, and change includes changing an organisation's

- Systems,
- Processes,
- Policies,
- Values,
- The way it does things.

In other words, changing anything can help an organisation perform better and be more sustainable.

The gap between "Where we are today" (the current state) and "Our vision of us as a sustainable organisation" (the destination) represents the length of this journey and its degree of difficulty.

Every organisation's journey will be different; however, there will likely be some generic steps or milestones to help signpost the way forward. Experience shows that the journey will include dead ends and wrong turns – it is typically an iterative and hugely enjoyable process.

There is great value to be had in the journey itself.

Begin With the End in Mind (a word about the destination)

Before looking at the journey (the transformation process), some ideas about the destination are worth exploring. We are interested in the specific **organisational capabilities** that a sustainable organisation of any type or size will likely need to possess: the things it needs to be good at and does as a matter of course rather than exceptionally.

In a rapidly changing world driven by free market economies with increasing societal and environmental influences, sustainable organisations need **an inherent ability to improve** and, when necessary, **radically change continually.** Put another way, a sustainable organisation will need an inherent **capability** to:

- Get better and better at understanding, meeting, and exceeding the expectations of its key stakeholders – *continually improve the things it does*; and
- Get better at getting better - continually increasing the rate of innovation, evolution and improvement.

The Transformation Process will need to put in place an enduring set of <u>principles</u>, <u>practices</u>, and <u>infrastructures</u> capable of continually aligning and mobilising the organisation to deliver products and services that meet the existing and future (perhaps as yet unknown) needs of customers, other key stakeholders, and the broader marketplace.

Principles

Some examples of the guiding principles that the organisation will use to underpin all efforts to build a sustainable organisation include:

- Deming's 14 points,
- Toyota's 14 Principles and
- ISO 9001 8 Quality Management Principles.

Principles should be based on tried and tested concepts/knowledge/theory that will not radically change with time. A fundamental principle is ***customer focus***.

The principles should address all elements of the MoSO becoming part of an organisation's DNA. Over time they embed themselves in the leadership and culture of an organisation and can be tested against an organisation's actions and behaviours.

Practices

A core set of common processes, tools, and techniques is used throughout the organisation to help implement the principles.

Common practices create a shared language and way of thinking (never underestimate the power of having common practices across all functions and at all levels of an organisation), reinforcing individual and organisational learning and continual improvement throughout the organisation.

Infrastructure

How an organisation governs and organises (manages) the change/transformation process is typically organised as a cascading 'management' team structure that touches all parts and all levels of an organisation.

The structure will likely need to be adapted to meet the needs of different parts of the organisation.

The Journey

There appear to be two main phases of any transformation process:

- Personal transformation and
- Organisational transformation.

Personal transformation is a prerequisite to organisational transformation.

Figure 43 shows the typical high-level, generic transformation steps:

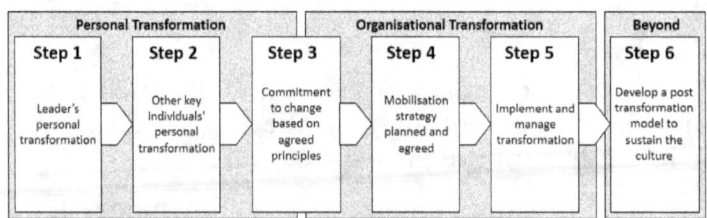

Figure 43: High Level Generic Transformation Process

Step 1. Leader's Personal Transformation

Before proceeding, leaders must change their thinking by embracing thoughts beyond present limitations or thought patterns.

Individuals need to be convinced, or more likely convince themselves, that the transformation journey is worth the effort. This effort is particularly true of individuals who will have leadership roles in the transformation process, such as:

- The CEO/MD/Owner
- Senior managers
- Change Agents/Local Managers
- Real Change Leaders (someone at any level in an organisation who uses their skills and drive to bring about improvements within their scope of influence).

Two things motivate leaders to lead a transformation:

- Learning
- Fear, Crisis or a jolt.

Learning occurs primarily outside the organisation from seminars, parent company, customers, suppliers, government agencies, communication with other leaders, personal experience (particularly influential), advisors, partners, consultants, and others.

However, learning alone is not enough to provide the necessary motivation. Learning only creates interest. Another trigger is needed – a second, perhaps more powerful, motivator.

Fear, Crisis or a Jolt. Major organisational change of any kind is usually precipitated by fear[40]. It could be fear that the organisation is "out of step" or falling behind competitors, market forces, societal influences or customer expectations. If something is not done, the organisation may not thrive or survive.

Delaying action until a full-blown crisis occurs may be acting too late. A Leader's job is to focus the organisation's thinking on the latent crisis that others cannot yet see.

A leader's personal transformation may take some or all of the following steps. It is unlikely to be a serial process – more likely to be iterative, taking place over time.

Fuzzy Issue Identified	An uncomfortable feeling or notion that a problem (which must be dealt with at executive level) exists.
Need for Change Identified	The fuzzy issue is more clearly defined. There is a feeling that the problem must be addressed sooner rather than later. Fear for my job, my future or the organisation's future. Fear sets in.

---

[40] According to a survey of Deming winners by Prof Noriaki Kano.

336

Moments of Truth across situations	Once aware of the problem, seek out and/or intuitively come across examples of the symptoms of the problem. Become aware of many other problems with the same/similar root cause. The "aha! or lightbulb" moments – many of them across the organisation - not isolated
Personal Learning Journey	Gain knowledge and understanding. Seek out those who potentially have skills associated with the same or similar problems. Perhaps other organisations; read books / articles; talk to trusted peers; go to seminars; meet with consultants.
Create Hypothesis & Vision	Based on increasing knowledge and understanding, articulate – perhaps with the help of others – a hypothesis of what's causing the symptoms and a vision of what needs to done.

Step 2. Other Key Individuals Personal Transformation

A leader cannot do it alone. Nothing will happen without the buy-in and commitment of other key individuals in the organisation. Just because the leader says so is not enough.

The leader will have to gain the buy-in of those key individuals who will have to drive or cooperate in managing the leadership for transformation. Key individuals could be other senior managers/peers.

These key individuals must go through their own personal transformation – possibly as a team – guided by the leader (possibly with outside help). The steps of Figure 2 still apply.

Some patterns of successful leader involvement in helping others to make a personal transformation include:

- **Holistic Personal Approach**: Spend personal time; convey passion; share own personal transformation process;
- **Strategy**: Lead by example; be open and accepting of different ideas; work in teams; do it again and again. Allow sufficient time and space.

Step 3. Commitment to Change Based on Agreed Principles

This crucial step is the first involving Organisational change. It is said that individuals learn naturally whereas organisations need a process or way to make it happen. It is a gating factor. If the leader cannot gain commitment from selected key individuals, no significant or lasting changes can occur. In this case, the leader has a major decision: whether to abandon the transformation or change the key players. This is perhaps an example of what Jim Collins, in his book *Good to Great*, calls 'Getting the right people on the bus in the right seats'.

This is such an essential step because the key individuals are already, or are likely to become, leaders in their own areas of influence. They need to be fully engaged – they cannot delegate to others.

Doing the 'transformation work' builds under-standing and skill and embeds the pro-cess/thinking to become the accepted way of do-ing things.

For this reason, these key individuals working with the leader as a team usually devise a set of enduring core principles that form the transfor-mation's bedrock. The set of principles addresses each of the MoSO Elements.

Step 4. Mobilisation Strategy Planned & Agreed

Regardless of type or size, organisations need a (mobilisation) strategy and a structure for intro-ducing and managing change initiatives. Mobili-sation Strategies typically have three integral parts:

1. **Leader as driving force for change**. This involves high visibility involvement, hands-on participation, making decisions, evaluating change processes and results, leading from the front, and not delegating

to 'experts'. The leader is committed to 'Walking the talk' and becoming the expert.

2. **Strategies for introduction.** Chosen to suit the style and culture of the organisation. Many different models are available, but typically phases include:

   a. **Initiating:** Goal setting, telling people what is coming and why, sharing the importance of the change, initial training;

   b. **Empowering or Mobilising:** Giving people the ability to act, setting to work, further training as required (e.g. action learning), organising teams;

   c. **Aligning:** Ensuring all the work is aligned to required results (e.g., Operational Excellence). The MoSO can be used for this purpose.

3. **Organisational infrastructure.** The organisation and processes that will be used to manage (govern) the transformation and beyond is typically a management team structure using standing teams to manage training programs, promotion of success stories, etc.

From the author's experience, the 7 Infrastructure model illustrated in Figure 44, which Professor Shoji Shiba helped develop, is an excellent way to manage change initiatives[41].

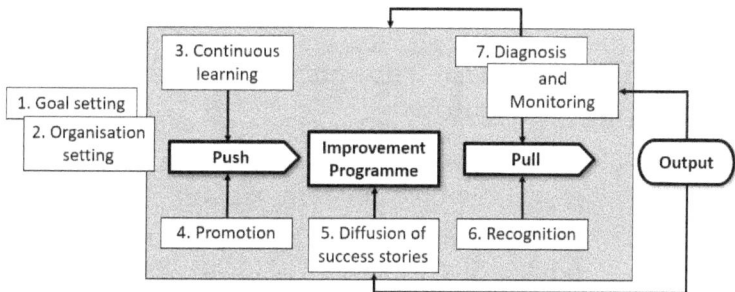

Figure 44: The 7 Infrastructure Model

Step 5. Implement & Manage Transformation

The organisational infrastructure implemented during Step 4 is used to manage the transformation mobilisation plan.

Basic project management principles can be used to manage both the process of transformation and individual improvement projects.

Step 6. Develop Post-Transformation Model to Sustain the Culture

Post-transformation, leaders must devote time and effort to determine how to sustain the changes. There have been many cases where the culture engendered during the transformation has become watered down or even replaced (perhaps out of sight of the leadership) due to new

---

[41] See also *'Leadership Principles of the New Six Sigma'* (Align, Mobilize, Accelerate, Govern) in the book The New Six Sigma published by Motorola University

people (including leaders and managers) joining the organisation.

Post-transformation activities are seen as an essential part of the transformation.

Some Additional Thoughts on Organisational Transformation

- Most likely to be a mass movement – reach/involve as many people in the organisation as possible (or everyone in the part of the organisation that is to undergo improvement).
- This is not easy – a (mobilisation) strategy needs to be implemented.
- A critical' success criterion' is the lack or absence of strong opposition. Opposition can gradually be reduced by building trust and realising the benefits.
- Without top management involvement, a strong culture of quality and business improvement is required (sufficient knowledge of the need for and the methods to achieve organisational improvement).
- Creating an 'Island of change' is possible if a local leader is reasonably autonomous.

Facilitators (external or internal) cannot be successful in driving change without the visible involvement of the leader and key individuals.

Some Recognised Transformation Processes

Step	Ford 6 Steps	Kotter 8 Step	Motorola New Six Sigma	MoSO Group
1	Benchmark	Increase urgency	Align	Fuzzy Issue
2	Management Commitment	Build the guiding Team	Mobilize	Need for change identified
3	Employee Involvement	Get the vision right	Accelerate	Moments of truth across situations
4	Participative Management	Communicate for buy-in	Govern	Change/Improvement starting point
5	Transforming Programs	Empower action		Change/Transformation process
6	Integrating & Systemising Continual Improvement	Create short-term wins		Post Transformation model to sustain the culture (at all levels in the organisation)

7		Don't let up		
8		Make change stick		

Note: The Deming Award process, the Baldrige criteria and the EFQM European Excellence model could also be transformation processes.

Self-Examination Questions

Some *initial* questions for a leader or a leadership team (and you will have others):

1. To what extent has your vision for the future been agreed between yourselves?
2. Have the imperatives for change (the Whys) been clearly set out and agreed upon?
3. To what extent has the gap between the organisation's 'current state' and the 'destination' been articulated?
4. Have the benefits of using MoSO as a comprehensive framework for sustainability been explored?
5. Has a defined set of principles (and values) that will form an enduring foundation for transformation and beyond been agreed upon?
6. To what extent are you (the leadership team) prepared to personally devote time and effort to building knowledge, understanding and skill in the practices that will drive change?

7. Developing an infrastructure for change throughout the organisation is essential. Has the team developed a suitable infrastructure for your organisation that involves all the leadership team playing an active role?

Bibliography

- Any of Dr W. F. Deming's books
- The following books by Shoji Shiba and David Walden:
    - *Four Practical Revolutions in Management*
    - *Breakthrough Management*
- *The New Six Sigma* published by Motorola University
- Jim Collins, *Good to Great*

Many others could be added, but why not start with those above?

Glossary of Terms

Transformation: A journey of significant change

Principles: The guiding principles that an organisation will use to underpin all efforts to bring about organisational change or transformation.

Practices: A core set of common processes, tools, and techniques that can be used throughout an organisation to help put the principles into practice

Infrastructure: The way an organisation governs and organises (manages) the change/transformation process

Breakthrough Management is a systemic approach to exploring significantly new directions or horizons needed to sustain the organisation. Breakthroughs could be in processes, technologies, how a business operates or a new business area.

Systems-Thinking

Author	Esther Ridsdale
Contrib-utors	Alan Clark, Alan Mossman, Patrick Hoverstadt, Terry Peterson, Tony Korychi

Overview

The Model of a Sustainable Organisation (MoSO) is based on a *systems-thinking* approach to organisational development.

What does this mean, and how does it work?

Systems-Thinking is a term increasingly relevant in various contexts relating to the environment, organisational life, private and, more recently, public sector, as well as in biology, engineering, and the social sciences, including management.

Many systems-based methodologies draw on systems principles and a handful of approaches closely related to the seminal thinking of the foundational thinkers[42].

This article aims to give an overview of ideas associated with Systems-Thinking to help those interested in supporting the development of organisations. It does not currently extend to psychodynamic approaches but draws mainly on the work of the thinkers in section The Origins.

---

[42] See The Origins, page 270.

This article summarises and considers how to acquire Systems-Thinking skills, gives a brief outline of some key concepts and concludes with some self-examination questions and a list of sources of further learning.

Summary

> *Everything is connected to*
> *everything else.*
> *(Leonardo Da Vinci)*

Most of us derive satisfaction from doing a good job, meeting or exceeding customer expectations, having good relationships with colleagues, and having opportunities to develop and learn. We want an enjoyable working environment where we are not continually 'fighting the system' and where various parts of the organisation work together, not against each other.

As customers, we want to be treated with respect, which means: not having to make five phone calls to different departments to obtain information, not getting off a train to find that the connecting bus left five minutes ago, or being sold products that work with 'compatible' accessories. We expect fast, efficient, easy-to-use, 'joined-up' service where all parts work together seamlessly.

You have your own examples, but those above typify what Systems Thinking is all about. It says that the complex interaction of many different factors impacts everything. We operate within systems of interconnected parts. Systems-Thinking acknowledges that 'improvements' made to one area of a system without proper attention to the broader system may result in a deterioration of overall 'performance' or 'experience'. An organisation has characteristics that cannot be understood merely by looking at the parts in isolation – i.e. by 'reduction' and using 'reductionist' approaches. To improve the experience or 'results', we need to consider the systemic nature of things, understand how things function as a whole, and consider different factors and perspectives.

> *Systems-Thinking focuses on how the individual (i.e. person, organisation or other entity) being studied interacts with the other constituents of the system. Rather than focusing on the individuals within an organisation, it prefers to look at a larger number of interactions within the organisation and in between organisations as a whole.*
> (Wikipedia section on Peter Senge)

Being a Systems Thinker

Systems-Thinking is arguably an invaluable competency for any human and particularly important for anyone in a leadership or management role.

How do we acquire this skill?

Simplistically, we need to improve our skills in understanding the *systemic* nature of the world, the joined-up-ness and how parts work in relation to the whole. We need to broaden our understanding of - and attention to - the many different factors that influence behaviour ('results' or 'outcomes') in areas of interest to us.

We need to increase our skills in examining and synthesising different perspectives to gain a rich picture of the whole. For example, in an organisation, the structure is not just determined by the organisational hierarchy but also by process flows, attitudes and perceptions, the quality of products and services, how decisions are made, and many other factors.

Our world is complex, and we need to find ways of assimilating enough of the complexity to intervene wisely without being swamped. Gaining this balance is the archetypal challenge of those attempting sympathetic action. Just as a picture speaks a thousand words, a set of pictures (diagrams or maps) can help develop a good individual understanding and, importantly, help gain a *shared* understanding. This is invaluable to gain the commitment to the collaborative action needed for sustainable change.

Pictures that are of particular help in considering human organisation include,

- *systems diagrams* defining a system of interest;
- *process maps* of the focus area in detail and also how it fits within the macro system in which it sits;

- *causal loop diagrams* that depict different influences and how these factors impact each other.

This understanding guides us to the appropriate use of other data. For example, some forms of statistics, such as Statistical Process Control (SPC), are particularly helpful for understanding the performance characteristics of given processes within a system. Such approaches consider performance over time rather than examining a static and meaningless snapshot. Moreover, we need to <u>collaborate</u> with others:

- to build useful mental models and 'pictures' to aid understanding and also, in order
- to effect any systemic change (change that is robust and sustainable).

In brief, we need to understand inter-relationships & connectedness, handle the complexity of holistic thinking, and link into broader purpose and higher-level goals and values. Developing our skills in this area will enable us to take action that achieves more robust, sustainable and far-reaching benefits. Systems-Thinking is about achieving 'wholeness' in all senses of the word.

The Origins

Commonly today, the term is used loosely. However, there is also a more defined science of Systems-Thinking building on foundational thinking by people such as Ludwig Bertalanaffy, Stafford Beer, Jay Forrester, Peter Checkland, Peter

Senge, Russell Ackoff, W.R.Ashby and Donella Meadows.

There is also a body of work on 'Systems-Thinking' from a psychodynamic perspective and related works on management cybernetics focused on conceiving organisations as 'systems'. Peter Senge talks of 'personal mastery', but several other works link the domains. Many systems-based methodologies draw on systems principles and a handful of approaches closely related to the seminal thinking of the foundational thinkers.

The Need For Systems-Thinking

In order to achieve better outcomes for more stakeholders, we often hear the call for more joined-up thinking, a more holistic approach, more sustainable solutions, greater collaboration and more common sense.

> *All we lack, perhaps, is the will to establish a more entire and connected perspective. Without such a systemic approach, I fear we will continue to deal with each individual crisis without seeing the connections between them.*
> *(Prince Charles, July 2009 Richard Dimbleby Lecture)*

Systems-Thinking responds to this call. It is a means of understanding the joined-up-ness, how things work together, what purposes are served and evaluating how effectively this happens. This understanding helps us discern high leverage from low leverage action. It provides us with a basis for taking informed, meaningful action.

> *The proper role of management is to lead people to understand business as a system of work, as a system that links each worker's capacity to serve with a specific customer's needs.*
> (Johnson and Broms, 2000)

Systems-Thinking Benefits and Concepts

Systems-Thinking involves understanding an area of interest systemically, that is, as a part of a system of interrelated parts. We can understand by considering an area's behaviour as a system and part or sub-system of a more extensive system or larger inter-related systems.

We can build up our understanding by considering, for example:

- What purposes are served?
- Who are the customers (and the customers' customers)?
- What are the outputs and outcomes?
- What are the inputs, and who are the suppliers?
- What other stakeholders are there, and what is their relationship with, role within and needs from 'the system'?
- What is the environment with which the system interacts?

It involves understanding the system's various drivers and influences and the consequential effect on behaviour or results. Systems-Thinking draws on social, biological science, engineering and management to help gain a broader and deeper understanding.

Systems-Thinking is a powerful discipline for seeing the structures that underlie complex situations. The fundamental tenet of systems theory is that systems have properties and behaviours that are not properties of their components. This is termed emergence, emergent behaviours, emergent properties or synergy. The implication is that to effect any change we need a broader understanding of how our area of focus works within the whole to avoid unanticipated and undesirable consequences. In other words, it follows that to understand, predict or design in these emergent properties, you must understand the system as a system, not just as a collection of parts. You can only do this using systems approaches. If you do not understand systems as systems, you are constantly surprised by how they behave and cannot manage them.

Systems-Thinking, therefore, aims to avoid sub-optimising, i.e. optimising one component or priority to the detriment of more over-arching goals and priorities and, for example, achieving cost reductions at the expense of quality and service hence losing customers to the point of becoming more unprofitable and similarly, adding features to the point of making a loss.

Systems-Thinking advocates considering the relationship with the wider world and bigger picture. It also advocates considering different perspectives on a problem e.g. the people, processes, variation and theory of knowledge, as in Deming's System of Profound Knowledge[43].

This differs from traditional analytical approaches, which are reductionist, narrowing focus and often losing sight of the significance of interconnections and emergent behaviours, which are lost sight of by narrow focus. Systems-Thinking combines analysis with synthesis by understanding the broader meaning, so retaining sight of the bigger picture.

Even when we understand areas of concern as a system, we are always limited by where we draw the boundaries and the examination angles taken. This is one of the reasons that advocates of the science of Systems-Thinking are critical of some systems and process-based approaches as not taking a sufficiently systemic perspective and understanding broader influences, perspectives and dynamics of the area of concern. Wherever we draw boundaries and narrow the focus, we invariably risk sub-optimising, losing sight of the bigger picture. To achieve a holistic understanding, we need to consider where best to draw boundaries to gain a good perspective of the whole.

---

[43] See System of Profound Knowledge, page 306.

The practitioner aims to understand how best to gain sufficient systemic understanding and determine appropriate action within their control and influence. (Specific debate on the merits and limitations of different approaches in achieving this is beyond the scope of this work to date but could be an interesting and useful development of it.)

> *Systems-Thinking is about whole. By understanding the whole, we learn how to foster health.*
> (Peter Senge)

Comparing Systemic Management and TQM

So how does Systems-Thinking differ from well-known and widely-deployed approaches such as Total Quality Management? A comparison was provided in Russell Ackoff's talk 'Beyond TQM', presented on 18th September 1992 at the University of Hull[44].

TQM	Systemic Management
Exceeding expectations of customers	Exceeding expectations of all stakeholders
Ask customers what they want	Stakeholders design what they want

---

[44] ref: SCIO website: www.scio.org.uk

Use continual improvement to get rid of what you do not want	Use continual improvement to get what you want
Use continual improvement to achieve incremental changes	Use discontinuous improvement to create leaps in performance
Efficiency	Effectiveness
Reductionism	Whole system
Optimisation of parts	Optimisation of the total system
Start solving the current problem	Start to design what you want and work backwards
No theoretical basis	Use proven relevant theory or create a new theory to understand the phenomena being controlled
Practice-based on knowledge and intuition	Practice-based on understanding
Unintended weakening of controls that drive quality through	Align incentives with the self-interests of all stakeholders with that of the organisation

inappropriate incentives	
Assumes that more communication must lead to improved solutions	Align information flow to total system performance

This does not suggest that organisations should not pursue TQM, 6-sigma, lean engineering or other approaches to help them improve. However, if management and leadership wish to embed changes within a holistic way of working that leads to sustained success, then Systems-Thinking has clear advantages.

Some Self-Examining Questions

Systems-Thinking involves <u>understanding</u>, so it may be worth asking for your organisation:

- What is the identity/purpose of your organisation (consider customers, suppliers and any other stakeholders)?
- Who is your customer, and their customers? How do those relationships work?
- What are your key outputs and desired outcomes? How does your organisation add value, and are there any critical outcomes within your organisational system that need particularly close attention?
- What are the inputs to your organisation, and which suppliers provide these? How well do your input processes work?

- What other stakeholders does your organisation have? What is their relationship, role and needs from 'your system'?
- What environment does your organisational system interact with (political, social, regulatory, economic)?

Sources of Further Learning

Introductory Texts

- Peter M Senge (1990) *The Fifth Discipline - The Art & Practice of The Learning Organisation.* (Currency Doubleday) ISBN 0-385-26095-4
- Peter M. Senge (1994) *The Fifth Discipline Field Book: Strategies and Tools for Building a Learning Organisation.* (Currency Doubleday) ISBN 0-385-47256-0
- Barry Oshry (1995) *Seeing Systems, Unlocking the Mysteries of Organisational Life.* (Berrett Koelher) ISBN 1-881052-99-0
- Peter Checkland (1981) *Systems-Thinking, Systems Practice.* (Wiley) ISBN 0-471-27911-0.
- Russell L. Ackoff (1999) *Ackoff's Best: His Classic Writings on Management.* (Wiley) ISBN 0-471-31634-2.
- Stafford Beer, *Heart of Enterprise* (Wiley)
- Bela H. Banathy (1996) *Designing Social Systems in a Changing World (Contemporary Systems-Thinking).* (Springer) ISBN 0-306-45251-0

- Bela H. Banathy (2000) *Guided Evolution of Society: A Systems View (Contemporary Systems Thinking).* (Springer) ISBN 0-306-46382-2
- Ludwig von Bertalanffy (1976 - revised) *General System Theory: Foundations, Development, Applications.* (George Braziller) ISBN 0-807-60453-4.
- Peter Checkland, Jim Scholes (1990) *Soft Systems Methodology in Action.* (Wiley) ISBN 0-47192768-6.
- Peter Checkland, Jim Sue Holwell (1998) *Information, Systems and Information Systems.* (Wiley) ISBN 0-471-95820-4
- Peter Checkland, John Poulter (2006) *Learning for Action.* (Wiley) ISBN 0-470-02554-9.
- John Seddon (2008) *Systems-Thinking in the Public Sector.* (Triarchy Press) ISBN 978-0-9550081-8-4.
- Barry Oshry, *Leading Systems, Lessons from the Power Lab.* (Berrett Koelher) ISBN 978-1-57675072-8
- C. West Churchman (1984 - revised) *The Systems Approach.* (Delacorte Press) ISBN 0-44038407-9. John Gall (2003) *The Systems Bible: The Beginner's Guide to Systems Large and Small.* (General Systemantics Pr/Liberty) ISBN 0-961-82517-0.
- Jamshid Gharajedaghi (2005) *Systems-Thinking: Managing Chaos and Complexity*

- A Platform for Designing Business Architecture. (Butterworth-Heinemann) ISBN 0-750-67973-5.

- Charles François (ed) (1997), *International Encyclopaedia of Cybernetics and Systems*, München: K.G. Saur.

- Charles L. Hutchins (1996) *Systemic Thinking: Solving Complex Problems* ISBN 1-888017-51-1

- Bradford Keeney (2002 - revised) *Aesthetics of Change.* (Guilford Press) ISBN 1-572-30830-3.

- Lars Skyttner (2006) *General Systems Theory: Problems, Perspective, Practice* (World Scientific Publishing Company) ISBN 9-812-56467-5.

- Gerald M. Weinberg (2001 - revised) *An Introduction to General Systems-Thinking.* (Dorset House) ISBN 0-932-63349-8.

- Brian Wilson (1990) *Systems: Concepts, Methodologies and Applications, 2nd ed.* (Wiley) ISBN 0-471-92716-3.

- Brian Wilson (2001) Soft Systems Methodology: Conceptual Model Building and its Contribution. (Wiley) ISBN 0-471-89489-3.

- Alan Clark (2007) *Picture Your Business: the way to extraordinary performance and quality.* (Word4Word) ISBN 978-09551677-5-1

- Robert Pirsig (1974) *Zen and the Art of Motorcycle Maintenance: An Enquiry into Values* (The Bodley Head) ISBN 0-370-10338-6

- Robert Pirsig (1991) *Lila: An Inquiry into Morals* (Bantam Press) ISBN 0-593-02507-5
- Robert Louis Flood (1999) *Rethinking the 5th Discipline.* (Routledge) ISBN 0-415-18530-0.
- Elliott Jaques with Wilfred Brown (1965) *Glacier Project Papers* (Heinemann) ISBN 0435851020.
- John Gall (1978), *SystemAntics: How systems work and especially how they fail* (Pocket) ISBN 0671819100
- Stephen Haines, *Becoming a Strategic Thinker on a Daily Basis: Raise Your Strategic IQ for 21st Century Success.* Published paper as pdf on Stephen Haines.com website.
- Eliyahu Goldratt (2004 – 3rd edition), *The Goal - A Process of Ongoing Improvement* (Gower) (TOC) developed by Goldratt. TOC[45] as a concept is closely aligned to aspects of Systems-Thinking, therefore showing a practical application of ST on management thinking in a manufacturing environment. Also read *The Critical Chain* by the same author, which uses TOC in a project management environment.
- William J (Bill) Schwarz (2006), *Building a Generative Organisation from Reactive Behaviour to Inspired Performance.* (Ardvark Global Publishing) ISBN 159971647X.

---

[45] Theory Of Chaos

- Patrick Hoverstadt, (2008) *Fractal Organisation: Creating Sustainable Organisations with the Viable System Model,* (Wiley) ISBN 978-0-470-06056-8.
- O'Connor and McDermott (1997), *The Art of Systems-Thinking – Essential skills for Creativity and Problem Solving.* (Thorsons).

Web Resources

www.scio.org.uk *the website of SCiO: Systems and Cybernetics in Organisation is a community of practice for systems practitioners with* a table of systems approaches. It also contains further reading lists and recommendations at: http://www.scio.org.uk/toolbox

www.deming-network.org – the Deming Electronic Network or 'The DEN', The DEN website and companion discussion list were created in 1994 as a focal point for sharing resources, discussions, learning, and research on the Deming Philosophy. These currently have more than 1,000 papers, essays, files, and programs and more than 1 million archived discussion list messages freely accessible on the website.

www.managementkybernetik.com/en/index1.html - Carel Isaf Institute was set up by Stafford Beer and Fredmund Malik and named after the cottage where Stafford lived in Wales. The website provides first-hand information on management cybernetics or, as it is also called, the science of effective organisation.

www.pegasus.com – Pegasus Communications Inc offers an array of resources and opportunities for advancing your knowledge and skill in Systems-Thinking and other innovative approaches to management.

www.fieldbook.com - home to The Fifth Discipline Fieldbook Project, currently featuring Schools That Learn & The Dance of Change: The Challenges of Sustaining Momentum in Learning Organisations,

http://www.idea.gov.uk/idk/core/page.do?pageId=11216560 - Local Government Improvement & Development, Innovation, Deming & Systems-Thinking discussion threads in UK Local Government

The Deming Approach

Author	Alan Clark
Reviewers	Tony Brown, Terry Rose, Alan Hodges, Val Thomas, Kate Kelly, Ros Allcott, Tony Korycki

Overview

This article aims to draw out the essence of Deming's approach to management and its continuing relevance to managers. The Deming approach is a reasoned, wide-ranging management system that delivers consistently high performance over the long term. It views an organisation as a whole system focused on meeting the needs of customers and other stakeholders, which means quality is the central value. Improving quality reduces waste and hence improves productivity. There is a brief insight into the sort of person he was and a Deming Timeline.

Summary

The writing, teaching and lecturing of Dr W Edwards Deming inspire the Model of Sustainable Organisation (MoSO). It is, therefore, appropriate that this article provides some information about Deming.

Deming was possibly one of the world's most influential 20th-century figures, as we know it economically and organisationally. His contribution will continue long after his death through his thinking about management.

This article aims to draw out the essence of Deming's approach to management in private, public and not-for-profit sectors of society and its continuing relevance to managers. The Model of Sustainable Organisation (MoSO) diagram is rooted in the Deming flow diagram[46], which is critical for understanding and applying his approach.

As outlined below, Deming Management follows Deming's own lecturing, teaching and writing. It is intended to complement the MoSO Principles, which are written in more up-to-date and widely applicable terms.

Appendix 1, page 387, contains some impressions about the sort of man he was. There is a brief insight into Deming's personality.

Main Content

The Heart of Deming Management

During his long life, Deming developed an approach to achieving enduring success for organisations and their managers and people. Its origins were in his life experiences, education and, significantly, the work of Dr Walter A Shewhart on quality and statistical methods. A manager, said Deming, is primarily a manager of **People**. This aligns with many thinkers, teachers and

---

[46] Found in *Out of the Crisis* p.4 and *The New Economics* p.58.

writers on organisations and management, including Douglas McGregor, Frederick Herzberg and William Ouchi. People, given respect, the context and freedom to contribute, make the difference in achieving enduring organisational success. More radically, he said management should ensure **joy in work and in learning for everyone**!

People are born with the potential for intrinsic motivation, self-esteem, dignity, cooperation, curiosity, innovation and joy in learning. Intrinsic motivation means inherently wanting to do a good job. Unfortunately, this can all be destroyed by life, education and work experiences such as ranking and rating, competition, trying to look good and extrinsic motivation. Extrinsic motivation is the complete reliance on external pressures, such as rewards and punishment – "If you do this, you will get that." Deming Management, therefore, advocates the removal of extrinsic motivation and creating conditions in which intrinsic motivation, self-esteem, dignity, cooperation, curiosity, innovation and joy in learning flourish.

Deming's approach is distinctive because of its far greater range of principles, knowledge and understanding. The seven themes below seem to be at the heart of this difference. It is the **combination** of these themes with the people aspects that achieves enduring organisational success.

The Customer

The Customer is the most essential part of the 'production line' or service provision. Consequently, the focus must be on customer satisfaction. Deming often referred to customers as consumers, highlighting that the users of the outcomes are the focus and not necessarily those who pay the bill.

His fundamental principle is research and understanding the customer's needs, now and in the future. Deming taught this to Japanese management in 1950, which still holds today. The second principle, which follows from this, is that it is impossible to estimate the future losses resulting from dissatisfied customers.

Correctly understanding the needs of the customer should lead to **innovation**. Deming is often misrepresented as promoting only continual improvement of products and processes. Time and again, he emphasises the need for innovation, which is the responsibility of the supplier or provider.

Quality

Only the customer can define **_Quality_**. Everything flows from quality. Quality is not an incidental or support issue but the central issue for management.

Deming referred to his approach as **Management for Quality**[47], quite different from the familiar Management by Results or Objectives, which often ends up as just setting targets, often arbitrar-

---

[47] See pp 27, 255 & 408 in *Deming Dimension* Dr Henry Neave

ily. Management for Quality focuses on customers' needs and the methods used to produce outcomes to satisfy them.

Chain Reaction

The Chain Reaction was used by Deming to assert that quality and productivity can coexist. Quality is fundamental to achieving the best productivity. His chain reaction may be summarised as: Improve Quality ➔ Costs Decrease ➔ Productivity Improves ➔ Prices Decrease ➔ Market Increases ➔ Stay in business ➔ Create jobs and more jobs[48].

Quality had also been identified earlier in the 20th century by Henry Ford (he called it accuracy) as being essential for productivity. This was one secret that Toyota learned from Ford and Deming. Lean management, which derives from the Toyota Production System, is thus also based on quality.

PDSA

The Deming Wheel or Plan-Do-Study-Act (PDSA) Cycle is how to put quality into practice daily and strategically. It includes looking at any organisation as a system serving the customer. It is a learning cycle based on **Scientific Method[49]**,

---

[48] Adapted from *Fourth Generation Management* by Brian Joiner

[49] Scientific Method is the investigation of observable events (sometimes extraordinary ones), the acquisition of new knowledge or the correction and integration of previous

which applies to individuals, organisations and society. Every employee and manager should use PDSA to drive continual improvement and innovation. Kerridge (2008) suggests Deming's management approach was based on Scientific Method, as laid down by Walter A Shewhart, and process improvement, though relevant, was a minor part.

Improving quality starts by observing the whole situation. Deming later used "Study" rather than the previous "Check" (PDCA), since "check" could imply holding back or a tick in a box. "Study", on the other hand, implies a more thorough observation and review of the situation consistent with the Scientific Method. Study in PDSA initiates feedback in the learning cycle.

System-Thinking

Systems-Thinking provides an end-to-end view of an organisation's activities flow from supplier to customer. Meeting the customer's needs must be the **aim** of an organisational system. To maintain that aim, the *Systems-Thinking view of an organisation recognises that* **feedback** is required to

---

knowledge. It features the collection of data through observation and experimentation, and the creation and testing of possible explanations, known as hypotheses. Possible explanations are proposed for the observed events. Experiments are then designed to test these possible explanations, the results of which must be repeatable. Scientific inquiry often includes significant original thinking and creativity. Crucially scientific inquiry also involves much social interaction. Explanations are useful when they enable predictions to be made. For more information look up "Scientific method on Wikipedia.

adapt the outcomes to continually meet ever-changing customer needs.

Systems-Thinking understands that outcomes, results and performance emerge from the inter-action of all the elements that make up the system. Any system is defined by its chosen bound-ary. There will also be influence from outside the system boundary.

Deming recognised the importance of viewing any organisation as a whole. The people and the parts of the system are all important and work together. His **flow diagram** shows the integration of all parts of an organisation. *The critical feature of the flow diagram is that it models a* **feedback** system that continually adapts the outcomes to keep them in line with customer needs. The management's job is to **Optimise the System** with everyone's help.

Here 'optimise' means delivering products or services as well as possible to meet customer needs. This is achieved by balancing or making trade-offs between all factors such as human needs, suppliers and partners, returns for investors, impact on society, the environment and natural resources. Eliminating waste from the system, maximizing human contribution and planning sustainability through a long-term commitment to innovation help to achieve optimisation.

Financial engineering or control, appraisal systems, extrinsic motivation (such as incentives), measuring only outputs and not throughputs and short-term thinking are some factors that **sub-optimise** the system's performance.

The MoSO diagram has its roots in the Deming flow diagram, which is critical for understanding and applying his approach.

Variation

Understanding Variation is essential to 'Study' when using PDSA in continual improvement and innovation. 'Study', which means understanding the whole situation, requires measurement. Measurement of any aspect of an organisation provides objectivity to counterbalance human nature. Measurement also lets us know whether and how much change has been achieved. This is Scientific Method.

In the real world, measurements are subject to random variation. Furthermore, Deming stated that there is no actual value of anything since it depends on how it is measured. The random variation comes from the complexity of the interactions in any organisational system or process. There will also be significant exceptional or special causes of variation from time to time.

Deming advocated using Shewhart's Control Chart to accommodate this variation in measured data to enable proper action. This method puts the measurement data into a graph against time and adds three decision lines calculated from the variability of the data. It is then possible to:

1. decide if the system or process is stable enough for it to be safe to take action based on the measurements (Shewhart's main innovation),

2. distinguish exceptional events from chance variations,
3. show if a change has been an improvement.

Donald J Wheeler is one of the leading writers and teachers of this technique for understanding variation. He calls it **Process Behaviour Charting**. The author of this article prefers it to the common alternative: Statistical Process Control (SPC). The reason is that apart from being more descriptive, it avoids the misunderstanding that the chart can control the data in some mysterious way. The chart indicates the stability of the process, changes in the process and whether extraordinary events have occurred. Operators and management must act to **change the process** to achieve stability.

Process behaviour charting should be applied to **all** organisations' boardroom, management, process and quality data. Indeed the technique has far greater application outside the field of manufacturing in which it originated.

Leadership

Effective ***Leadership*** inspires and engages people in ongoing change. It works through the six themes above, particularly the system's leadership. Thinking systemically does not appear to come naturally to many managers, who either think linearly or become lost in the detail of daily life. Only leadership from management can initiate and sustain changes to the system in organisations and achieve the outcomes.

The Customer, Quality, Chain Reaction, PDSA Cycle, Systems-Thinking, Understanding Variation and Leadership can be seen to run consistently through Deming's writing and teaching. The combination of these seven distinctive elements with the people aspects is essential. You cannot cherry-pick the ones you 'fancy'. The approach is developed in the following section.

The Transformation of Management Style

Transformation starts with the individual, particularly individual leaders and managers. True transformation takes place slowly.

The prevailing way organisations are managed is ineffective in achieving consistently high performance in the long run and requires radical change or transformation of management style. This is Deming's stark message.

Too many conventionally managed organisations cannot endure in the long term and produce all sorts of unintended consequences and side effects. Currently, there is the new challenge of creating environmentally friendly organisations.

The evidence is all around us. In his book, *The Living Company: Growth, Learning and Longevity in Business,* Arie de Geus states,

> *The average life expectancy of a multinational company... is between 40 and 50 years. [...] A full one-third of the companies listed in the 1970 Fortune 500, for instance, had vanished by 1983 – acquired, merged or broken into pieces.*

He goes on the quote Ellen de Rooij of the Satrix Group, whose research suggested that the average life expectancy of companies in Japan and Europe was only 12.5 years!

Toyota Motor Corporation is perhaps one of the most visible examples of an exception, and after World War 2 was influenced by Deming, being revered there still. Even though it has been affected by economic cycles, it has outperformed its competitors worldwide over the long term. It has become the World benchmark for manufacturing companies.

Other articles in these pages and in the *CQI Body of Quality Knowledge* go into more detail on all aspects of Deming's thinking and approach for managers. However, for completeness, mentioned below are the well-known elements of the Deming approach from which this article has drawn out the above distinctive elements of his approach.

The most important is the **System of Profound Knowledge** (SoPK), which identifies the balanced structure of four essential fields of knowledge that managers require for the most effective, transformed management style. In *The New Economics for Industry, Government, Education,* he listed them as:

- Appreciation for a system – performance comes from parts working together;
- Knowledge about variation – proper measurement and use of statistics;
- Theory of knowledge – conscious domain knowledge about the business;
- Psychology – understanding people's needs - and why they behave as they do.

He called this a *System* because each field is related to the others and cannot be considered in isolation. This has profound implications for the education and training of management, which rarely considers all of these elements and almost never as a complete system.

Using this wide range of knowledge provides what he called a **lens** to view and understand an organisation in its context, thereby facilitating the transformation from the prevailing Western management style to one of optimisation, and achieving what we call a sustainable organisation. This distillation of the knowledge managers require came in his final book. It is, however, consistent with his teaching throughout his life.

The famous 14 Points or Obligations for Managers, the Deadly Diseases and the Forces of Destruction all flow from SoPK.

It is important to understand that these approaches were aimed at management and were in the form of principles. Ironically although one of his most famous questions of managers was, "By what method?" he hardly ever told managers a method or how to do something. The outstanding exception is the use of the Shewhart control chart to understand variation in the measurement of system and process characteristics.

Are There Benefits for Managers from Using this Approach Today?

Arguably, Deming Management is more important today than it ever was. Customers have new priorities, and the World is moving ever faster under the influence of rapidly developing information and communications technology. For managers and their customers, the global economic recession, triggered by the 2007 sub-prime mortgage collapse, is undoubtedly a crisis, harking back to the 1980s crisis addressed in the title of his book *Out of the Crisis* and the one faced by Japan after World War 2. Added to this, the spectre of global warming is still with us, increasing the complexity of the operating environment for every organisation.

Systems-Thinking and leading an organisation as a whole system are better ways to handle this complexity and emerge stronger from these crises. Making the most of the abilities of everyone in the organisation to improve and innovate continually can deliver better processes and products or services.

People interacting within any organisation and externally with customers and wider society form a system. The enduring success of an organisation depends upon the quality of the outcomes from the organisation as perceived by the customers. How the people working in an organisation feel depends on how much they can engage with and contribute to its aims. How they engage with it will determine the quality and economic success of the organisation. There is also the impact an organisation makes on the outside world in addition to the products or services it supplies, including the impact on the environment and society.

Managers, by whatever name, appear to have been part of most organisations throughout recorded history. A manager's job is to optimise or balance or seek trade-offs to satisfy customers, investors and society at large. Deming's approach facilitates this balancing act.

People working together encounter problems achieving the outcomes their organisation strives to deliver to customers. Some of the problems derive from human nature, and some from the sheer complexity of what they are trying to achieve and how they are trying to achieve it.

Managers, especially senior managers, are challenged by Deming that they are not doing and do not know their job! This was based on his direct experience combined with his knowledge of statistics and science.

Senior management, both in companies and the Public Sector, appeared to Deming to believe, and unfortunately continue to believe, that all they have to do is set near impossible standards or targets, so-called "stretch targets". They give the impression of having no interest in whether the

378

standards are attainable, the changes necessary to methods and equipment to achieve these targets, and even whether their policies must also change. They seem content to employ specialists to handle performance and quality's "technical" details. Deming firmly believed that quality is made in the Boardroom. In the Red Bead Experiment[50], Deming demonstrated management setting impossible targets without attempting to determine if the targets can be met or making any system changes.

Certainly, Deming has contributed to the World as the statistical expert he was through his books and over 170 academic papers. However, he was not purely an academic, as witnessed by a "hot" online debate that ensued at the end of 2007 on the Deming Electronic Network (DEN) after one contributor's suggestion.

> The consensus was that he was interested in using scientific methods and statistics, particularly his emphasis on theory (proven explanations of observed events), *to find practical ways to solve business problems*. Del Nelson and John Dowd's Contributions to the DEN at that time show that Deming also genuinely cared about people and improved the quality of life of everyone in the world of work — something many managers have yet to do.

Today, Deming's emphasis on verified **knowledge**, based on evidence obtained through

---

[50] see *The New Economics*, Chapter 7

ongoing scientific inquiry, is the key to sustainable organisations. Such organisations endure in
the long term whilst minimising their environmental impact through continual improvement
and innovation.

You Say This is Based on his Direct Experience?

Deming worked his way through school and
higher education and knew what it was like to be
a worker. One of his vacation jobs was at Western Electric in the summers of 1925 and 1926,
ironically at the same time as Dr Walter A
Shewhart, although they did not meet until a
year later. Perhaps with the worker's life in mind
in his book *The New Economics,* he related the
warning from his new boss at Western Electric
not to get caught on a stairway when the whistle
blows for fear of being trampled to death. It
seems he understood only too well how bad the
work experience was for many people.

He also knew what it was like to be a manager.
According to Bill Cooper, in a posting to the DEN
on 20-Dec-2007, Deming corrected the view of
him only as a statistician and consultant, "I managed 450 people when I worked at the Census
Bureau, and together we developed the methods,
procedures and processes that are used by the
Census Bureau today".

When he went to Japan in 1950, he was keen to
talk to senior management, for it was already his
experience as a consultant that management
would not willingly get involved in the detail. Instead, they would delegate quality matters to the
quality specialists. Thus in 1981, triggered by

the groundbreaking 1980 NBC TV documentary *"If Japan can, why can't we?"*, when the Ford Motor Company asked for his help, he insisted on only working with the CEO, Don Petersen. His experience in World War 2 and Japan showed that the leader must personally lead the change, and the change must come from within each person.

Yes, But is This All Still Relevant Today?

Definitely.

Whilst quality has improved in many organisations, the original approach has been lost. One only has to look at the media to see the current preoccupation with targets, particularly in the public sector. Politicians want the quick-fix "instant pudding" of demonstrating that they are 'doing something' by setting a target. No consideration is given to how the target can be achieved.

Targets, in a more subtle way, bedevil the private sector. The myopic focus on shareholder benefits and the expectations of the returns on investment by stock markets is just another manifestation of the target mentality. Deming was not against targets *per se*. He understood that there were facts of life (survival) numbers. He railed against arbitrary, externally imposed targets that lack planning or method and the exhortations that accompany them.

Deming Management is Not Just About Statistics, Then?

No! Categorically not.

In the Deming approach, management is responsible for the whole system, which includes people, methods, processes, and suppliers. Statistics is just one of the four essential fields of knowledge that enables managers to take a balanced, outside-in view of the whole system.

Conclusion

The Deming approach is a reasoned, wide-ranging management system that delivers consistently high performance over the long term. It views an organisation as a whole system focused on meeting the customer's needs, which means quality is the central value. Improving quality reduces waste and hence improves productivity.

Organisations comprise people working together to achieve this aim. It is the management's job to create the conditions within the organisation where people can maximise their intrinsic motivation, self-esteem, dignity, cooperation, curiosity, innovation and joy in learning. Intrinsic motivation means inherently wanting to do a good job.

Management must lead the organisation as a system that continually improves and innovates using the PDSA Cycle. An essential part of PDSA is the measurement of performance, which is then analysed using Shewhart's statistical methods.

Parts of the approach are seen throughout current management practice. However, where the entire management system is applied over the long term, the result is enduring high performance.

Adopting this approach to management starts with you, the individual manager, really wanting sustainable high performance, wanting things to be different and being willing to start doing things differently. The starting point is to ask yourself where you are now.

MoSO Health Check

Deming inspired questions to ask yourself and your fellow managers

- To what degree are we an organisation that thinks in terms of the whole system of operation, stakeholder interests, process flow and quality?
- Who are our customers, the consumers of our outcomes?
- How focused are we on our customers?
- What research do we do on the needs of our customers?
- In what ways are we pushing for innovation?
- How do we create the conditions in which creativity and innovation can thrive?
- What evidence do we have that quality is a central issue for us as managers?
- How does the Board of Directors use quality as a basis to set policy?
- To what extent do Directors (Executives) and all managers set an example about the importance of quality?
- What proportion of our focus is on productivity, and how much is on quality?

- To what extent is the PDSA cycle central to how we run our organisation?
- How much performance management and appraisal of individuals are there, and how is this consistent with Systems-Thinking?
- What evidence do we have to show how we concentrate on continually improving and innovating the flow in the end-to-end series of activities that are our value-adding chain?
- How can we demonstrate that the way we apply measurement is based on a proper understanding of process behaviour, variation and the use of statistics?
- How are we continually improving our leadership and that of everyone in our organisation?

Bibliography

References
- http://www.deming.org/theman/biography.html
- http://deming-network.org/mailman/listinfo/den.list_deming-network.org
- http://en.wikipedia.org/wiki/W._Edwards_Deming
- http://en.wikipedia.org/wiki/Scientific_method
- Kerridge, David (2008) http://deming-network.org/pipermail/den.list_deming-network.org/2008-December/000912.html in a posting to the DEN

Books by W Edwards Deming:

- Deming, W E, (1943) *Statistical Adjustment of Data.* New York: John Wiley & Sons
- Deming, W E, (1960) *Sample Design in Business Research.* New York: John Wiley & Sons
- Deming, W E, (1966) *Some Theory of Sampling.* New York: John Wiley & Sons
- Deming, W E, (1982) *Quality, Productivity & Competitive Position.* Cambridge, MA: CAES - MIT
- Deming, W E, (1986) *Out of the Crisis.* Cambridge, MA: CAES - MIT
- Deming, W E, (1993) The New Economics for Industry, Government, Education. Cambridge, MA: CAES - MIT
- In addition, according to the Deming Electronic Network, Deming published over 170 articles, some of which may still be available through The W Edwards Deming Institute at
- http://www.deming.org/resources/publications.html.

Books About W Edwards Deming and his Approach to Management

- Delavigne, Kenneth T, & Robertson, J Daniel (1994) *Deming's Profound Changes: When Will the Sleeping Giant Awaken?* Englewood Cliffs, NJ: PTR Prentice Hall ISBN

- Joiner, Brian L (1994) *Fourth Generation Management: The New Business Consciousness.* New York: McGraw-Hall
- Kilian, Cecelia S (1992). *The World of W. Edwards Deming* - 2nd Edition. *SPC Press, Inc. ISBN 0-945320-29-9*
- Latzko, William J & Saunders, David M (1995) *Four Days with Dr. Deming: A Strategy for Modern Methods of Management.* Reading, MA: Addison-Wesley ISBN 0-201-63366-3
- Mann, Nancy R (1989). *Keys to Excellence: The Story of the Deming Philosophy* - 3rd Edition. Prestwick Books. ISBN 1-85251-097-8
- Neave, Henry R (1990). *The Deming Dimension.* Knoxville, TN: SPC Press, Inc. ISBN 0945320-08-6
- Salsburg, David (2001) *The Lady Tasting Tea: How Statistics Revolutionized Science in the Twentieth Century.* New York: W H Freeman & Co
- Scherkenbach, William W (1986) *The Deming Route to Quality and Productivity: Road Maps and Road Blocks.* London: Mercury Books ISBN 1-85251-082-X
- Scherkenbach, William W (1991) *Deming's Road to Continual Improvement.* Knoxville, TN: SPC Press ISBN 0-945320-10-8
- Shewhart, Walter A (1930). *Economic Control of Quality of Manufactured Product / 50th Anniversary Commemorative Issue.* American Society for Quality December 1980. ISBN 0-87389076-0

- Shewhart, Walter A (1939). *Statistical Method from the Viewpoint of Quality Control.* Dover Publications December 1, 1986. ISBN 0-486-65232-7
- Voehl, Frank, Ed. (1995) *Deming: The Way We Knew Him,* Boca Raton, FL: St. Lucie Press. ISBN 1-884015-54-9
- Walton, Mary (1986). *The Deming Management Method.* The Putnam Publishing Group. ISBN 0-399-55000-3

Appendix 1 What Sort Of a Man Was Deming?

In an insightful posting to the DEN on 20-Dec-2007, Bill Cooper, who worked with Deming, said that he defied categorisation. Cooper says he was many things, including an academic, a theorist, a practical person interested in systems and their effect on organisations and their successes or failures, a mathematician, a physicist and, reading further, the best kind of teacher: one who made you think.

He was a stern-looking tall old gentleman in a three-piece suit to many people. He could be critical and did not suffer fools gladly. Earning perhaps the "glare" remarked upon by Cooper in his posting. Possibly he was entitled. Having been scientifically educated and become eminent in statistics, he might not be expected to consider kindly partially thought out or ill-conceived questions.

One has a deep sense of a respectful, highly ethical stance emanating from his faith. In his books, he was scrupulous in crediting those who had contributed. His respect manifested itself in his approach to the Japanese, starkly contrasting the arrogance of many Americans in the occupation forces after World War 2.

In 1950, The Deming Award was formulated by JUSE with the funds accumulated from reprints of his lectures propagating his philosophy across Japanese industries. Possibly this was his most important legacy. The recognition it conferred encouraged Japan to take these ideas forward. Good examples are Taguchi and, latterly, Shiba, plus the list of company transformations recognised, including Toyota in 1965.

Among his friends, he was known for his kindness and consideration for those with whom he worked. He had a robust if very subtle, sense of humour. Deming knew how to have fun. He was also a musician and composer.

Further insight into Deming as a person can be gained from reading an article by Lisa D McNary, found at http://www.spcpress.com/pdf/deming_memorial_essay.pdf. Lisa was the last postgraduate student to be mentored by Deming. We get a picture of Deming as the challenging teacher contrasted with how his humour and humanity shone through. This humanity is as important as any part of his approach.

System of Profound Knowledge

Author	Malcolm Gall
Reviewers	Terry Rose, Alan Clark

Overview

The system of profound knowledge is the thought processes we use to help us understand

- the world in which we live,
- the family to which we belong,
- the organisation in which we work, even
- the team in which we work.

Fundamentally it is about viewing any organisation from the outside through four lenses which often interact with one another:

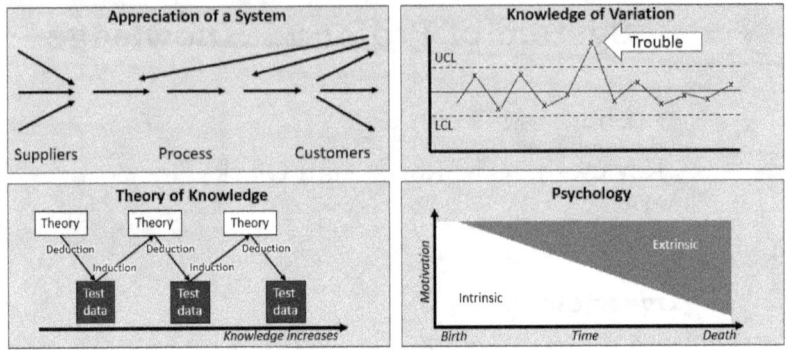

Figure 45: The Four Lenses of SoPK

Main Content

SoPK is a valuable approach with which to view a problem and any proposed solutions.

The four lenses of the system are inextricably linked. However, one does not have to be an expert in any of them in order to use the system.

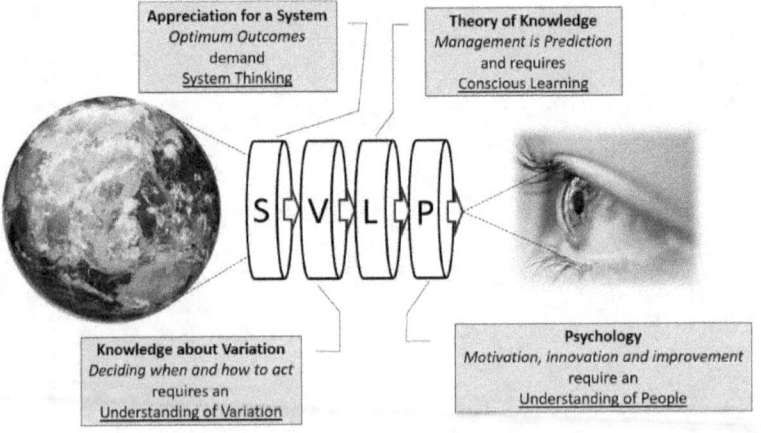

Figure 46: System of Profound Knowledge

Usually, organisations need a view from the outside to understand themselves. The system of profound knowledge can provide this.

The system of Profound Knowledge can be considered a compound lens to view the world as depicted on the next page supplied by Alan Clark.

Appreciation of a System

A system involving people must have an aim; otherwise, it has a destiny of negative, or at best, ineffectual action or collapse. The system is a network of interdependent components that work together to accomplish the aim. A human example would be a football team. Lack of appreciation of the system leads to silo thinking and sub-optimisation in its elements, to the detriment of the aim of the whole, eg. "My department has got to win" is not an attitude focussed on the customer and may lose the organisation's business. The results of failing to recognise a system are often described as "the law of unintended consequences".

The appreciation of a system also includes an understanding of the relationship between the organisation and its environment.

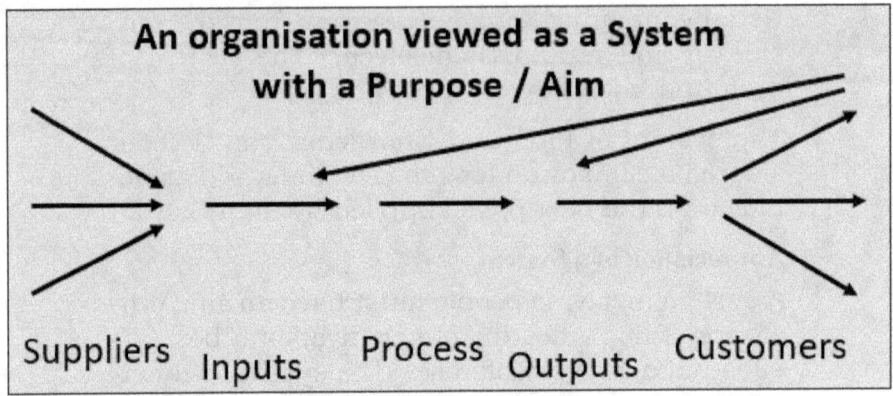

Figure 47: SoPK System

The process diagram raises our awareness of how our involvement and our department (or our project) contribute, interact or influence the achievement of the organisation's aims.

Knowledge of Variation

Knowledge of variation allows us to predict, in some circumstances, the outcome or result of a process and series of measurements.

For any process, the measures we use to monitor the acceptability of the work can be recorded/plotted on a process behaviour chart (also called a Shewhart or control chart). The charts show changes over time or batches, which helps identify whether materials, people, methods, or equipment have changed and affected the process.

The average and range results can be plotted by analysing the data, and then the upper and lower control limits can be calculated. The limits on the chart are calculated empirically from the data. They are set from economic criteria, not any statistical model, giving us the fingerprint or signature tune of the process, the voice of the process:

- Points recorded outside the process (control) limits are termed special causes;
- Points recorded between the process (control) limits are termed normal causes.

Use of Charts

Extra-ordinary variation comes from special causes of variation. These can be detected as sig-

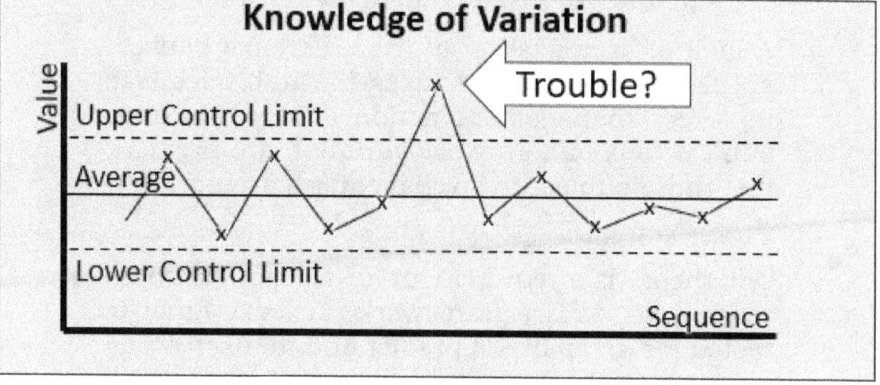

Figure 48: Process Behaviour Chart

nals on a process behaviour chart and tend to be localised in time or sequence. It is usually economically worthwhile investigating and removing them to make the process stable and predictable.

The output of a stable process shows results between the process limits. This output can be predicted to an extent. The following individual point cannot be predicted, but the average and spread can be. The spread stays within the limits. A stable process can do no better. It is subject only to common causes of variation. This is *the Voice of the System*. This can be compared with what the customer wants, *the Voice of the Customer*, which may or may not be expressed as a specification.

If a different average or smaller output spread is required, then the process must be subjected to improvement or innovation. This is likely to be a management responsibility. Tampering (adjusting a stable process) can increase variability.

A lack of appreciation of the difference between special and common causes inevitably leads to incorrect management action. Only processes subject to common cause variation are predictable; those subject to special causes are not.

Theory of Knowledge

The theory is a requirement for the application of reasoning. It is a framework. Theory must be tested for its ability to predict and its usefulness.

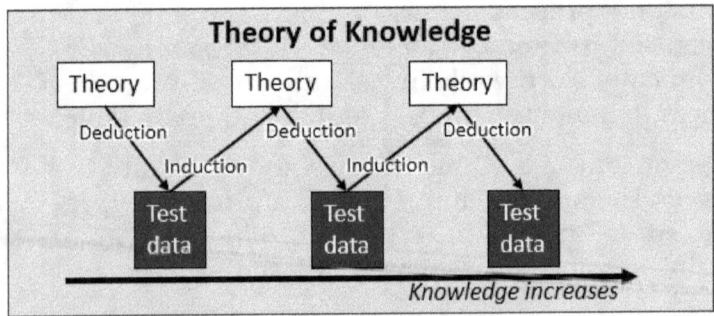

Figure 49: SoPK Theory of Knowledge

The PDSA cycle is a shorter, more focused version of the applied scientific method.

PDSA cycle can be used for learning, improvement or innovation, provided the system is stable while going around the cycle.

The job of management inevitably involves prediction. Prediction comes from theory. Without theory, examples and experience are unreliable guides. Initiatives based on "common sense" can produce counter-intuitive and counter-productive results.

Another area where confusion and damage can be reduced is using Operational Definitions. Operational Definitions (comprising a test for the concept, a criterion for passing the test and a decision on whether the test has been met) are helpful in communicating a concept or even a word, thereby reducing variation between people who have to use the concept together. If a concept is

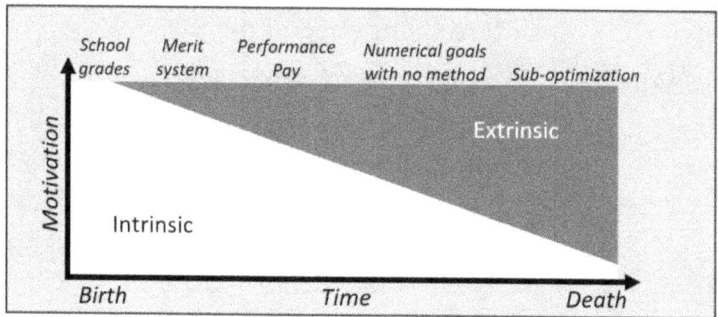

Figure 50: Forces of Destruction

395

important enough, it is worth the effort to set up an operational definition. An example of an operational definition would be a standard test method. Operational definitions can be improved by using devices such as the PDSA cycle if necessary.

Psychology

Human motivation is of two types: extrinsic and intrinsic. Extrinsic motivation uses external stimuli, e.g. rewards and punishments, which can be material (e.g. money) or emotional (e.g. status or fear), as found in command and control organisations. Intrinsic motivation comes from within the person. It shows itself as self-regard and a desire to learn, leading to pride in workmanship.

Some Examples of Interactions of the Four Lenses

Psychology

System   Failure to use the strengths and opportunities arising from the interdependence of people.

Variation   Fear generates wrong figures.

Ranking people without understanding natural variation.

Setting performance targets without understanding the difference between average and extreme values.

Theory of People learn in different ways. They
Knowledgeacquire knowledge differently. In the
absence of operational definitions,
people ascribe different meanings to
words.

Theory of Knowledge

System The application of learning to only
one component of a system.

Variation In PDSA cycles, the Study phase is
curtailed due to a lack of appreciation
of variation.

Variation Process charts on a small part of the
system do not reveal the full benefits.

System Not recognising that wrongly timed
feedback increases variability.

Using a performance measurement
target that assumes a single number
tells you all you need to know about a
system.

Looking more deeply into cases will often reveal
interactions between three or four of the elements
of Profound Knowledge.

More?

Dr W E Deming first presented this system in
1987-90 to explain the basis of what he was saying in his Four-Day Seminars, looking back to his
Fourteen Points for Management, as defined in
"Out of the Crisis". The System of Profound

Knowledge was expounded in "The New Economics", and a more extended account is given in "The Deming Dimension" (H R Neave).

Some Frequently Asked Questions

What use is knowledge of variation?

> Without appropriate knowledge, the numbers might mislead you – it is difficult to evaluate the possible effects of chance or to sort signal from noise. If you are studying a process without current knowledge of variation, you will not know whether it is stable or not.

Why is the Theory of Knowledge useful?

> Do not be put off by the terminology, which sounds very philosophical and therefore of questionable relevance to people in the real world. Theory of Knowledge is about learning and knowing which facts are helpful and reliable in a given set of circumstances. For example, the output of a stable process is predictable in the future, provided circumstances do not change.

Why have an appreciation for a system?

> Because processes, operations and people are often linked, changes in one can easily affect another, often with unpredictable consequences. This applies to physical systems as well as to organisations of people.

What use is psychology?

> This is a vast subject, so for a start, just consider people's motivation. Their motivation directs their behaviour and actions. Organisations benefit from constructive and cooperative behaviour.

Why have these four been linked together?

> Because in real life, where people are involved, not just one, but often all four aspects can be found if you look hard enough into a problem.

Where does SPC come in?

> SPC stands for "Statistical Process Control". It is the state that a process is in when a "control chart" (today, it is more likely to be called a "Process Behaviour Chart" or a "Shewhart Chart") of a critical process characteristic shows no signals indicating the presence of a special cause of variation. Achieving this state was often the first step in improvement since it is achieved by removing unnecessary variation.

Is Six Sigma all about Variation?

> No. It is usually a programme of improvement based upon projects which follow a methodology like the PDSA cycle. There are many different "Six Sigma" types, depending upon the provider or organisation involved. It can involve many formal sta-

tistics. One key question for potential users is whether the requirements of their customers can be expressed as conventional, independent specifications, e.g. ranges of values with upper and lower limits. If so, then capability indices are extensively used.

What is "Lean"?

"Lean" describes an organisation that has successfully applied improvement, say by using SoPK, to reduce waste generation in the organisation's activities. Lean is about driving out all forms of waste: wasted time, wasted effort, wasted resources, wasted materials, wasted finance and more. For example, the massive reduction of inventories (stock) in a set of processes reduces waste (money tied up in these stores) and uses the economies of flow. The adjective "lean" can also be applied to individual processes.

Self-Examining Questions

1. Can you measure the variability of your key processes or production?
2. Have you used clear operational definitions for the items you have measured or counted?
3. Do **all** your processes and systems support your organisation's aims, or do some frustrate them?
4. Which of your processes are stable and, therefore, predictable?

5. What motivates your people?
6. How do you solve problems and establish improvements?

Values

Author	Terry Rose
Reviewers	Alan Clark, Terry Peterson

Introduction

The subject of values (some would include ethics) applies to all aspects of organisational conduct and is relevant to individuals and organisations. Values remain consistent over the long haul, even as markets, strategies and goals change.

Many organisations develop values to which they expect everyone who works on their behalf to adhere or aspire. The intent is to guide individuals on good/desirable/ethical behaviours. Each organisation's values statements are likely to be different - or at least worded differently.

Organizational Values

Business does not operate in a vacuum. Organisations of all types and sizes operate in the social and natural environment and, therefore, (from a MoSO perspective) are duty-bound to be accountable to the natural and social environment in which they survive - irrespective of the demands and pressures upon it.

However, the need for or efficacy of values in an organisational setting is disputed. For example, Milton Friedman held that corporations are amoral and CEOs have only one duty: to maximize a company's profits. He also said in an interview that business cannot have social responsibility. Peter Drucker said, "There is neither a separate ethics of business nor is one needed". Drucker also observed that the ultimate responsibility of company directors is not to harm. Everybody is a member of society. Why would it be acceptable to behave ethically, principled as a partner in a relationship, parent or community member and then in a selfish or immoral way when working for an organisation?

So why do organisations spend time and effort formulating and training their people on non-economic social values? Some might say to strengthen a corporate identity (core values reflected in the brand) or for compliance reasons. Others believe policies are developed mainly to limit legal liability or curry public favour by appearing to be good corporate citizens.

One common problem is for an organisation to allow, through culture and policies, a disconnect between their published code of values and actual practices. This disconnect can put individuals in difficult situations, making them feel like they must choose between their conscience and their job or career. For example, an organisation that includes 'respect' as a core value whilst a culture of senior managers bullying subordinates to meet monthly sales goals. Alternatively, they have included 'honesty', yet feel that it is acceptable to be less than frank with a customer about the likely delivery date of a critical order. A senior partner of a law firm that espouses strong ethical values when signing a new client knows that, in certain circumstances, the junior partner working with the client will be under pressure to put the firm's self-interest above that of the client.

And you will know of many other examples. How can employees be held to, or expected to, apply the stated values in such situations?

So what is required to make a values policy successful? Would you agree with the following?

- The unequivocal support of top management, by both word and example;
- Involvement of stakeholders in their development;
- Be explained in writing and orally, with periodic reinforcement;
- Be feasible - something employees can both understand and perform;
- Be monitored by top management, with routine inspections for compliance and improvement;
- Backed up by clearly stated consequences in the case of disobedience.

How do organisations develop a set of values or core beliefs? We believe that organisations that enjoy enduring success have core values developed and articulated by the people who work there rather than handed down from on high. The core values are then much more likely to be embraced by all as part of the institution's fabric.

Specific Organizational Values That Support MoSO

There are values which could be listed by most, if not all, organisations, such as; honesty, integrity, trust, and respect. However, our focus here is to ask whether any values *specifically* support MoSO – and to articulate why. We have made a start below, deliberately using different styles of wording.

Trust

MoSO is predicated on Systems-Thinking, which often relies on implementing cross-functional or multi-agency solutions or programs over an agreed period. You have to be able to trust other people/functions/agencies to do their best to fulfil their part of an agreement and not to revert to the usual 'silos of self-interest' when the opportunity arises. For teamwork to achieve results at any level in an organisation, an environment of trust must exist.

Customers can count on us

This means that an organisation does whatever it takes to satisfy the customer – to go the extra mile to do what is right for them because, ultimately, individual customers must be able to rely on the organisation to come through for them.

Openness to learning

Reflecting a high value placed on creating a learning and continual improvement environment throughout all levels and departments of an organisation.

Transparency

Some might use the phrase 'open door', reflecting the value placed on open and candid discussions throughout the organisation and with partners and customers. When all the cards are on the table, and all information is available, the right decisions can be made.

Sharing success equally

All stakeholders share equally and fairly in the organisation's success and place very low value on bureaucracy and perks like special executive offices and bonuses only for a select few (i.e. the things that get in the way of doing what is right for the customer).

Respect for the environment in which we live and work

As you might expect, a value statement that goes to the heart of MoSO.

And you may have more.

Section 9. Self-Examining Questions

The purpose of this section is to bring together all the Self-Examiming 'powerful' questions from throughout the other sections of the book into one place for ease of access and to allow the big picture to emerge.

The list is not a comprehensive list of questions – it is more of a starting place.

Questions you might ask about your organization

1. To what extent is our organisation sustainable?
2. What would our MoSO look like?
3. What strategies do we have in place for each of the elements?
4. Do they work together as a whole, focused on a common aim?
5. Are there gaps and inconsistencies?

MoSO Benefits

1. Does your organisation understand the difference between "Cutting Costs" and "Removing the Causes of Costs" and does it know where the causes of costs are to be found within it?
2. What is the result of your constructing the Chain Reaction for your organisation?
3. How will you tackle the essential first step of the chain reaction? Without it, the remainder is just a wish list.
4. How does **WIN-WIN** help your organisation?

5. In what way can **WIN-WIN-WIN** emerge from your organisation's activities ?

Customers

1. To what extent is the primacy of the customer recognised within our organisation?
2. What evidence do you have that you use your customers to align both people and policy?
3. What evidence is there that you are really striving to achieve customer delight?
4. Where are customer perceptions of your products or services relative to the three types of quality: Attractive, More-is-better and Must-be? Be honest!
5. How much support does management provide front-line staff in moments of truth?
6. Give examples of ways customer-facing staff can resolve issues on the spot.
7. What active steps are you taking to build trust within your organisation and with your customers?

Your operations

1. To what extent are you ready for this journey? What help or support do you need?
2. To what extent is your organisation ready for change – who will be the change champions who will work you? What constraints have to be overcome to gain initial momentum versus continued momentum?

3. How does the big picture of your organisation align with the MoSO model? Are the differences significant in terms of sustainable performance?
4. If the differences are real, what can be done to introduce the missing elements or improve ineffective areas?
5. To what extent are the three voices to renew and sustain the organisation (VoC, VoS, VoP) used systematically and continually improved?
6. Looking at the MoSO model, what important influences are affecting, or likely to affect, your operations, and how are you recognising and managing these influences?

PDSA

1. To what extent is the PDSA Learning and Improvement Cycle understood in your organisation?
2. To what extent do you use a PDSA cycle in strategy and plan deployment?
3. Do you have a consistent process to improve your core operating processes to achieve better performance, reduce variability, and keep the processes current with business needs and directions?
4. Do improvement teams have a consistent method based on PDSA?
5. Do you have a consistent process to improve your support processes?
6. How do you translate data from organisational performance reviews into priorities

for continuous and breakthrough improvement and opportunities for innovation?

7. How are these priorities and opportunities deployed to workgroup and functional-level operations throughout your organisation?

8. How are improvements shared with other organisational units and processes?

9. When appropriate, how are the priorities and opportunities deployed to your suppliers, partners, and collaborators to ensure organisational alignment?

People, Culture, Leadership and Management

1. On reflection, what more might you do?
2. How could you engage and encourage others to do likewise?
3. What responsibility can you take for designing the system?
4. How capable are the processes?
5. How will you avoid 'tampering'?
6. Where does PDSA apply?
7. How do you lead by example?

The Environment

1. Does our management structure empower all levels of our organisation to eliminate waste? Does our theory/self-image fit the facts?

2. What are we doing to introduce 'co-opetition' to share approaches and reduce costs

with competitors to address common environmental concerns?

3. What are we doing to change from a focus on maxima or minima to one where we continually improve the system/process in order to eliminate waste?

4. Does our system encourage or discourage innovation and the adoption of new ideas?

5. Are we driving out fear to encourage heartfelt feedback from every level of our organisation? What is this feedback's quality and frequency, and how do we measure it?

6. Are our targets self-interested and short-term, or are they sustainable and stable over time, outside management initiatives and fads? What exactly are we measuring, and why?

7. Do we genuinely encourage our creative thinkers and recognise that their new ideas may solve tomorrow's problems? How and how can this be improved?

8. Do we have a cooperative relationship with our community, or do we view them as an obstruction and a nuisance we would rather ignore - if so, how do we change this relationship for the common good and mutual benefit?

9. Do we have a separate environmental function within our organisation - or is our view of the environment and sustainability something every single member of our organisation participates in and takes pride in, from the very top to the very bottom?

10. Are we running an organisation that will make the world a better place for our communities and children? If not, what should we do now and on an ongoing basis to address the issues?

11. Do politics and self-image obstruct our attainment of a genuinely sustainable, efficient and environmentally friendly organisation? Are we being faithful to these goals? Does our aspiration in this area equal our self-image in other areas of organisational performance? (i.e. if we view ourselves as a world leader, are we also a world leader in our environmental policy?)

12. Are we really a zero-waste organisation? How do we continually move towards this goal by creating a sustainable, organic system - and what exactly are we measuring when we make our policy?"

Voice of the Customer

1. Do I/we know who our customers are (both internal and external)?

2. Do I/we truly know our customers' needs and expectations– now and in the future?

3. What is the predominant culture in my/our organisation – Product-Out or Market-In?

4. Do I/we have the basic language skills to capture the Voice of the Customer accurately?

5. Do I/we have the appropriate Voice of the Customer processes in place?

6. Do I/we understand that, to deliver excellent performance, it is necessary to align the Voice of the System with the Voice of the Customer? (See Voice of the System)

Voice of the System

1. When trying to make sense of numerical data, do I/we have a binary view of the world – always either "Doing OK" or "In trouble"?
2. Do our management reports simply compare two values (for example, where we are now compared with last week/month/quarter or compared to an average value) and use that comparison to drive actions?
3. Are our management reports 'eye charts' of tabular data from which people are expected to extract vital trends and unexpected values?
4. To what extent do our current data reporting systems allow us to distinguish between normal behaviour of the process/system, and identify exceptional (special) events and causes for investigation and improvement action?
5. Do I/we know the consequences of not understanding data?
6. What checks would we need to carry out to know whether our data is sufficient to assess System behaviour?
7. Have I/we made the progression from reporting data in tabular or graph formats to using Process Behaviour Charts?

8. Do I/we know the difference between the Voice of the System and the Voice of the Customer?
9. Do I/we understand that, to deliver excellent performance, it is necessary to align the Voice of the System with the Voice of the Customer?
10. Do I/we realise that setting goals does nothing to improve the system?
11. Is being in control the same as being on target? Discuss.
12. To what extent am I/we using Voice of the System thinking to drive continual improvements and innovation?

Innovation

1. Have senior management in your organisation shown leadership in innovation?
2. Is there a support infrastructure for innovation in your organisation?
3. In your organisation's terms, what is the difference between innovation and improvement?
4. Do you know where to start?

Sustainability

1. To what extent do you think your organisation is currently sustainable as a business?
2. How can you measure the vitality of your organisation? Do you dare?
3. Which of the silent killers stalk your corridors?

4. How do you rate your organisation's capabilities against each of the items in the list above?

Transformation

1. To what extent has your vision for the future been agreed between yourselves?
2. Have the imperatives for change (the Whys) been clearly set out and agreed?
3. To what extent has the gap between the organisation's 'current state' and the 'destination' been articulated?
4. Have the benefits of using MoSO as a comprehensive framework for sustainability been explored?
5. Has a defined set of principles (and values) that will form an enduring foundation for transformation and beyond been agreed?
6. To what extent are you (the leadership team) prepared to personally devote time and effort to building knowledge, understanding and skill in the practices that will drive change?
7. Developing an infrastructure for change throughout the organisation is essential. Has the team developed a suitable infrastructure for your organisation that involves all the leadership team playing an active role?

Systems-Thinking

1. What is the identity/purpose of your organisation (consider customers, suppliers and any other stakeholders)?
2. Who is your customer, and their customers? How do those relationships work?
3. What are your key outputs and desired outcomes? How does your organisation add value, and are there any critical outcomes within your organisational system that need particularly close attention?
4. What are the inputs to your organisation, and which suppliers provide these? How well do your input processes work?
5. What other stakeholders does your organisation have? What is their relationship, role and needs from 'your system'?
6. What environment does your organisational system interact with (political, social, regulatory, economic)?

The Deming Approach

1. To what degree are we an organisation that thinks about the whole system of operation, stakeholder interests, process flow and quality?
2. Who are our customers, the consumers of our outcomes?
3. How focused are we on our customers?
4. What research do we do on the needs of our customers?
5. In what ways are we pushing for innovation?

6. How do we create the conditions in which creativity and innovation can thrive?
7. What evidence do we have that quality is a central issue for us as managers?
8. How does the Board of Directors use quality as a basis to set policy?
9. To what extent do Directors (Executives) and all managers set an example about the importance of quality?
10. What proportion of our focus is on productivity, and how much is on quality?
11. To what extent is the PDSA (or PDCA) cycle central to how we run our organisation?
12. How much performance management and appraisal of individuals are there, and how is this consistent with Systems-Thinking?
13. What evidence do we have to show how we concentrate on continually improving and innovating the flow in the end-to-end series of activities that are our value-adding chain?
14. How can we demonstrate the way we apply measurement based on a proper understanding of process behaviour, variation and the use of statistics?
15. How are we continually improving our leadership and that of everyone in our organisation?

System of Profound Knowledge

1. Can you measure the variability of your key processes or production?

2. Have you used clear operational definitions for the items you have measured or counted?
3. Do **all** your processes and systems support your organisation's aims, or do some frustrate them?
4. Which of your processes are stable and, therefore, predictable?
5. What motivates your people?
6. How do you solve problems and establish improvements?